COST A

A. J. Tubb is Senior Lecturer in Accounting at Ealing Technical College. He has
previously been employed as a company
secretary and an accountant and so has
been able to draw on both theoretical and
practical experience in writing this book.

TEACH YOURSELF BOOKS

# COST ACCOUNTING

**A. J. Tubb,**

BSc.(Econ.), FCMA, FAAI, AMBIM

Editorial Adviser: Ronald Chappell,
Dean of the Faculty of Social Sciences,
Harrow College of Technology and Art

TEACH YOURSELF BOOKS
Hodder and Stoughton

*First printed 1977*

*Copyright © 1977*
A. J. Tubb

ISBN 0 340 21904 1

*Printed and bound in Great Britain for*
*Hodder and Stoughton Paperbacks, a division*
*of Hodder and Stoughton Ltd, Mill Road,*
*Dunton Green, Sevenoaks, Kent*
*(Editorial Office 47 Bedford Square, London WC1 3DP)*
*by Richard Clay (The Chaucer Press), Ltd.,*
*Bungay, Suffolk*

# Preface

This book has been written as a result of a great deal of encouragement from my academic colleagues and many kind comments from students.

It has its beginnings in the lectures I have given, revised and developed over the years, to professional accounting and other students required to write first examinations in cost accounting. Those lectures were, and are still, conducted on the basis that to learn is to understand and appreciate. There is thus, I hope, an absence of rules and the regurgitation of so-called principles, but rather a concentration on the need to absorb the basic framework on which the fabric of this and the wider subject of management accounting is to be hung.

This book is appropriate for foundation stage students of the major United Kingdom accounting bodies as well as for those who are being examined for the first time in the subject area on such courses as Ordinary and Higher National Diplomas and Certificates, and for members of other non-accounting professional bodies. It is also useful background reading for all those in any way involved in the development or use of cost-accounting systems at work.

A full list of acknowledgments would prove to be too extensive. I must content myself with the bare minimum. To all my colleagues in the Division of Accounting at Ealing Technical College, for their forbearance with my sometimes outrageous and provocative theories. To Tony Platzer, for reading my extensive drafts and providing valuable comments. To Shirley Ellis, who valiantly transcribed my handwritten manuscript. To the publishers in the guise of Lydia Greeves for her valuable appraisals and help. To the professional accounting bodies for permission to use past examination questions, fuller details of which are given elsewhere. Last but by no means least, to Eileen, Linda and Wendy—my wife and two daughters—for minimum distraction and maximum encouragement, without which the pen would probably not have reached the end of the manuscript.

I nevertheless accept full responsibility for any errors of omission, commission and principle.

A. J. Tubb.

# Acknowledgments

I wish to acknowledge the permission to use past examination papers granted by the following bodies. The initials in parenthesis are used at the end of each question to identify the body from whose examinations that particular question was taken.

- (ICA)—The Institute of Chartered Accountants in England and Wales
- (ACCA)—The Association of Certified Accountants
- (ICMA)—The Institute of Cost and Management Accountants

A. J. Tubb.

# Contents

# 1

# Introduction

Accounting is concerned with recording, measuring and reporting the incomes and expenditures of an organisation to two distinct groups of people—owners and managers. The basis of accounting is bookkeeping, which is defined as

> 'The analysis, classification and recording of financial transactions in books of accounts.'[1]

It is generally accepted that financial accounting is used to record, measure and report to owners, whilst management accounting is used to record, measure and report to managers. Financial accounting is defined as:

> 'The analysis, classification and recording of financial transactions and the ascertainment of how such transactions affect the performance and financial position of a business' (ICMA).

Management accounting is defined as:

> 'The application of professional knowledge and skill in the preparation of accounting information in such a way as to assist management in the formulation of policies and in the planning and control of the operations of the undertaking' (ICMA).

---

[1] *'Terminology of management and financial accountancy'*, The Institute of Cost and Management Accountants 1974. This reference will be used throughout the text and denoted by (ICMA) when a definition is given.

In order to establish a basis for the concept in the last definition, a system of cost accounting will be needed. Cost accounting is defined as:

> 'The application of accounting and costing principles, methods and techniques in the ascertainment of costs and the analysis of savings and/or excesses as compared with previous experience or with standards' (ICMA).

Glancing back through these definitions we observe that all forms of accounting are related. We note that bookkeeping is the basis of the recording system and that cost accounting is the basis of reporting to managers.

### What is cost?

It may be defined in two ways: firstly as a noun—'The amount of expenditure (actual or notional) incurred on, or attributable to, a specified thing or activity' (ICMA). For example, we may talk of the *cost* of a bar of chocolate. Secondly, it may be defined as a verb—'To ascertain the cost of a specified thing or activity'. For example, how much will it *cost* to make a bar of chocolate?

We note that, in both cases, cost implies two features, price and quantity. We could thus say that cost may also be defined as being the product of price and quantity.

### Cost accounting and the organisation

Students of cost accounting should be aware of the management function and the organisation within which it operates. For our purposes a manager could be defined as a person who has effective control over a group of people for the purpose of achieving given objectives. This definition necessarily includes every type of manager from the managing director to the chargehand with six operatives under his control. It is to this range of people that we are reporting. They are all concerned with management within an organisational structure. A simple example in chart form is given in Figure 1.

This only shows how a business may be organised. It is not intended to be complete: the expansion of one department has been shown as an inset, and for clarity, the functional lines of co-ordination between, say, the cost accounts department and production sections have also been omitted.

None the less, to be aware of the functions of managers and their place in the organisation will help us to understand what we are attempting to record and report on, and make it more valid.

## The characteristics and behaviour of costs

There are three discernible characteristics of cost:

1 Variability
2 Normality
3 Controllability

### Variability

Costs may be described as being variable or fixed. A variable cost is defined as:

> 'A cost which, in the aggregate, tends to vary in direct proportion to changes in the volume of output or turnover' (ICMA).

An example of such a cost is the timber used to make chairs. If each chair requires £3 worth of timber then 1000 chairs will need £3000 worth of timber. Note carefully that if there is no production of chairs there will be no expenditure on

A typical organisation chart for a small/medium Limited Liability Company

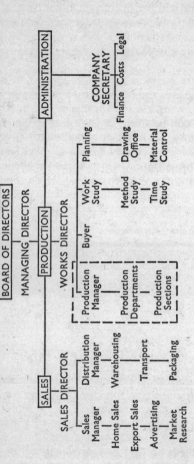

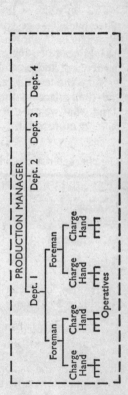

FIGURE 1

timber. For this reason variable costs are sometimes referred to as avoidable costs. A fixed cost, on the other hand, is defined as:

'A cost which accrues in relation to the passage of time and which, within certain output or turnover limits, tends to be unaffected by fluctuations in volume of output or turnover' (ICMA).

An example of such a cost is rates. For irrespective of the number of chairs produced, the total rates demand for the year is unaffected. For this reason fixed costs are sometimes referred to as unavoidable costs.

We now consider a numerical example. Let us suppose that the only expense the firm has is £2000 in rates and that it only uses £3 worth of timber per chair. Then, for varying ranges of output we could produce the following table:

|  | *Production of Chairs* | | | |
|  | 1 | 100 | 1 000 | 10 000 |
| --- | --- | --- | --- | --- |
| Rates (F) | £2 000 | £2 000 | £2 000 | £2 000 |
| Timber (V) | £3 | £300 | £3 000 | £30 000 |
| Total Cost (TC) | £2 003 | £2 300 | £5 000 | £32 000 |
| Cost per chair | £2 003 | £23 | £5 | £3·20 |

Here we can observe the importance of distinguishing between variable (V) and fixed (F) costs. As production increases, fixed costs remain at the same value, whilst variable costs increase directly in proportion to production. Thus, the cost per chair decreases as production increases.

Whilst this is a simple example, the concept of the variability of cost and its behaviour under varying conditions is fundamental. It will be examined more rigorously as our study proceeds.

## Normality

A normal cost has been defined as one which is normally incurred at a given level of activity under conditions in which that level of activity is normally obtained. This is a rather roundabout way of saying that a normal cost is one which can be anticipated from past experience. The essence of normality is thus one of individuality, not generality. It may help in deciding whether a situation is normal to consider, conversely, whether or not it is abnormal. Clearly, loss of materials by theft may be abnormal, whilst an 'acceptable' level of wastage or scrap may be normal. What is regarded as acceptable will be based on technical knowledge and past experience. A great danger in setting levels of normality is the insidious effect of the gradual deterioration of acceptable levels.

## Controllability

A controllable cost is one which is influenced by the action of a given employee. We remember that cost has two facets, price and quantity. It is doubtful whether any person or group of people in an organisation is really in a position to influence to any great extent the price of goods or services obtained from outside the organisation. However, that same person or group of people will be in a position to decide how the goods or services will be used. Indeed, they may well be in a position to decide whether the good or service is required at *any* price or whether it is the best type of good or service for the needs of the organisation.

We can thus see from this first look at cost accounting that it forms a vital basis of the reporting system necessary to keep managers informed and able to make decisions.

This text will consider the subject-matter in three stages: the elements of cost, cost ascertainment and control techniques. A fourth stage concerned with decisions is also introduced.

# Part I

# The Elements of Cost

# 2

# The Elements of Cost and their Relationship

The inputs of goods or services required to produce a final product can be divided into three distinct elements of cost: materials, labour and expenses.

We should be quite clear about the expression 'produce the final product'. It should not be assumed that the product is always in a tangible form, for the word 'produce' implies not just changing the form of, say, a sheet of steel into a car door, but may also mean the provision of some service such as drawing up an insurance policy. In our highly complex society there are four types of business operation: manufacturing, wholesaling, retailing and servicing. All four 'produce a final product' out of the three elements of cost. The physical transformation may not be immediately apparent, but it exists.

Of the three elements, materials and labour are perhaps the more tangible, whilst expenses are less so. We see materials being used in factories, shops and offices. We could think of many of them without difficulty—steel, timber, coal, oil, flour and cement being a few examples of what are usually referred to as 'raw materials'. We note that the motor-car industry regards steel as a raw material to produce cars whilst the steel industry regards steel as a final saleable product.

There are other forms of material inputs, such as springs, nuts, bolts, bandages, chemicals, pens, pencils and so on, which are usually referred to as 'bought in materials'.

An example may be the spark plugs bought in for inclusion in a car engine manufactured by one of the motor-car firms.

The second element, labour, is also tangible. This term covers everyone who is receiving a monetary reward for due effort, and it includes managing directors, road sweepers, professional footballers, cost clerks, machine operators, bank managers and so on. It is usually true to say that without this element the material element remains inanimate. Thus transformation or production is effected by the application of labour.

The third element, expenses, is the least tangible. It covers the acquisition of all the things which are needed in the running of a business—electricity, water, gas, telephones, insurance, rates, and advertising being some that come to mind. Without them the transformation process with labour and materials would be difficult if not impossible.

A relationship of interdependence is therefore established between our three elements, for all the elements are present to a greater or lesser degree in everything that is available.

### Direct and indirect cost

We may observe that there are some elements of cost that are readily identifiable with a product and some that are not. Consider, for example, a suit or dress. It consists of cloth, thread, buttons and so on, which have been cut and assembled by cutters, sewers and pressers in a factory which is lit, heated, equipped with machines and organised by managers.

If we organise a table listing the inputs under two columns, headed 'identifiable' where an input can be specifically visualised as being part of a particular suit or dress, or 'unidentifiable' where we cannot be so specific, the following would result:

| Input | Identifiable | Unidentifiable |
|---|---|---|
| Cloth | x | |
| Thread (?) | | ← x → |
| Buttons | x | |
| Cutting labour | x | |
| Managers | | x |
| Electricity bills | | x |
| Machine lubricating oil | | x |
| Stores labourers etc. | | x |

The term used to classify the identifiables is *direct* costs whilst the unidentifiables are referred to as *indirect* costs.

A reasonable working definition of a direct cost would be: 'a cost which becomes a directly identifiable part of the finished product or service.'

Direct material would include:

(a) Raw material purchased specifically to be transformed into a saleable product or service, e.g. steel, timber, plastic.

(b) Products made completely by other companies and totally incorporated in saleable products or services, e.g. springs, electric motors.

(c) Products made partially by other companies to specific order and totally incorporated in saleable products or services.

Direct labour would include:

(a) Wages and other remuneration paid to all employees who directly contribute to the conversion of direct materials into saleable products or services.

(b) All the associated expenditure paid by the company in employing people, including social security contributions and overtime premium.

Direct expenses would include:

(*a*) Royalties payable by an organisation to use a process which is the property or right of another organisation.
(*b*) Special tools used in manufacture.
(*c*) Hire charges for special equipment used in manufacture.

The foregoing should not be considered as exhaustive, but as indicative of the manner in which we need to think about direct and indirect costs.

Having defined direct costs, we can now define indirect costs as 'all those other expenditures which are not classified as direct'.

It is now possible to draw up a chart, to show the interdependence of the direct and indirect elements of cost in a more visual form and to point out one or two other matters which will demand attention at a later stage.

We see from Figure 2 that a new term, 'overhead', has appeared in the chart. This term is defined as 'the total cost of indirect material, indirect labour and indirect expense costs' (ICMA), and it will give rise to some problems to be considered later; but for the moment we can ponder on how we are going to collect the information for future addition to the direct or prime cost where there is more than one product or service being produced in the same organisation.

Another matter that should be carefully noted is that this presentation ends with a box entitled *Total Cost*. It should not be assumed that by adding a percentage for profit to that figure we can arrive at selling price. To do so would be to assume, mistakenly, that

1  the method and manner in which we have ascertained costs is perfect and without question
2  the manner in which we have produced the good or service has been efficient and effective

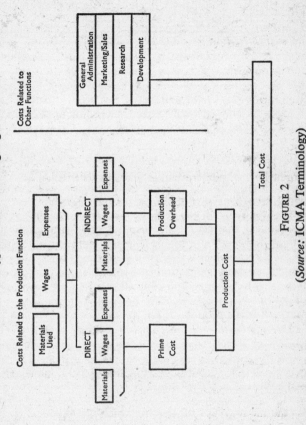

THE ELEMENT OF COST
related to a typical manufacturing organisation

FIGURE 2
(*Source*: ICMA Terminology)

3 the market for the product or service is willing to pay the price we have decided, bearing in mind the two previous comments.

More properly, the presentation can be used for management information. On the assumption that the information is made on a reasonable basis, answers can be formulated to such questions as:

1 Can we stay in the market for this product or service?
2 Can we enter the market for this product or service?
3 Why is the market price for our product or service lower than cost?

### Production, administration, selling and distribution

The *production* function has the main responsibility for producing the saleable goods in the most efficient, effective and economical manner at its disposal and within the constraints imposed on it by the availability, the type, the price of the direct elements of cost and the conditions of operation facing the organisation as a whole. To do this, production must be planned and controlled with a specified policy or set of objectives which are probably constrained by the market for the product or service.

The *administration* function will have an overall responsibility for the effective control and operation of office procedures, paperwork and data flow and will include such departments as accounting, secretarial, general management and so forth.

The *selling* function will be responsible for all aspects of marketing, market research and advertising, that is, obtaining and retaining customers.

The *distribution* function will be responsible for the efficient and effective warehousing and delivery of all goods, including packaging, where it has not already been carried out as part of the manufacturing process.

The general tenets discussed so far and those that are to follow apply equally to the four broad divisions of the organisation mentioned above. All cost is to be accounted for.

### Exercises

1 Variability, normality and controllability are three characteristics into which costs may be classified. Describe these three characteristics and, with examples, comment upon the purposes of these classifications.
(ACCA)

2 Define and give examples of the following terms:
   (a) Direct and indirect costs
   (b) Overhead
   (c) Prime cost
   (d) Variable cost
   (e) Fixed cost
   (f) Normal and abnormal

3 What do you understand by the term 'overhead'? What are its characteristics? How may it be classified?

4 What is cost accountancy? What do you consider to be the major objectives?

5 'No system of cost accountancy can function effectively unless the business organisation is sound.' Discuss this statement from as wide a viewpoint as possible.

6 'Costing is an instrument of management control.' 'Costing is nothing more than a detailed analysis of expenditure.' Reconcile these two statements, quoting examples to illustrate the truth of each. (ACCA)

# 3

# Materials

Recent statistics of the UK economy show that in general terms some 50% of total cost is material cost. However, it may represent a significant input in quite large numbers of organisations and yet be insignificant in others. It would not do to ignore the fact that this element of cost represents money's worth and as such, careful consideration must be given to its acquisition, storage and use.

The acquisition of materials by an organisation will be governed by its requirements, the availability of the materials, the cash available or credit limits, and the storage facilities. The storage facilities will be governed by the amount of space that can be made available out of total available space. The use of materials will be governed by production capacity and the consumption of materials through that production capacity. The production capacity is dependent on the market for the goods produced by the firm.

From this we observe the interplay between quantity and price. How much material is needed? At what price will it be acquired and used?

It is clear that a carefully defined and effectively operated system of material planning and control is necessary to maintain the delicate balance necessary to produce profits.

**Categories of materials**

Materials used in organisations can be classified as:

(*a*)  raw materials such as metal sheets and bars, timber, flour, plastic powder, bricks, cement, paper and so forth; that is, any basic constituent of any manufactured product;

(*b*)  bought out components such as springs, electric motors, switches, castings and so forth—'bought out' because the organisation using them does not have the expertise or resources to manufacture them internally;

(*c*)  consumable materials such as small tools, cleaning materials, oil and grease and all the other incidental requirements necessary for the efficient operation of an effective production process;

(*d*)  stationery and office supplies such as paper, pens, paperclips, catalogues, advertising materials, drawing office supplies and a hundred and one other items without which an organisation would not be able to operate effectively.

In the remainder of this chapter it may seem that emphasis is given to the first three categories and particularly to manufacturing industries. But the points made and the systems outlined are equally applicable to all forms of commercial operation in both the private and public sector.

**Material control**

Five stages can be recognised:

1  the design stage, when the availability and range of possible materials is considered and standard items used where possible;

2  the planning stage, when design is translated practically

and a compromise reached between the designers' artistic flair and the production planners' practical requirements;

3　the acquisition stage, when the goods are ordered;
4　the receiving and storage stage, when it must be ensured that the delivery is in accordance with order and that materials are stored in suitable conditions;
5　the production stage, where goods are issued from stores for use in the production process.

We shall not be concerned in this text with the first two stages but we must understand the last three.

## Material classification

The use of a classification and codification system will make a control system more effective, since it:

1　describes by alphabetical and/or numerical means the various materials and components in use and thus
2　eliminates errors of description;
3　shortens descriptions and speeds up transmission and recording of information;
4　simplifies the clerical effort required in a material control system.

To consider a simple demonstration:

(*a*)　Metal can be steel, brass or copper.
(*b*)　It may be obtained in strips, round bars, hexagonal bars or tubes.
(*c*)　It may have varying dimensions of length measured in metres, and width, thickness or diameter measured in millimetres.

In the above example we see that the classifications (*a*), (*b*), (*c*) can be carefully codified (1 steel, 2 brass and so forth). In doing so a simple, flexible system can be evolved, from which numerical notation can be applied to material description.

To take a simple example consider the description: 'Brass Strip 12 millimetres × 3 millimetres.' This could be condensed to a numerical notation by referring to the classification and coding instruction, to obtain:

> 2 for Brass
> 1 for Strip
> 12 for width in millimetres
> 03 for thickness in millimetres

giving the number 211203. The flexibility of the system can be noted:

(*a*) The classification of metal can take in up to 9 basic descriptions.

(*b*) The classification of the shape of the material being used—round, strip, tube and so forth—also allows for up to 9 basic shapes.

(*c*) The measurement in millimetres formed in the last four figures of the code clearly allows for measurement of materials up to 99 millimetres wide and 99 millimetres thick, or, 99 millimetres in diameter.

To take an extreme example, the code 99999999 may be the numerical description of Solid Oak (the first two nines), of a three-sided shape (the third and fourth nines), one side of which is 99 millimetres, (fifth and sixth nines), with the other side also of 99 millimetres (the seventh and eighth nines).

From this very basic example it could be seen that a great range of description and flexibility can be incorporated into a classification and codification system.

## Materials ordering

The ordering or acquisition of materials must be considered in two quite distinct stages.

*Stage 1* commences when the need for supplies of certain materials is triggered by some known event; for example, Production Control are setting up the manufacture of a new component or model. To do so they must make sure that sufficient quantities of the correct materials are acquired and held in stores before the production programme can commence.

*Stage 2* is triggered by *Stage 1* and is the action to be taken to acquire those supplies of materials. This stage is usually the concern of the Purchasing or Buying Department.

It should be clear from this that *Stage 2* can only be activated by some instruction arising from the events in *Stage 1*. *Stage 2* can never be activated by the direct action of the Purchasing Department, firstly, because that department would not be in possession of all the facts with respect to the planned production programme (although they may be aware of it in general terms), and secondly, because they would not have the technical expertise needed to formulate in specification and quantity terms a purchasing order without instruction or technical directive.

## Purchasing procedure

To overcome the difficulties outlined above it is necessary to evolve a basic procedure of information transmission, so that every department, section or person in the organisation who is required to know, will know what is required.

This will require the use of three important documents:

1   *The purchase requisition*
This is originated by the department or section requiring the

goods and authorised only by a specified person within that department. The requisition is the *Stage 1* trigger which will activate the purchasing officer and authorise him to make the purchase. Control over buying is thus limited to persons having authority to sign purchase requisitions. Those persons may only be authorised to sign requisitions for certain classes of materials. For example, Production Control

| | PURCHASE REQUISITION | | No. | |
|---|---|---|---|---|
| From | | | Date | |
| Material Code | Material Description | Quantity | | Purchase Order | |
| | | Req'd | Ordered | Date | Number |
| | | | | | |

Raised by _____ Date ___  Order initiated by _____

Authorised by _____ Date ___  Dated _____

Charge Reference _____  Buyer _____

FIGURE 3

would only have authority to sign requisitions for direct or production materials. An accountant would only be authorised to sign requisitions for Accounts Department supplies. Control then, is exercised through limiting authority to sign requisitions to those persons having knowledge of the requirements, and the purchasing function is restricted until such duly authenticated documents are in their possession. The requisition should show the fullest possible details of specifications, sizes, quantities and, possibly, recommended suppliers and prices, especially where consultation with such suppliers has already formed part of the requisitioning process. The format of the requisition will vary from organisation to organisation and from industry to industry but generally will be more or less as shown in Figure 3.

In some industries, where mass-production or large-scale batch production is undertaken, detailed forecasts of material requirements are made well in advance of need and usually in the form of material schedules, the master copy of which is constantly amended and updated. It is a simple matter to use this master copy to duplicate copies of requirements as needed and send this to the buying department, attached to a 'blanket' requisition as covering authority. In any event the requisition would be raised in duplicate, the original being sent to the purchasing office and the duplicate being retained by the originator.

## 2   *The purchase order*

This should be in writing, on a standardised form containing all possible detail, since it will form the basis of a legal contract between the organisation and the supplier. The format for such a document will vary from organisation to organisation and from industry to industry but generally will take the form of Figure 4. This document will be raised with at least five copies, the first two printed as in Figure 4, the remainder on plain paper. Copies 1 and 2 go to the supplier who will be required to sign and return one copy as acknowledgement and acceptance of the order. Copy 3 is sent to the originator to indicate that his requisition is now on order. Copy 4 is sent to Goods Inwards Department as an indication of what to expect and when, and copy 5 will be retained by the Purchasing Department for progressing the order and linking with and passing the suppliers' invoice for payment.

## 3   *Goods received note*

This will be raised by the Goods Inwards Department after

PURCHASE ORDER

Newtown Engineering Ltd.
Newtown Wharf Estate
Shuffle Road
Easthampton EA4 2AX

┌To:

No. _____

Date _____

Charge a/c _____

Ref. _____

V.A.T. Ref. No.

Delivery by:

└

Delivery Instructions _____

| Material Code | Description | Your Reference | Unit Qty. | Unit | Unit Rates | Total Value |
|---|---|---|---|---|---|---|
|  |  |  |  |  |  |  |
|  |  |  |  |  |  |  |
|  |  |  |  |  |  |  |
|  |  |  |  |  |  |  |

All prices quoted are inclusive of V.A.T. Our order number and references must be quoted in full on all invoices and communications. Invoices must be rendered in duplicate.

Please supply the above goods in accordance with your estimate/price list No. _____ dated _____ and with the conditions printed on the reverse of this order.

For Newtown Engineering Ltd. _____

BUYER

FIGURE 4

the delivery has been inspected by competent and qualified persons. In order to maintain control and impartiality this department would not be under the direct responsibility of either production or purchasing management but is more likely to be under a completely independent Chief Inspector.

Because Goods Inwards Department are in possession of a copy of the detailed purchase order they can confirm that the goods are as required, and can set the minimum standard to be expected. The physical specifications and quantities will be checked and if they are found to be in order, a goods received note will be raised with a minimum of four copies. The format of the goods received note will vary from organisation to organisation and from industry to industry but generally will be as shown in Figure 5.

| | GOODS RECEIVED NOTE | | | No._____ |
|---|---|---|---|---|

Delivery received from_____ Date_____
_____ Order No._____
_____ Charge a/c_____

| Material Code | Description | Quantity | | Comments |
|---|---|---|---|---|
| | | Ordered | Received | |
| | | | | |
| | | | | |
| | | | | |
| | | | | |

Carrier_____ Date_____ | Inspection Stamp
Received by_____ Date_____ |
Sent to_____ Date_____ | Date_____

FIGURE 5

Copy 1 is sent to the originator of the requisition to indicate that his goods have been received. Copy 2 is sent to purchasing department for attachment to the purchase order. When the suppliers' invoice is received the documents will serve to validate that invoice. Copy 3 will accompany the goods when they are physically moved from Goods Inwards to the person or department for whom they are intended. Copy 4 is retained by Goods Inwards Department and attached to their copy of the purchase order.

If the delivery only partially completes the purchase order then the fourth copy is held against future deliveries. If the delivery was complete in itself or was the final delivery to complete an order, the fourth copy and its accompanying purchase order can be removed to a completed orders file or scrapped.

If the goods as delivered do not match up to the order and, on investigation, are not acceptable to the originator, a goods received note will not be raised and the system reverts to its original position, as if the goods had never been delivered. However the delivery must be kept in a safe place whilst the matter is being raised with the supplier by the Purchasing Department and settled to everyone's satisfaction.

If partial acceptance of the goods is made, the goods received note will only record the portion that has been accepted. Clearly, short deliveries will fall into this category.

## Stores and stores control

The storage of goods requires not only adequate facilities in the form of space and equipment, but also an understanding of the nature of the materials and their requirements.

The stores must be properly laid out. The point has already been made that goods must be capable of easy identification and location. Goods must be stacked, racked or binned properly. Protective measures such as greasing, wrapping and inhibiting corrosion must be carried out as soon as the goods are received.

It should be clear that the physical storage of materials constitutes a separate study of its own. The aspiring accountant should always take the opportunity of examining this important aspect of any manufacturing and commercial operation by reading some of the excellent literature that is available on the subject.

The more immediate problem concerns the quantity and price aspect of cost. That is, how much material should be held in stock? And at what price should it be held and issued from stock?

## How much should be held in stock?

A manufacturing process requires at least a bare minimum of stock around which production schedules may be planned. At the same time, to hold too much stock would involve the organisation in additional storage costs and tie up more cash than necessary.

Conversely, to operate at the bare minimum of stocks and constantly re-order may decrease the cost of holding stocks but increase the cost of ordering them. The problem is then:

1 What shall be a minimum stock?
2 What shall be a maximum stock?
3 What should be the best or most economic re-order quantity?
4 When or how often should the goods be re-ordered?

*Minimum stocks* are regulated by:

1 the rate of consumption;
2 the rate of delivery by the supplier.

*Maximum stocks* are regulated by the conditions for a Minimum Stock Level together with:

3 storage space available;
4 the funds available for investment in stocks;
5 the political and economic factors operating which may determine shortages or protracted delivery cycles;
6 deterioration or perishability of the material;
7 the risk of obsolescence.

## The Economic Order Quantity

A tabular arrangement of information relative to a particular component would help to formulate ideas on this matter.

| | |
|---|---|
| Estimated requirements per year | 5000 units |
| Price per unit charged by supplier | £1 |
| Ordering cost per order | £4 |
| Stock carrying cost as a percentage of average stock value | 10% |

Based on this information an approximate Economic Order Quantity could be determined as follows:

| | | | | | | | |
|---|---|---|---|---|---|---|---|
| Possible order size in units | 200 | 500 | 625 | 1000 | 1250 | 2500 | 5000 |
| Number of orders $\left(\frac{\text{Total requirement}}{\text{order size}}\right)$ | 25 | 10 | 8 | 5 | 4 | 2 | 1 |
| Average stock $\left(\frac{\text{Order size}}{2}\right)$ | 100 | 250 | 312 | 500 | 625 | 1250 | 2500 |
| Average stock value (Average stock × unit cost) | £100 | £250 | £312 | £500 | £625 | £1250 | £2500 |
| **TOTAL CARRYING COST** | | | | | | | |
| Stock carrying cost (10% × average stock value) | £10 | £25 | £31 | £50 | £62 | £125 | £250 |
| Ordering cost $\left(\begin{array}{l}\text{Number of orders} \times \\ \text{order cost per order}\end{array}\right)$ | £100 | £40 | £32 | £20 | £16 | £8 | £4 |
| | £110 | £65 | £62 | £70 | £78 | £133 | £254 |

The table shows that, of the range of possible order sizes, an order for 625 units placed 8 times per year would give the 'least cost' total carrying cost of £62.

This is, however, only approximate. There may be a better order size—say, between 500 and 625 units, or between 625 and 1000 units. We are aware, however, that, given reasonable accuracy in the estimates, it is better to order 625 units 8 times per year than 1250 units 4 times per year.

A graphical presentation of this table is shown in Figure 6.

The graph shows in more illustrative form a low point on the 'total cost to carry and order' curve. Reading off the

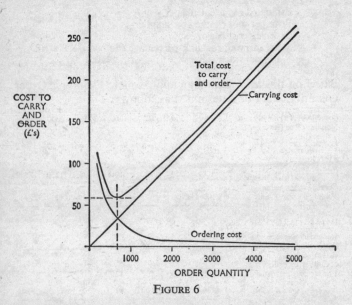

FIGURE 6

unit value against that low point gives an Economic Order Quantity of between 625 and 650.

Determining the EOQ in tabular or graphical form is lengthy and may not provide an accurate solution. Mathematically it is possible to obtain the Economic Order Quantity by a formula which is:

Economic
Order
Quantity = $\sqrt{\dfrac{2 \times \text{Annual Required Units} \times \text{Cost per order}}{\text{Cost per unit} \times \text{Carrying Cost}}}$
(EOQ)

Taking the information previously used in the table and graph above we would obtain:

$$EOQ = \sqrt{\frac{2 \times 5000 \times £4}{£1 \times 10\%}}$$

$$= \sqrt{\frac{40\,000}{0 \cdot 10}}$$

$$= \sqrt{400\,000} = \text{approximately 632 units}$$

—which is very close to the answer of 625 units obtained by the table method. That fact should not be considered as proof that the table method is as accurate as the formula.

It should be understood that the use of both the table and the formula assume that:

1 there is a reasonably steady or average requirement for the material;
2 the production/sales patterns are uniform with steady or average demand;
3 the price per unit is constant regardless of order size;
4 the errors in estimating the basis are small, consistent and acceptable.


## When should goods be ordered? The Re-order Level

This is controlled by three factors:

1 The lead time, that is, the interval between the placing; of an order and its delivery;
2 The rate of usage;
3 The minimum safety or 'buffer' stock to be held.

If the first two factors can be calculated with reasonable certainty the need to hold minimum stocks decreases. Whilst it may be argued that the Rate of Usage should be known by the organisation, it must be remembered that external influences will affect the demand for the products of the firm in much the same way as it affects the supply of materials to make those products. Consider the effect of a change in, say, the Rate of Usage as illustrated in Figure 7.

The full line represents a normal condition. If the usage increased (the dotted line), stock would run out—a 'stock-out'—and would remain so for a short while before the

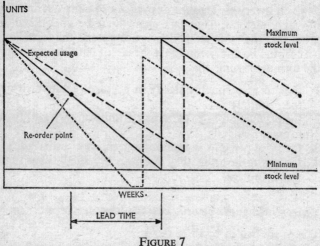

FIGURE 7

re-order quantity was received. If no adjustment were made, the out-of-stock time would increase over subsequent periods. If the usage decreased (the dashed line), the re-order quantity would be delivered before the minimum level was reached and the stock level would increase above maximum at the point of delivery. If no adjustments were made, the stock levels would continue to rise above the maximum levels, causing an increasing over-investment in stock.

Similar graphical analysis can be carried out for changes

in the Lead Time (holding Usage Rate constant). From a combination of the two factors we can see that forecasting material stock points is a complex and specialised subject.

It is none the less essential to establish a trigger point to act as the signal for a re-order purchase. For present purposes we accept that the re-order level point can normally be established as

Lead Time Usage + Minimum Stock Level

Lead Time Usage is calculated as the product of Normal Usage and Normal Delivery Period.

*Illustration*
Normal Rate of Usage — 200 units per week
Normal Lead Time (delivery period) — 5 weeks
Minimum Stock Level — 300 units

Then Re-order level = Lead time usage + Minimum stock
$$= (200 \times 5) + 300$$
$$= 1300 \text{ units}$$

We shall find at a later stage, when considering the calculation of Minimum Stock Levels, that such a calculation requires the use of known Re-order Levels. To use the foregoing method may result in a stalemate. An alternative solution could be found by using the formula:

Maximum Usage per week × Maximum Lead Time

## Minimum Stock Level

Opinions differ as to the exact nature and characteristics of Minimum Stock. It would be correct to assume that it is basically a safety margin or 'fail-safe' device to ensure that if usage does unexpectedly increase or suppliers take longer than expected to deliver, there is at least something in stock to keep production going.

If we accept this concept then a Minimum Stock Level can be calculated by considering:

1   A possible rate of usage. It may be appropriate to consider the highest rate of usage that could occur.
2   A Lead Time; that is to say, how much longer a supplier could take to deliver the order.

These however are basically the traditional rule-of-thumb methods that have been established by experience. Statistical techniques are now used to a greater extent, giving greater protection at lower costs against a possible stockout.

This always assumes that an organisation has time, money, expertise and the relevant information to be able to carry out statistical analysis for every component. There are always situations where this may not be so convenient. For those instances an alternative may be useful. One formulation is:

Re-order level — (Normal Usage × Normal Re-order Period)

*Illustration*

|  |  |
|---|---|
| Re-order level | 4000 units |
| Re-order Period | 4 weeks |
| Normal Usage | 300 units per week |

then Minimum Stock level would be

$$4000 - (300 \times 4)$$
$$= 4000 - 1200 = 2800 \text{ units}$$

which we see as being a re-arrangement of the Re-order Level approach. We recall that Re-order Level could be calculated by Lead Time Usage × Minimum Stock where Lead Time Usage was the product of Normal Rate of Usage and Normal Delivery Period. Thus

Re-order Level = (Normal Usage × Normal delivery) + Minimum Stock

Re-arranging our terms this would give:

Minimum Stock = Re-order Level — Lead Time Usage

Clearly, the use of such an approach could not give the same degree of accuracy as a statistical method.

**Maximum Stock Level**

This should be regarded as the highest level at which stocks are held, consistent with the matters discussed with respect to Re-order Quantity and Minimum Levels. There are, however, other influences to be considered. Under current conditions the more important factors are probably the economic and political influences which may bring about future shortages and cause an organisation to consider increasing its stocks. Conversely, those influences could also indicate a future fall in the demand for certain goods, the result being that an organisation will cut back its investment in stocks.

Linked with the economic and political influences, consideration must also be given to the funds available to pay suppliers, the amount of storage space available and the risks of deterioration or perishability of the goods in store. It has been shown that an Economic Order Quantity can be calculated, given an acceptance of reasonable assumptions. From this we accept that a Maximum Stock Level could be established as Economic Order Quantity *plus* Minimum Stock Level.

There is some sense in accepting that although there is protection built into the calculation of Minimum Stock, an organisation might be prepared to modify such protection and increase the risk of stockout by reducing its Maximum Stock Level by the equivalent of the bare minimum stock holding. This bare minimum could be called Minimum Lead Time Usage and is calculated as the product of Minimum

Usage and Minimum Lead Time. Thus an alternative solution to the Maximum Stock Level could be: Re-order Quantity + Minimum Stock — Minimum Lead Time Usage.

*Illustration*

| | |
|---|---|
| Re-order Quantity | 8000 |
| Re-order Level | 4000 units |
| Normal Usage | 300 units per week |
| Normal Lead Time | 4 weeks |
| Minimum Usage | 100 units per week |
| Minimum Lead Time | 2 weeks |

*Method 1*

Re-order Quantity + Minimum Stock
= 8000 + 4000 − (300 × 4)
= 8000 + 2800 = 10 800 units

*Method 2*

Re-order Quantity + Minimum Stock
  − Lead Time Usage
= 10 800 − (100 × 2) = 10 600 units

The question of which approach is adopted is entirely in the hands of the organisation and will depend on its knowledge of the industry and the material supply market. It should be noted that the calculation is really a starting point which may be modified by experience.

## Stock control records

Calculating Minimum and Maximum Stock Levels, Re-order Quantities and Re-order Levels, serves to establish some predetermined boundaries or limits around or within which we expect a control system to operate. They may be regarded as triggers which activate the whole or part of a system. For example, a Re-order Level might be established at 2000 units. When that point is reached it triggers off an action for a purchase requisition to be raised for the Re-order Quantity units.

Such an activity requires correct recording of the actual situation for comparison with the desired or predetermined situation. The activity trigger for stock control is the stock balance. Two documents constitute the basis for this: the bin card and the stores ledger card. The bin card is maintained as a storekeeper's record within the stores office. It records every transaction, in and out, as soon as possible after the physical receipt and issue of goods.

```
+-------------------------------------------------------------+
|                        BIN CARD                             |
|  Material Classification Number_____      |
|  Material Description_____     |
|  Maximum Stock_____        Re-order Level _____    |
|  Minimum Stock_____        Re-order Qty. _____    |
+----------+------------------+-------------------------------+
|          |                  |    Quantity in units of____   |
|  Date    |    Reference     +----------+---------+----------+
|          |                  | Received | Issued  | In Stock |
+----------+------------------+----------+---------+----------+
|          |                  |          |         |          |
|          |                  |          |         |          |
|          |                  |          |         |          |
```

FIGURE 8

With the current move towards more integrated systems and a wider use of more sophisticated recording systems, the bin card may seem a somewhat unnecessary duplication of work. But the usefulness of such a record will be seen when we come to consider stock audits and perpetual inventory. Figure 8 shows the form of the bin card.

We note that all the necessary information on material classification, description and stock levels, is shown, together with the means of recording the date, the reference document and the amount of actual physical movement. Given reasonable clerical efficiency there is no reason why

the right-hand column of quantity in stock should not be
regarded as the trigger activating a re-ordering process. The
problem, however, is that the storekeeper is unlikely to
know, except in very small organisations, whether the
material in question will continue to be used in the future.

The second document in the system, the stores ledger card
is shown in Figure 9. The major difference between this

| | | Received | | | Issued | | | Stock | | |
|------|-----------|------|------|-------|------|------|-------|------|------|-------|
| Date | Reference | Qty. | Rate | Value | Qty. | Rate | Value | Qty. | Rate | Value |
| | | | | | | | | | | |

STOCK LEDGER CARD

Material Description _____ Code _____

Maximum Stock Level _____ Re-order Level _____

Minimum Stock Level _____ Re-order Qty. _____

FIGURE 9

record and the bin card is that it enables us to record the
unit price and total value of stock receipts and issues. This
will provide the basis for completion of the right-hand section for stock in hand. In other words, receipts — issues =
stock.

## Stock balances

It is necessary to establish a closing stock balance. In
exercises, such a figure usually appears as part of the notes
and adjustments attached to a trial balance. We are now
required to make a more detailed study of how such a figure
is calculated and of the checks that are necessary to support
it.

Two courses are open to us: we could simply go into the stores at the end of the year or period of account and physically count and list every item of stock. Alternatively, we could list and extend all the balances on the stores ledger cards. But before we look at both methods we need to consider what differences could occur which may not be recorded anywhere at all. If this is happening in an uncontrolled manner then neither method of calculating a closing stock balance will be effective or accurate.

Such differences may be caused by one or all of three basic factors: clerical, physical or natural.

Clerical differences may arise due to:

1 Incorrect recording
2 Omitting to record
3 Miscalculations
4 Complete loss of all documents.

Physical differences may arise due to:

1 Incorrect location of goods
2 Issue of incorrect quantities
3 Correct issue of incorrect material.

Natural differences may arise due to:

1 Breaking from bulk
2 Shrinkage and evaporation
3 Breakages, deterioration, pilferage.

We should not regard all such differences as losses; some may be gains. For example, incorrect recording on the stock ledger card may have created a lower balance in the records than the stock which physically exists.

These matters constitute good reasons for having a physical count of the items in stock. For, by so doing, any losses or gains arising as a result of the three basic causes noted above will clearly be taken into account. But the demerits of adopting such a system are:

1  It is usually a lengthy and tedious operation.
2  It requires more staff to perform stock-taking than are usually employed in stores.
3  Because the extra staff employed on stock-taking are unfamiliar with the items, greater errors can occur.
4  It tends, for the above reasons, to be expensive.
5  Because of this it is usually only done once a year. It therefore cannot be regarded as a worthwhile operation unless carried out by a firm of professional valuers, which may prove to be more accurate but also more expensive.

## Perpetual inventory and continuous stocktaking

Under this system the book record of stock is accepted as an accurate record of the physical existence of materials in stores. Listing the value for each item of stock directly on to a stock sheet is a quick way of obtaining a necessary closing stock balance. Indeed, we may see that it would not even be necessary to list the individual values of each item at all but simply to accept the closing balance of the stock account contained within the accounts ledger.

To do so, however, we must be sure that two important tasks are being carried out:

1  There should be a continuous means of updating the record of every item of stock by means of a flow of documents on a day-to-day basis. After every receipt of materials, the item stock balance should be increased and after every issue of materials the item stock balance decreased. The balance of each item of stock is therefore continuously brought up to date—or, to give it the accepted title, there is a system of perpetual inventory.

2 To support the practice of perpetually updated stock or inventory balances there must be a system of physical checking. This has become known as continuous stock-taking. This entails a daily check of items in stock to verify or disprove the stock balances as recorded on the various records—bin cards, stock ledger cards and so forth. It will be seen that by carrying out such a check, many of the errors that occur could be located and corrected soon after they happen.

It would be impossible to check every item every day, but it is possible to check some items every day or even twice a day. The problem is how to establish which items should be counted daily and which, say, every other month.

Selection is based on the '80/20' or 'Pareto' phenomenon. Simply, this theory states that 80% of the value of stock is represented by 20% of the items. If we accept this then, clearly, it would be of value to check the small number of items that represent the largest value more frequently than the larger number of items whose total value is small.

To implement such a system requires an intense clerical and statistical effort.

### Stock check responsibility

In order to make the foregoing method valid it would be necessary to operate a formal reporting system. The basic requirements would be twofold—impartiality and documentation. Impartiality requires that the team of people carrying out the continuous stock-taking be members of an Internal Audit Section. If this were not possible then at least the responsibility should be attached to accounting management. Documentation is necessary to ensure that differences between actual and book values of stocks are properly recorded and incorporated into the accounting system. The basis of this would be a stock checking report as displayed in Figure 10.

With the detail contained in such a report it will be possible to record the relationship between the actual stocks and the book value of those stocks as recorded in the accounts ledger in a more meaningful and accurate manner. The con-

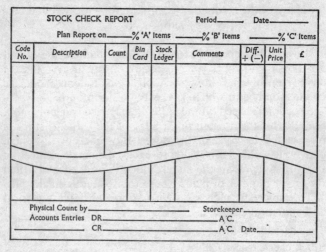

FIGURE 10

tinuous stock-taking system and the resulting reports would thus enable the closing stock balance as shown in the stock account in the ledger to be extracted as a reliable closing stock balance for the purpose of producing final accounts and balance sheets. In time, and with continuous vigilance, this procedure will negate the need for an annual physical count. Indeed it is fundamental to the production of more up-to-date control accounting at relatively short intervals.

## The issue of materials from stock

We now consider two fundamental matters, firstly, the physical transfer of materials from stock and, secondly, the value at which that transfer is to be made.

The physical issue is concerned with security and documentation. If the continuous stock-taking system described is to have any value it is clear that good storekeeping can only be as good as the physical control exercised over that

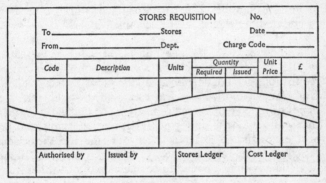

FIGURE 11

stock. Since stock represents money's worth it is reasonable that it should be kept in an enclosed space, that only authorised employees should be allowed within that area, and that the area should be secure against unauthorised entry and so forth.

The physical issue of goods should only be made against properly authorised stores requisitions as shown in Figure 11.

This document, which would be pre-numbered, would be raised in at least three copies. One copy would be retained by the originator, who would send the other two copies to stores to allow authorised withdrawal of goods from stock.

Of those two copies, stores would retain one to update their own records and, having completed the 'quantity issued' section, would then send the other copy to the stock ledger section. Here it would be priced and used to update the relevant item stock card before being forwarded to the cost accounts section.

Cost accounts are now in possession of a priced document which would enable them to charge the job, product, process or unit in question. The same document will also be used to update the balances in the accounts ledgers.

We now consider the question of the value of the issue. In the above description, it was mentioned that stores requisitions would be priced in the stock ledger section. Unfortunately, pricing is less easy than this suggests, for prices of individual items are likely to be fluctuating rather than constant. It is only when prices are constant that no problem exists and, as this is never really the case, the pricing of issues from stores has always created a problem; stock of an item is almost bound to be made up of quantities from two or more deliveries of goods supplied at slightly different prices. This does not complicate the *storage*, since goods ordered against a specification or drawing or catalogue reference look the same physically even if ordered months apart.

The problem arises when considering the accounting context: if there are two or more prices for an item of stock, which one will be used to price the stores requisition? The method chosen may affect the cost charged to the job, product, process or service and the closing value of stock, or, indeed, may affect both.

To examine the problem and be aware of its implications it is necessary to consider the three bases on which issue prices may be formulated and the variations possible within each basis:

1 Actual price basis

    (*a*)  First In First Out (F.I.F.O.)
    (*b*)  Last In First Out (L.I.F.O.)
    (*c*)  Next In First Out (N.I.F.O.)
    (*d*)  Highest In First Out (H.I.F.O.)

2 Based on actual prices

    (*a*)  Simple average
    (*b*)  Weighted average

3 Notional prices

    (*a*)  Standard price
    (*b*)  Replacement price

In order to make clear the individual effect of using each method we shall use the same information throughout. The following information relates to Material Code 27525 during the month of October.

Hardwood Battens 75 mm wide × 25 mm thick    Code 27525

October 1 — Opening Stock 500 metres at £0·40 per metre

| | Receipts | | | Issues |
| Date | Quantity in metres | Price per metre | Date | Quantity in metres |
| --- | --- | --- | --- | --- |
| Oct  1 | 1000 | £0·45 | Oct  2 | 800 |
| 4 | 1500 | £0·60 | 12 | 900 |
| 14 | 2000 | £0·80 | 20 | 1800 |
| 25 | 2000 | £1·00 | 29 | 2200 |

*First In First Out—F.I.F.O.*

The basis is that the issue price will be the same as the price of the goods first taken into stock from which the material to be priced could be drawn. That is, the first price is used until the quantity of the first receipt is exhausted, then the price of the second receipt is used, and so on.

*Illustration*

HARDWOOD STRIP Code 27525

| | Receipts | | | Issues | | | Closing Stock | | |
|---|---|---|---|---|---|---|---|---|---|
| Date | Qty | Unit Price | Total Value | Qty | Unit Price | Total Value | Qty | Unit Price | Tota Value |
| Opening Balance | | | | | | | 500 | £0·40 | £200 |
| Oct 1 | 1000 | £0·45 | £450 | | | | 1500 | | £650 |
| 2 | | | | 500 | £0·40 | | | | |
| | | | | 300 | £0·45 | £335 | 700 | | £315 |
| 4 | 1500 | £0·60 | £900 | | | | 2200 | | £1215 |
| 12 | | | | 700 | £0·45 | | | | |
| | | | | 200 | £0·60 | 435 | 1300 | | £780 |
| 14 | 2000 | £0·80 | £1600 | | | | 3300 | | £2380 |
| 20 | | | | 1300 | £0·60 | | | | |
| 25 | 2000 | £1·00 | £2000 | 500 | £0·80 | 1180 | 1500 | | £1200 |
| | | | | | | | 3500 | | £3200 |
| 29 | | | | 1500 | £0·80 | | | | |
| | | | | 700 | £1·00 | 1900 | 1300 | | £1300 |

From the illustration we note that for the issue of 800 items on October 2 it was necessary to price 500 items at the 'First In' price of £0.40 per unit, thus exhausting the stock of opening balance prices. The remaining 300 were then priced at the next 'First In' price of £0.45 per unit from the delivery of 1000 units on October 1.

The points to be noted about the use of F.I.F.O. are:

1   Issues are made at the earliest price and thus production costs tend to be undervalued in periods of rising prices and overvalued in periods of falling prices.
2   The closing balance of stock reflects a valuation approximating to the best known up-to-date value.
3   The clerical routine of pricing requires a precise cross-check between receipts and issues and a clear identification between a particular receipt and a particular issue.
4   As the basis is one of actual price, the question of whether profits or losses are made against issues does not arise.

## Last In First Out—L.I.F.O.

The basis is that the issue price will be the same as the price of the goods last taken into stock from which the material to be priced could have been drawn. That is, the last received price is used until the quantity of the last receipt is exhausted, then the price of the previous receipt is used, and so on.

*Illustration*

HARDWOOD STRIP Code 27525

| | Receipts | | | Issues | | | Closing Stock | | |
|---|---|---|---|---|---|---|---|---|---|
| Date | Qty | Unit Price | Total Value | Qty | Unit Price | Total Value | Qty | Unit Price | Total Value |
| *Opening Balance* | | | | | | | 500 | £0·40 | £200 |
| Oct 1 | 1000 | £0·45 | £450 | | | | 1500 | | £650 |
| 2 | | | | 800 | £0·45 | £360 | 700 | | £290 |
| 4 | 1500 | £0·60 | £900 | | | | 2200 | | £1190 |
| 12 | | | | 900 | £0·60 | 540 | 1300 | | £650 |
| 14 | 2000 | £0·80 | £1600 | | | | 3300 | | £2250 |
| 20 | | | | 1800 | £0·80 | 1440 | 1500 | | £810 |
| 25 | 2000 | £1·00 | £2000 | | | | 3500 | | £2810 |
| 29 | | | | 2000 | £1·00 | 2160 | 1300 | | £650 |
| | | | | 200 | £0·80 | | | | |

where the closing balance of 1300 units is made up as follows:

*Opening Balance* 500 units at £0.40 = £200

*Oct 1* Receipt 1000 less 800 issued on Oct 2

at 0·45 = 90

*Oct 4* Receipt 1500 less 900 issued on Oct 12

at 0·60 = 360

£650

This illustration demonstrates the mechanics of the system. For example the issue of October 2 for 800 units was priced at the 'Last In' price of £0·45 per unit from the receipt of October 1. With respect to the issue of 2200 units on October 29, 2000 were priced at the 'Last In' price of

£1·00 per unit which completely exhausted the receipt of October 25. The remaining 200 were priced from the next 'Last In' price of £0·80 from the receipt of October 14. The issue of 1800 units on October 20 had left just 200 units at £0·80 remaining. If another issue is to be made after October 29 and before another delivery is made, the price to be used will be £0·60 for 600 units remaining from the October 4 delivery.

The points to be noted about the use of the L.I.F.O. system are:

1 Issues are made at the latest price and thus production costs tend to reflect the best known up-to-date value.
2 The closing balance of stock is made up of the earliest prices. In a situation of rising prices, stocks would be undervalued and, in periods of falling prices, stock values tend to be overvalued.
3 The clerical routine of pricing requires a precise cross-check between receipts and issues and a clear identification between a particular receipt and a particular issue.
4 As the basis is one of actual price, the question of whether profits or losses are made against issues does not arise.

*Next In First Out— N.I.F.O.*

This system rests on the ability to predict the price of the next delivery to be taken into stock from which the material to be priced can be drawn. The basis is that of the purchase order next awaiting delivery, and the assumption is that the delivery will be made at the price quoted there.

However, because prices recorded on the stock card are likely to be different, price adjustments will be required at the point of material issue. Failure to make such adjustments, could, under conditions of violent price rise, result

*Illustration*

HARDWOOD STRIP Code 27525

| | Receipts | | | Issues | | | Closing Stock | | |
| Date | Qty | Unit Price | Total Value | Qty | Unit Price | Total Value | Qty | Unit Price | Total Value |
| --- | --- | --- | --- | --- | --- | --- | --- | --- | --- |
| *Opening Balance* | | | | | | | 500 | £0·40 | £200 |
| Oct 1 | 1000 | £0·45 | £450 | | | | 1500 | | £650 |
| 2 | | | | 800 | £0·60 | £480 | 700 | | £170 |
| Price Adjustment | | | | | | | | | |
| 2 | 800 | £0·15 | £120* | | | | — | | £290 |
| 4 | 1500 | £0·60 | £900 | | | | 2200 | | £1190 |
| 12 | | | | 900 | £0·80 | £720 | 1300 | | £470 |
| Price Adjustment | | | | | | | | | |
| 12 | 900 | £0·20 | £180* | | | | — | | £650 |
| 14 | 2000 | £0·80 | £1600 | | | | 3300 | | £2250 |
| 20 | | | | 1800 | £1·00 | £1800 | 1500 | | £1450 |
| Price Adjustment | | | | | | | | | |
| 20 | 1800 | £0·20 | £360* | | | | — | | £810 |
| 25 | 2000 | £1·00 | | | | | 3500 | | £2810 |
| 29 | | | | 2200 | £1·20 | £2640 | 1300 | | £170 |
| Price Adjustment | | | | | | | | | |
| 29 | 2000 | £0·20 | £480* | | | | — | | £650 |
| | 200 | £0·40 | | | | | | | |

in a negative value for closing stock. This would result in an absurd closing value of stock position.

You should note that without the total price adjustments of £1140 shown at * in the receipts section, the closing balance of stock shown here at £650 would, in fact, have been a negative figure of £490 (+£650−£1140)—which would be an obvious nonsense.

This illustration demonstrates that the stock value shown using this system and a simple price adjustment is exactly the same as if we were using L.I.F.O. The merit is, however, that the costs charged to the job, product, process or unit are higher than with the L.I.F.O. system. These production costs thus tend to resemble a replacement cost basis.

The points to be noted about the use of the N.I.F.O. system are:

1 Issues are made at a future price and thus tend to be inflated with respect to current known cost.

2   The closing stock value tends to reflect earlier out-of-date prices. When prices are rising, stocks would thus tend to be undervalued, and in periods of falling prices, to be overvalued.

3   The clerical routine of constantly adjusting issue prices tends to be tedious and complicated.

4   As the basis of issue is future price there is an assumption of profit against the issue of stock in periods of rising prices, and consequently distortion of profits through the accounting system. This could be overcome by an independent closing stock valuation incorporating the price adjustment, but this tends to be a complex matter.

## Highest In First Out—H.I.F.O.

The basis is that the issue price will be the highest unit price of a delivery taken into stock from which the material to be priced could have been drawn. That is, the highest unit price of a delivery is used until the units in that delivery have been exhausted, then the next highest unit price will be used, and so on.

*Illustration*

HARDWOOD STRIP Code 27525

| | | Receipts | | | Issues | | Closing Stock | | |
|---|---|---|---|---|---|---|---|---|---|
| Date | Qty | Unit Price | Qty Value | Unit | Unit Price | Total Value | Qty | Unit Price | Total Value |
| Opening Balance | | | | | | | 500 | £0·40 | £200 |
| Oct 1 | 1000 | £0·45 | £450 | | | | 1500 | | £650 |
| 2 | | | | 800 | £0·45 | £360 | 700 | | £290 |
| 4 | 1500 | £0·60 | £900 | | | | 2200 | | £1190 |
| 12 | | | | 900 | £0·60 | £540 | 1300 | | £650 |
| 14 | 2000 | £0·80 | £1600 | | | | 3300 | | £2250 |
| 20 | | | | 1800 | £0·80 | £1440 | 1500 | | £810 |
| 25 | 2000 | £1·00 | £2000 | | | | 3500 | | £2810 |
| 29 | | | | 2000 | £1·00 | £2160 | 1300 | | £650 |
| | | | | 200 | £0·80 | | | | |

Given that prices are rising and issues are always less than deliveries, the results obtained will be the same as with the L.I.F.O. system. One will also see that this system allows for the absorption of the highest prices into production soon after the delivery of the highly priced goods. The comments made about L.I.F.O. are thus applicable to H.I.F.O.

## Simple average

The price of the material issue is calculated by dividing the total of the prices of materials in stock from which the material to be issued could be drawn, by the number of prices used. For example there may be a stock of 100 units at £1·00 per unit, 300 units at £1·20 per unit, and 200 units at £1·40 per unit. By adding the prices together, i.e. £1·00 + £1·20 + £1·40 we obtain £3·60. By dividing by the number of prices, 3, we arrive at the simple average: £3·60/3 = £1·20. To use the mechanics of this with our standard demonstration shows:

*Illustration*

HARDWOOD STRIP Code 27525

| | | Receipts | | | Issues | | | Closing Stock | |
|---|---|---|---|---|---|---|---|---|---|
| Date | Qty | Unit price | Total value | Qty | Unit price | Total value | Qty | Unit price | Total value |
| Opening Balance | | | | | | | 500 | £0·40 | £200 |
| Oct 1 | 1000 | £0·45 | £450 | | (a) | | 1500 | | £650 |
| 2 | | | | 800 | £0·425 | £340 | 700 | | £310 |
| 4 | 1500 | £0·60 | £900 | | (b) | | 2200 | | £1210 |
| 12 | | | | 900 | £0·525 | £472·50 | 1300 | | £737·50 |
| 14 | 2000 | £0·80 | £1600 | | (c) | | 3300 | | £2337·50 |
| 20 | | | | 1800 | £0·70 | £1260 | 1500 | | £1077·50 |
| 25 | 2000 | £1·00 | £2000 | | (d) | | 3500 | | £3077·50 |
| 29 | | | | 2200 | £0·90 | £1980 | 1300 | | £1097·50 |

Simple Average unit rate calculatio :

$$(a) \quad \frac{£0·40 + £0·45}{2} = £0·425$$

$$(b) \quad \frac{£0·45 + £0·60}{2} = £0·525$$

$$(c) \quad \frac{£0·60 + £0·80}{2} = £0·70$$

$$(d) \quad \frac{£1·00 + £0·80}{2} = £0·90$$

The issue of October 2 is priced at (£0·40 + £0·45)/2 because 800 can be issued from the 1500 in stock. But for

the issue of October 12, the 500 prices at £0·40 each in opening stock must be assumed used at October 2, and thus only
the prices of £0·45 and £0·60 per unit can be used to calculate the simple average for the issue. From this explanation you will also perceive that the calculation of the average
requires that some sort of F.I.F.O. or L.I.F.O. decision will
need to be made. It is also quite clear that the simple average
may also be based on a N.I.F.O. or H.I.F.O. concept. If
this were done it would seem that the simple average was
being used in a more accurate and sophisticated manner. A
simple average is only as good as the components making
up the hidden bias.

To demonstrate let us look at another example. There are
in stock 1000 units at £0·80, and 10 units at 0·50, from
which the simple average would be calculated as £0·80 +
£0·50/2 = £0·65. The question should then be asked, is
£0·65 per unit a price representative of the whole stock?
Under the biased conditions in the example, it cannot be.
This, then, is the great danger of simple averages. The other
points to be noted about the use of this system are:

1  Issues are made at an average which, in the nature of
   averages, will be lower than current price in periods of
   rising prices and higher than current price in periods of
   falling prices.
2  The closing stock valuation will tend to reflect the same
   characteristics as noted for issue price.
3  The clerical routine will require precision of calculation
   together with an accurate and clear identification
   between particular receipts and particular issues.
4  As the calculations are based on actual prices the question of whether profits or losses are made against issues
   does not arise. Nevertheless the point made above with
   respect to biased simple averages must always be remembered.

*Weighted average*

The price of the material issue is calculated by dividing the total cost of the material in stock from which the material to be priced could be drawn, by the total quantity of the units of material in that stock. For example, there may be in stock:

100 units of stock at £1·00 per unit = £100
300 units of stock at £1·20 per unit = £360
200 units of stock at £1·40 per unit = £280

600 units of stock costing £740

The weighted average is £740/600 = £1·23

This should now be compared with the figure of £1·20 per unit that was obtained with the same unit prices under the section headed 'simple average'; the comments that were made with respect to the bias that should be avoided when calculating that simple average also apply here.

The use of this system is shown with the standard demonstration:

*Illustration*

HARDWOOD STRIP Code 27525

| | | Receipts | | | Issues | | | Closing Stock | |
| Date | Qty | Unit price | Total Value | Qty | Unit price | Total value | Qty | Unit price | Total value |
|---|---|---|---|---|---|---|---|---|---|
| *Opening Balance* | | | | | | | 500 | £0·40 | £200 |
| | | | | | | | | (a) | |
| Oct 1 | 1000 | £0·45 | £450 | | | | 1500 | £0·43 | £650 |
| 2 | | | | 800 | £0·43 | £346·67 | 700 | £0·43 | £303·33 |
| 4 | 1500 | £0·60 | £900 | | | | 2200 | | |
| | | | | | | | | (b) £0·54696 | |
| | | | | | | | | (c) | £1203·33 |
| | | | | | | | | £0·54 | |
| 12 | | | | 900 | £0·54 | £486 | 1300 | | £717·33 |
| 14 | 2000 | £0·80 | £1600 | | | | 3300 | | |
| | | | | | | | | (d) £0·7022 | |
| | | | | | | | | (e) | £2317·33 |
| | | | | | | | | £0·72121 | |
| 20 | | | | 1800 | £0·72121 | £1298·18 | 1500 | | £1019·15 |
| 25 | 2000 | £1·00 | £2000 | | | | 3500 | | |
| | | | | | | | | (f) £0·86261 | |
| | | | | | | | | (g) | £3019·15 |
| | | | | | | | | £0·91428 | |
| 29 | | | | 2200 | £0·91428 | £2011·41 | 1300 | | £1007·74 |

(*a*)    Calculated by £650/1500 = £0·43.
(*b*)    Calculated by £1203/2200 = £0·54696. But since 800
        have been issued there can be none of the 500 items at
        £0·40 left in stock. Therefore it is more correct to use:
(*c*)    £900 + £450/1000 + 1500 = £0·54 or some other
        basis which must clearly imply the adoption of a
        L.I.F.O./F.I.F.O./N.I.F.O./H.I.F.O. method.
(*d*)    Calculated by £2317·33/3300. But the question arises
        as to how the 3300 units are made up. Are they all the
        receipt of October 14 together with some of the deli-
        veries of October 1 and 4, or are they composed of
        some other combination? Some type of L.I.F.O./
        F.I.F.O. decision may be required, to enable us to cal-
        culate as follows:
(*e*)    For example, on a F.I.F.O. basis:

Oct.  1 delivery—none in stock
Oct.  4 delivery—1300 in stock at £0·60 per unit =      780
Oct. 14 delivery—2000 in stock at £0·80 per unit =     1600

          3300 in stock costing                        £2380

          Weighted average = £0·72121 per unit

(*f*)    £3019·15/3500 = £0·86261
(*g*)    Oct. 1 delivery—none in stock
Oct. 4 delivery—none in stock
Oct. 14 delivery—1500 in stock at £0·80 per unit = £1200
Oct. 20 delivery—2000 in stock at £1·00 per unit = £2000

          3500 in stock costing                        £3200

          Weighted average = £0·91428

There is some attraction in simplifying the situation and
saying, to calculate the weighted average, divide the total
units in stock into the total value of stock somewhat in the

manner of calculations (*a*), (*b*), (*d*) and (*f*) above. The great danger is the possibility of eventually calculating the weighted average of the weighted average. The alternative is to adhere rigidly to the definition given above, which will involve deciding whether rotation will be by L.I.F.O., F.I.F.O. or some other method.

1 Issues are being made at an average, which, in the nature of averages, will be lower than current price in periods of rising prices and higher than current price in periods of falling prices.
2 The closing stock valuation will tend to reflect the same characteristics as noted for issue price.
3 The clerical routine will require precision of calculation together with an accurate and clear identification between particular receipts and particular issues.
4 As the calculations are based on actual prices the question of whether profits or losses are made against issues does not arise.

*Periodic averages*

We may observe from the demonstration of averages that the calculation has been carried out on a rotating or moving basis. We also observe that as early deliveries are used up, their price or units and price are dropped from the calculations, and, as new deliveries are made, their price or units and price are brought into the calculation. The system thus requires tedious but precise clerical routine. This may be overcome and simplified to a great extent by adopting a 'periodic average', that is, an average calculated on prices and units in stock at a predetermined point and used for a defined period of time, such as one month, irrespective of price changes in that month.

We are now able to summarise the results obtained from

the six methods explained and demonstrated above. The following table illustrates these results.

SUMMARY   Code 27525

| Method | Receipts | | Issues | | Closing stock value | |
|---|---|---|---|---|---|---|
| | Qty | value | Qty | value | Qty | value |
| (Opening stock-balance common to all methods **500 £200**) | | | | | | |
| F.I.F.O. | 6500 | £4950 | 5700 | £3850 | 1300 | £1300 |
| L.I.F.O. | 6500 | £4950 | 5700 | £4500 | 1300 | £650 |
| N.I.F.O. | 6500 | £4950⎫ | | | | |
| N.I.F.O. | | ⎬ | 5700 | £5640 | 1300 | £650 |
| price adj | | £1140⎭ | | | | |
| H.I.F.O. | 6500 | £4950 | 5700 | £4500 | 1300 | £650 |
| SIMPLE AVERAGE | 6500 | £4950 | 5700 | £4052·50 | 1300 | £1097·50 |
| WEIGHTED AVERAGE | 6500 | £4950 | 5700 | £4142·26 | 1300 | £1007·74 |

It is clear from this table that the six methods illustrated using the same basic facts of 500 units of opening stock valued at £200, 6500 units received at a total value of £4950 and with 5700 units issued to production, have given fairly wide variations of costs charged to production and of the closing stock value. One may then be tempted to ask which is best and which is correct, questions to which there is no simple answer. The following points should be noted:

1 Given that an organisation has good material and stock control, the wide variations demonstrated in the foregoing illustrations may tend to become insignificant.
2 Organisations will have been using one or other of these systems over a considerable period. Thus the relationship between the start and finish of an accounting period may tend to be a constant.
3 Materials purchased for stock may be thought of as an anticipation of the future and are only replenished as other anticipations occur. The price of the supply is regarded as a future price.

4 Alternatively, materials purchased may be thought of as replacing stock. The price of the supply can then be regarded as 'today's' rather than 'yesterday's' price.

From these comments it may be possible to formulate an issue price policy in conjunction with consideration of the industry, the product, the process and so on. It is reasonable to suppose that these considerations, when added up, will give vastly different answers in, say, a food-producing firm whose stocks are highly perishable and where stock turn-round is quick, and a shipbuilding firm, where some goods may have been in stock for a considerable time and many items have a slow turn-round. This leads us to investigate the bases, possibilities and uses of some notional price for material issues.

Two such bases are 'replacement price' and 'standard price', both of which, in slightly different ways, assume that materials are purchased against a controlled and anticipated future use, while at the same time recognising that replenishment is necessary to fill the gap left by present use.

## Replacement price

This is based on the idea that issues from stock will be made at the market price for the materials ruling on the day of issue. It will be seen that there is a marked similarity between this basis and Next In First Out—N.I.F.O. The difference is that with N.I.F.O. we are at least in a position to judge the 'Next In' price by having in our possession the details of a replenishing order. No such document would be used for replacement price except by sheer coincidence. Theoretically, the replacement price would need to be obtained through the buying price guide published or available for that commodity. Where catalogues and price lists are available, whose constancy is acceptable between given datelines, no great problem arises. However, where material prices are subject to daily fluctuation, as in the commodities market for cocoa, cotton, gold, copper and so on, there may be extreme difficulties. The difficulties may be noted as:

1　ascertaining 'today's' prices today;
2　the complication of updating price lists on a daily or some other agreed short-term basis;
3　the complication of constantly adjusting stock values in the short term.

None the less, given some indications of price performance, for example, the Retail Price Index published in statistical tables issued by the Government, there may be a certain attraction in this system under current inflationary conditions.

## Standard price

This is a predetermined price, fixed on the basis of a specification of all the factors affecting price, fixed in advance of use, and fixed for use over a given period of time. It is usually associated with the technique of standard costing which will be examined later.

The preliminary work that goes into establishing standard prices for each individual item of stock is usually quite considerable and of a statistical nature. The setting of price requires:

1　the extraction of the range of prices paid for each individual item of material or component over a given number of previous periods;
2　establishing the relationships within that range and over the period of analysis;
3　some prediction of the possible future movements of those prices taken in conjunction with a forecast of future shortages or surpluses.

Let us use the same basic information used in illustrating the other systems, that is, Hardwood Battens—75 mm wide by 25 mm thick—Code 27525.

If we assume that in the three previous years ending September 30 the price per metre has been £0·70, £0·77, and £0·88 respectively, which displays a 25 % shift between £0·70 and £0·88. Under a condition of price change, it may be reasonable to assume a 25 % shift in price for the next year. Market demand and supply remaining constant, we would increase the £0·88 price by 25 % to £1·10 per metre and use that price as the standard price for two purposes; firstly, to re-price all the deliveries of that material and secondly, to price all issues of that material from stock to production.

Taking the first point and referring to the example used to illustrate the other systems, we see that there were 4 deliveries, on October 1, 4, 14 and 25. These would need to be re-priced as follows:

| Date | Quantity Received | Unit Delivery Price | Delivery Price Total | Unit Standard Price | Standard Price Total | Difference Standard |
|------|------|------|------|------|------|------|
| Oct 1 | 1000 | £0·45 | £450 | £1·10 | £1100 | +£650 |
| 4 | 1500 | £0·60 | £900 | £1·10 | £1650 | +£750 |
| 14 | 2000 | £0·80 | £1600 | £1·10 | £2200 | +£600 |
| 25 | 2000 | £1·00 | £2000 | £1·10 | £2200 | +£200 |
|  |  |  | £4950 |  | £7150 | +£2200 |

From this we see that during October we are committed to paying our supplier £4950 but that stores will be charged £7150. Clearly the difference of £2200 must be taken into account. More formally, the bookkeeping entries will be:

DR Raw Material Stock     £7150
CR Creditors (Supplier)     £4950
CR Material Price Variance     £2200

It may seem from this that we are going to build up credit

balances, and thus profits, in the Material Price Variance account. But remember, during the following months we are likely to pay more than the standard price of £1·10 per unit for future deliveries. This will mean that the difference or Material Price Variance will be debited to Material Price Variance account. If the forecasts about unit price have been correct, then theoretically there should be a zero balance on Material Price Variance account at the end of the year.

We note that materials are being held in stock at a constant or standard price. The second matter mentioned above should become apparent. That is, all issues from stock can be priced at standard. This means that the stores ledger or stock card recording system can be greatly simplified because we can dispense with all notation of value and unit price columns. We simply record in quantities columns, because all movement in and out of stock is happening at standard price.

Because value and price recording is no longer required, the information on the stock card can be concentrated into a smaller area and directed at quantity control—which is really the important basis of good stock control.

It should however be borne in mind that although a standard price system gives constancy of product costs per unit of usage throughout the period of validity of that standard price, it is still only a forecast or estimate. It must therefore be constantly reviewed during the period of validity and, if circumstances warrant, it should be amended.

## Stock valuation

We have now seen the basic methods by which material deliveries to and issues from stock can be recorded. We have seen the effect that each system may have on production costs and closing stock values. It has been said that if we can constantly check the physical state of the stock, and have confidence in the monetary values attached to those movements, then stock valuation could be obtained by listing the closing values of each stores ledger or stock card.

It must also be recognised that stock valuation has been approached by the accountant in a conservative, even pessimistic manner for a considerable number of years. Over this time a convention of valuation has been established i.e. valuing stock at cost or net realisable value, whichever is the lower.

The question of whether the convention conflicts with the systems described here would require another chapter. In general terms it is reasonable to accept that the convention would tend to give lower values under normal conditions. But the question arises as to what *is* a normal condition.

It should be remembered that in reporting to management we will be aiming at consistency, accuracy and speed. Thus if the same basis of valuation of any element of cost has been applied consistently throughout the period under review, then it is reasonable to assume that final values, including closing stocks, will be as accurately valued as the system allows and that profit reporting will be of the same consistency and quality.

## Exercises

1  MC Manufacturing Company Limited's system of material control is relatively inefficient. As management accountant to the company you have been requested by the managing director to recommend an economic system of stock levels to improve the control of material stocks. These comprise a large range of items of varying values. In preparing your report to the managing director you should:

(a) state your approach to establishing stock levels and the major factors to be considered in setting them;
(b) explain how these levels would operate;
(c) indicate briefly the main advantages to be derived from the system. (ICMA)

2 The following information is given for material XYZ:

| Stock levels: | Maximum | 3000 units |
| | Minimum | 500 units |
| Re-order level: | when free balance reaches | 800 units |
| Re-order quantity: | | 1000 units |

Opening balances at February 1 included:

| Stock in hand | 800 units |
| Ordered from supplier awaiting delivery | 1100 units |
| Allocated to jobs | 600 units |

Transactions for the three months ending April 30 included:

| | February | March | April |
| --- | --- | --- | --- |
| Received | 600 | 1200 | 1800 |
| Issued | 700 | 1800 | 1100 |
| Allocated | 900 | 2300 | 700 |
| Returns to stores | 300 | 200 | 100 |
| Returns to supplier (not replaceable) | 100 | 400 | 200 |
| Transfers from Production Department A to Production Department B | 300 | — | 400 |

You are required to:

(a) design a stores record card to provide for the information given above;
(b) enter on the stores record card the transactions for the three months for material XYZ using the details given, and show the respective balances at each month-end. (ICMA)

3 Y Limited has recently appointed a new stores controller, who has decided to introduce a new stores control system. He has asked you, as cost accountant, to design for him a new materials code. You are required to prepare a report to the stores controller in which you should briefly:

(a) explain the principles to be observed in designing a materials classification code;

(b) state the advantages of such a coding system in a system of stores control.

Assume that the design of your system of coding has been completed. Included in the range of Y Limited's products is a series of flat sections of varying dimensions and in four different raw materials: aluminium, brass, copper and stainless steel. Examples of coding of two of these are:

| Material | Dimensions | | | Code Number |
| | length | thickness | width | |
| --- | --- | --- | --- | --- |
| Stainless Steel | 4 ft 0 ins | 7 ft 8 ins | 3¾ ins | 04081415 |
| Brass | 8 ft 6 ins | 1⅜ ins | 2 ins | 02172208 |

(c) Determine the code for the following:

Aluminium 6 ft 6 ins × ¼ in × 3½ ins
Copper      1 ft × ⅜ in × 4¼ ins

(d) Describe the type of bar as defined by these codes:

03112903
01071721

(ICMA)

4 During the last year, your company has installed a system of stock control which includes the maintaining of stock levels. As cost accountant to the company, you have been requested by the managing director, who is

not an accountant, to explain briefly and clearly how the system of stock levels works. To illustrate your report, use the data given below for material H and:

(a)  show how the maximum, minimum, re-order and average stock levels would be calculated;

(b)  calculate the stores turnover rate.

| Month | Budget consumption in units |
|---|---|
| January | 600 |
| February | 600 |
| March | 1000 |
| April | 1200 |
| May | 1600 |
| June | 2000 |
| July | 2000 |
| August | 2000 |
| September | 2000 |
| October | 1800 |
| November | 1200 |
| December | 800 |

Delivery period from suppliers:

Maximum — 4 months
Minimum — 2 months
Average  — 3 months

Re-order quantity—4000 units.                    (ICMA)

5  The stores ledger account for a certain material for the month of October includes the data given below. You are to assume the following alternative methods are being considered and are required to calculate the values of:

(a)  the stores loss at October 31 using the First In First Out system;

(b)  issues of five of the following:

  1  October 27 using Last In First Out system

2 October 22 using Highest In First Out system
3 October 14 using Next In First Out system
4 October 27 using simple average system
5 October 9 using weighted average system

| | | Ordered | | | Received | | | Issued | | | Stock | |
|---|---|---|---|---|---|---|---|---|---|---|---|---|
| | Q | P | A | Q | P | A | Q | P | A | Q | P | A |
| October 1 | | | | | | | | | | 420 | £1·20 | |
| 2 | 500 | £1·25 | | | | | | | | | | |
| 5 | | | | | | | 200 | | | | | |
| 7 | | | | 300 | £1·25 | | | | | | | |
| 9 | | | | | | | 400 | | | | | |
| 10 | | | | 200 | £1·25 | | | | | | | |
| 12 | 500 | £1·20 | | | | | | | | | | |
| 14 | | | | | | | 200 | | | | | |
| 15 | 500 | £1·30 | | | | | | | | | | |
| 16 | | | | 400 | £1·20 | | | | | | | |
| 19 | | | | | | | 300 | | | | | |
| 20 | | | | 100 | £1·20 | | | | | | | |
| 21 | | | | 200 | £1·30 | | | | | | | |
| 22 | | | | | | | 300 | | | | | |
| 23 | 500 | £1·35 | | | | | | | | | | |
| 24 | | | | 300 | £1·30 | | | | | | | |
| 26 | | | | 200 | £1·35 | | | | | | | |
| 27 | | | | | | | 400 | | | | | |
| 28 | | | | 300 | £1·35 | | | | | | | |
| 29 | 500 | £1·25 | | | | | | | | | | |
| 30 | | | | | | | 200 | | | | | |
| 31 | Actual stock in hand | | | | | | | | | 380 | | |

*Key*

Q = Quantity
P = Price
A = Amount

(ICMA adapted)

# 4

# Labour

## Introduction

The second element of cost, labour, represents the human input to production and its associated activities. Its importance as a cost can be gauged by the amount of control and analysis that organisations are prepared to devote to its measurement.

We find some industries where the input of labour is large relative to total cost, for example in the hand-assembly of intricate and delicate instruments. In others the proportion of labour cost to total cost would be quite small, for example, in a mass-production firm where large, expensive units of machinery are operated by one person.

In Chapter 1 we discussed the characteristics of cost and cost behaviour. If we apply this to labour cost, in general terms, there is a certain portion of wages paid that is constant irrespective of work done, that is, the fixed portion of wages. The remainder, the variable wage, will tend to move more or less in proportion to changes in production.

For example, given a guaranteed weekly wage payment of £10·00, with additional payments at £1 per unit produced, inspected and passed, we demonstrate cost behaviour as follows:

*Illustration*

| Production (units passed inspection) | 1 £ | 4 £ | 10 £ | 20 £ |
|---|---|---|---|---|
| Fixed portion of wages | 10·00 | 10·00 | 10·00 | 10·00 |
| Additional production payments at £1 per unit | 1·00 | 4·00 | 10·00 | 20·00 |
| Total Labour Cost | £11·00 | £14·00 | £20·00 | £30·00 |
| Unit Cost (Total/Production) = | £11·00 | £3·50 | £2·00 | £1·50 |

—which may be shown graphically as in Figure 12.

We note the shape of the curve, which indicates a decreasing unit cost with increasing activity. Furthermore, as activity increases, the decrease in unit labour cost becomes less marked.

But even if we were to regard all wage payment as a fixed cost, or in other words the payment of a constant sum of money per period irrespective of the activity per period, then the greater the activity the lower becomes the unit labour cost. This can be illustrated using the same figures as above:

*Illustration*

| Production (units passed inspection) | 1 | 4 | 10 | 20 |
|---|---|---|---|---|
| Wages per period | £10 | £10 | £10 | £10 |
| Unit cost of labour: $\dfrac{\text{Wages Cost}}{\text{Production}} =$ | $\dfrac{£10}{1}$ | $\dfrac{£10}{4}$ | $\dfrac{£10}{10}$ | $\dfrac{£10}{20}$ |
| = | £10 | £2·50 | £1·00 | £0·50 |

With rising wage rates and the payment of more and higher fringe benefits, it would seem to be an advantage to consider, where possible, means of increasing production which reduce unit labour costs.

However, wage payments are still directly geared to the capability and skill of the operative. Productivity or output

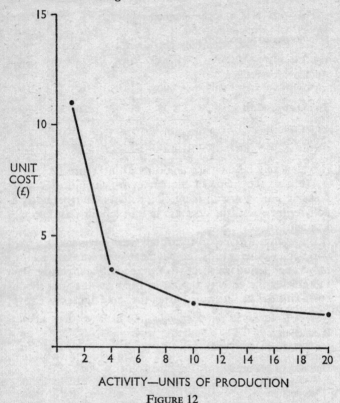

ACTIVITY—UNITS OF PRODUCTION

FIGURE 12

per real man hour is not just a matter of installing bigger, faster, or more sophisticated machinery. It is also necessary to employ properly selected staff, to see that staff are properly motivated, to be able to exercise control over factors such as these and finally to operate a system of monetary measurement and accountability to evaluate the outcome.

This text will not be concerned with the behavioural aspect of staff/management relations and motivations. Nevertheless the intending accountant should take every opportunity of finding out how these matters are dealt with.

## The personnel function

Although this work does not extend to a study of this specialist area, we should nevertheless be aware that the personnel function provides records on which a wages department can act.

Only properly inducted people will appear on the payroll; it is they who figure in the records produced by the wages department for subsequent incorporation into financial and cost accounting records. Those records must be quite explicit with respect not only to existing employees but also to new and terminating employees.

## Labour turnover

This term refers to the frequency and cause of termination of employment. The frequency is usually calculated as a percentage, in the form

$$\frac{\text{Number of Terminations}}{\text{Average Number on Payroll}} \times \frac{100}{1}$$

There may however be some sense in modifying this calculation slightly so as to consider only those terminations where replacement is necessary. Clearly, where reorganisation is taking place, and where a redundancy policy is being pursued, there will be some employees who become anxious about their job and seek alternative employment before any threatened unemployment affects them. It would only confuse the issue if this natural wastage factor were included in a calculation of labour turnover. The alternative form is thus:

$$\frac{\text{Number of Replacements Needed}}{\text{Average Number on Payroll}} \times \frac{100}{1}$$

The percentage for the firm as a whole would, if calculated, say, weekly or monthly, indicate a trend. It would be rather more informative if it could be calculated for each department or section, for then the trends between departments would be discernible and the figures would thus be more useful to those taking action.

However, the more important aspect is to attempt to discover causes, so as to give the firm, and its individual managers, the means of halting an increasing trend or lowering an existing figure.

To carry this out would require all persons terminating their employment to be routed through the personnel department, for two important reasons: firstly, so that personnel department records can be updated and the record card removed from records of current employees; secondly, so that all terminal documents can be checked and handed over to the terminating employee at an interview. At this interview, the personnel department attempts to discover the cause of termination.

The reasons given by the terminating employee can usually be classified either as 'controllable' (e.g. pay and conditions, relationships with superiors, or social and welfare reasons) or as 'uncontrollable' (e.g. transport, pregnancy, or domestic reasons).

If these causes can be established by the personnel department for each termination, a percentage of labour turnover can be calculated, and its causes incorporated in a report.

Such a report may take the form demonstrated in Figure 13. From this, discernible and recurrent causes and trends may be observed. In the case of 'controllable' causes, such as relationships with superiors, effective action can be taken in an attempt to obviate the cause and thus decrease the turnover. In the matter of 'uncontrollable' reasons, there may be some case to be made for adjusting the present policy for interviews and engagements: applicants with apparent travel

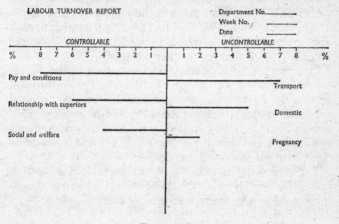

FIGURE 13

(With acknowledgements to *The Cost of Labour Turnover*, ICMA)

or domestic problems could then be diplomatically guided away from employment.

## Classification and coding

How do we differentiate between one employee and the next? In a small company of a hundred employees, visual differentiation by managers, supervisors and wages clerks may be possible. In an organisation with five thousand employees, the personnel department, or indeed any other administration department, would find it much harder to carry out such a visual identification. The supervisor of the department might be able to identify individuals but it is doubtful whether he could transmit such visual information to anyone else.

Aside from physical identification there is the very important matter of recording which employee performed which task. Thus, some means of identification is required. The problem is usually solved by assigning a number to each employee, normally referred to as that person's 'works number', 'clock number' or 'key number'.

One method of allocating clock numbers to employees would be to start with the number 1 and carry on through, so that the next person engaged would simply be assigned the next available number on some list or register. This system would be untidy and would not meet the requirements of a good classification system, which are that it should be flexible, expandable and descriptive.

Let us consider an example of an acceptable classification system for employees. It should be noted that we are assigning numbers in an attempt to classify every situation.

### Illustration

The firm, in general terms, knows that of every thousand employees 75% are male, 25% are female and that there are three grades, skilled, semi-skilled and unskilled. A table classifying these facts may be as follows:

|              | *Male*    | *Female* |
|--------------|-----------|----------|
| Skilled      | 1–100     | 751–800  |
| Semi-skilled | 101–600   | 801–900  |
| Unskilled    | 601–750   | 901–999  |

The firm also has five departments, each with two or more sections. These departments and sections could be listed and numbered as follows:

| DEPARTMENT | | SECTION | |
|---|---|---|---|
| *Number* | *Title* | *Number* | *Title* |
| 1 | Lathes | 1 | Capstan Lathes |
| | | 2 | Centre Lathes |
| | | 3 | Automatic Lathes |
| 2 | Drills | 1 | Single-Spindle Drills |
| | | 2 | Multi-Spindle Drills |
| 3 | Mills | 1 | Horizontal Mills |
| | | 2 | Vertical Mills |
| 4 | Assembly | 1 | Components |
| | | 2 | Sub Assembly |
| | | 3 | Main Assembly |
| 5 | Administration and Service | 1 | Managers |
| | | 2 | Supervisors |
| | | 3 | Clerical and Typists |
| | | 4 | Technical |
| | | 5 | Labourers |

The breakdown of people by grade and sex, and the listing and numbering of departments and sections can now be combined to give a classification or identification system, as in the following three examples:

1   A skilled male operative employed as a centre lathe-turner has a works or clock number 12046. The first and second numbers indicate department and section and the last three numbers his grade, i.e. 'male skilled'.

2   A female typist would probably have, as her personal works number, 53777, to indicate where she worked i.e. Administration, clerical and typists—53, and her grade—777—indicating 'female skilled'.

3   The managing director could be allocated number 51001!

In the five departments listed there are fifteen sections, i.e. 11 to 55. In each of those fifteen sections it is possible to classify 1000 employees. Thus this simple system is capable of identifying 15 000 different people. It would not require a great deal of thought to see that it would be possible to classify in a much more sophisticated and wider manner, in such a way as to identify employees, not just with a particular section, but even with a particular machine or office location.

## Time recording

Having discovered something about labour input and its classification it is now time for us to look at the price or value aspect of labour cost.

The method of finding out such values depends on the means available to record labour time. It is necessary to establish two quite distinct elements:

1　Attendance time. That is to say, how many hours did the employee spend in the organisation in a particular period?
2　Work or job or activity time. That is to say, how was the employee used during the hours he attended in a particular period?

It should be noted that the existence of both records for an employee provides a useful way of comparing attendance with activity time. From this comparison it may then be possible to establish a relationship and discover the degree of labour utilisation.

There are two criteria for time recording: reliability and accuracy; and there are two ways in which such time recording may be carried out: manually and mechanically.

### Manual methods

These require employees to complete some form of time or work sheet, as in Figure 14, or to make entries in some form of time or work book. Such forms or books may be as simple or as complicated as circumstances dictate. They may be for attendance or work time or, as in Figure 14, a combination of both.

If we apply the two requirements, it would have to be admitted that this form of recording could not be readily acceptable as either reliable or accurate. This is not to say that the employees completing such documents are not to be trusted, but that it is human nature to record after the event rather than at the event. Thus heavy reliance is placed on

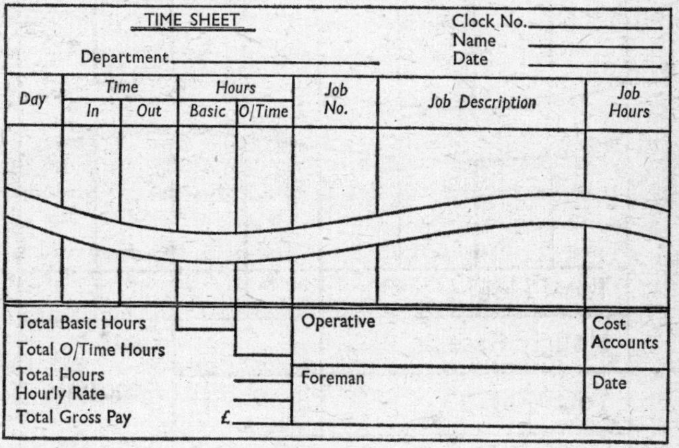

FIGURE 14

memory to complete time or work sheets. On that basis alone we must reject most manual methods as unreliable and inaccurate.

## Mechanical methods

These require the use of some mechanical time recorder in conjunction with a clock card such as displayed in Figure 15. There are several brands of recorders and cards all of which

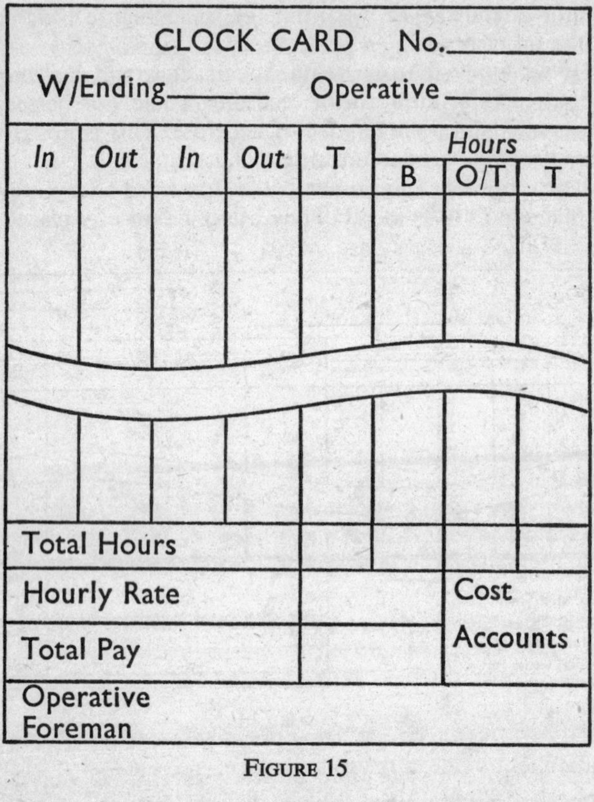

| | | | | | CLOCK CARD | No._____ |
|---|---|---|---|---|---|---|

The clock card figure:

| In | Out | In | Out | T | Hours | | |
|---|---|---|---|---|---|---|---|
| | | | | | B | O/T | T |
| | | | | | | | |

CLOCK CARD   No._____
W/Ending_____   Operative_____

| In | Out | In | Out | T | B | O/T | T |
|---|---|---|---|---|---|---|---|
| | | | | | | | |
| Total Hours | | | | | | | |
| Hourly Rate | | | Cost | | | | |
| Total Pay | | | Accounts | | | | |
| Operative Foreman | | | | | | | |

FIGURE 15

require a similar procedure. For recording attendance time, a clock card bearing the employee's name and identifying number is placed in a rack next to the clock recorder. The rack is usually in two parts, one labelled '*IN*' on one side of the clock recorder, another labelled '*OUT*' on the other side.

On entering the works the employee removes his card

from the '*OUT*' rack, inserts it into the clock recorder and either by exerting slight pressure on the card or depressing a lever on the clock recorder, is able to stamp the time shown by the clock recorder on to the face of his clock card. He then places the stamped card in the '*IN*' rack. The procedure is reversed on leaving the works.

The simplicity and rapidity of such a system has much to commend it. But, more important, the two criteria of reliability and accuracy are met.

## Work or job or activity time

In accounting for labour, the clock card showing attendance time is evidence that time has been purchased from the employee. In accounting for labour cost we need a system to show the specific task to which the labour time so acquired can be charged.

We could again consider a daily or weekly time sheet, but we would have to accept that there may be a great element of unreliability and inaccuracy.

Alternatively we may consider using individual job or work or activity cards or tickets, a new card or ticket being made out for each new job started by each employee; this however, may lead to a proliferation of job cards. The use of either system will, of course, be dictated by the needs and size of the organisation. The job card system requires more personnel to run, but the time sheet system will be slower and less accurate, and probably just as costly, if not more so, in the long term.

It may be possible to achieve economies by a combined record of both the attendance and the job time. This could be done by locating the clock recorder, together with a time clerk, at or near an appropriate production point or centre. The time clerk's duties would then be twofold; firstly, to keep the attendance clock card system in order, and secondly, to issue and receive job cards at the start and finish of each job.

Such a system would have to be completely integrated with the production control system which will always decide what work is to be done and in what order.

Word of mouth or informal information would not suffice. A clearly defined instruction must be an integral part of the system. This could be achieved by the use of a card as outlined in Figure 16.

| MATERIALS OR COMPONENTS USED | | | Job Card No.: _____ | |
| | | | Part or Drawing No.: _____ | |
| | | | Cost Code No.: _____ | |
| Operation No. | Job Description | | Time Allowed | Quantity Required |
| | | | | |
| | | | | |
| Start Date | Required by | Finish Date | Passed Inspection _____ Inspector _____ | |

FIGURE 16

It can be seen that the face of the card can be designed so as to give a set of fairly precise instructions to everyone concerned. It also allows for the completed work to be inspected and the outcome recorded. The reverse of the card would be ruled in a similar fashion to the clock card shown in Figure 15.

## Work study

The importance of work study cannot be over-emphasised, for two reasons: firstly it allows us to establish that the materials and components are being processed in the correct manner within an acceptable time scale; secondly, it enables us to co-ordinate the production resources in the most effective and efficient manner. The second matter has already been mentioned as being a sphere of specialisation and expertise that the avid student should follow up for himself.

The first matter is also a sphere of expertise that can be gainfully studied from a specialised text.

Work study covers two distinct but closely related areas: method study and work measurement. Method study sets out to ensure that, given that the materials and components to be used are acceptable, the method by which those materials and components are being processed is also the best.

Having obtained satisfaction on these points the work study engineer proceeds to work measurement, that is, the measurement of work performance by time. Every operation is broken down into elements and each element timed by a stop-watch. Checking and re-checking of these element times is carried out for the same elements of the same operation over a number of operatives. Allowances for fatigue, delay and personal time are incorporated so that after rigorous examination and re-examination a time allowance for an operation can be established.

This time allowance can then be incorporated in job records and will appear in the column headed 'time allowed' in Figure 16.

## Employee remuneration and incentive

A general theory of remuneration has evolved, requiring that a remuneration system:

1 Should be simple, that is to say, easy to understand and easy to calculate. Complex systems cause discontent among employees and a high work-load in wages departments.
2 Should be reasonable, that is to say, it must offer a fair

day's pay for a fair day's work. The fact that two divergent answers can be obtained to this requirement is probably the biggest single cause of disagreement between employer and employee.

3 Should take into account the relationship between quality and quantity of outputs required. It would be an unusual situation where high quality and large outputs were obtained simultaneously.

4 Should be based on an acceptable method of work measurement and unit of work definition.

5 Should take into account differences of training and occupation, that is to say, a recognition of skill differential.

6 Should recognise the values attached to skills and occupations by other employers in other industries and in other parts of the country.

## Bases of remuneration

It is clear from the foregoing that employees will be paid for the time that they are in attendance. There may however be other alternative or additional payments due to them when they achieve a particular output or production target. It is possible to formulate two distinct bases of remuneration: 'Time-based' and 'Incentive-based'.

### 'Time-based'

This is usually referred to as a time rate or day rate and is the oldest method of remuneration.

Payment is made by the hour, day, week, month or year. In many organisations production workers are paid hourly, clerical and junior supervisory staffs are paid weekly, senior staff and executives are paid monthly. It is a simple method requiring only a reasonable amount of clerical effort.

In many classifications of work it is usually the only workable method of payment, for example, for clerical staff, labourers, tool-makers and managing directors. In general terms we would find it difficult, if not impracticable, to attempt to set or assess times or rates within which certain types of operation could be performed or achieved.

'Time rates' are a simple, straightforward and well-understood method of payment which cause little dissatisfaction provided that skill differentials are recognised.

However, they offer no inducement towards increased productivity, and close supervision and keen management are needed to ensure that acceptable levels of work loads are maintained: the skilled and energetic employee will receive exactly the same pay as the skilled and less energetic employee. Setting aside the question of personal satisfaction, time rates offer no inducement for the skilled person to maintain output levels.

*'Incentive-based'*

In contrast with the time-based payment by the hour, week or month, 'incentive-based' methods measure an operative's output and pay him in accordance with some predetermined method of reward.

This overcomes some of the disadvantages of time-based systems of payment, for two distinct reasons: firstly, it rewards the employee in proportion to his effort; secondly, it can encourage greater effort as a means of achieving higher pay. It must also be noted that advantages accrue to the firm, in that the fixed costs are spread over increased outputs and thus lead towards decreased unit costs.

However, the success of such incentive-based rewards is almost completely dependent on the ability of someone in the firm to set acceptable standards of performance.

There are two bases for incentive payment—work and results.

## Work-based

The methods evolved in this area are usually referred to as piecework and can be classified as either 'straight piecework' or 'differential piecework'.

### 'Straight piecework'

There are two forms of straight piecework, 'money piecework' and 'time piecework'.

Money piecework implies the fixing of a stated price per unit of output produced, so that payment for work performed depends entirely on output and not time taken. The price per unit is established by the firm after consideration of the time involved, since otherwise the money piece rate would not be acceptable to the employee.

Fixing money piece rates requires experience, skill and sound judgement. An unduly low rate causes friction with employees, whilst an unduly high rate will cause loss to the firm.

To see how a money piecework system operates, consider the following data:

| | |
|---|---|
| Basic pay for 40 hour week | £20·00 |
| Money piece rate for operation 6 on Component T72 | £0·40 per unit |
| Hours clocked in a particular week | 40 |
| Output range of units | 10; 20; 30; 40; 50 |

A table showing the wages earned over a range of outputs would be as follows:

*Illustration*

| | | | | | |
|---|---|---|---|---|---|
| Attendance hours | 40 | 40 | 40 | 40 | 40 |
| Output units | 10 | 20 | 30 | 40 | 50 |
| Basic weekly wage | £20 | £20 | £20 | £20 | £20 |
| Money piecework earnings (Output × money piece rate) | 4 | 8 | 12 | 16 | 20 |
| Total wages | £24 | £28 | £32 | £36 | £40 |
| Unit Labour Cost (Wage/Output) | £2·40 | £1·40 | £1·06 | £0·90 | £0·80 |

Furthermore, if we assume that the foregoing earnings were made in a week of 40 hours, then the composite rate per hour can be calculated at £0·60, £0·70, £0·80, £0·90 and £1·00 respectively. These results are shown graphically in Figure 17. We note two effects; firstly, 'the straight line' effect of piecework earnings and hourly wage rate under the assumptions made; secondly, the drop in unit labour cost as productivity increases. But we again see that the drop is less dramatic at high levels of activity than at low levels.

We now turn to the other form of straight piecework known as time piecework. This requires the fixing of a standard time for an operation, and a standard rate per hour for the grade of labour usually used on that type of operation. As with money piecework it is also usual, under current conditions, to pay a basic weekly wage irrespective of piecework earnings. This guaranteed minimum basic rate is likely to be less than that encountered in money piecework systems.

To illustrate the mechanics of the system let us assume the following information:

| | |
|---|---|
| Guaranteed minimum for all hours of attendance clocked | £0·50 per hour |
| Time piece rate for operation 2 on job number 64 | 48 minutes |
| Output range of units | 10: 20: 30: 40: 50 |

Total weekly pay would be calculated as follows:

| | |
|---|---|
| Basic pay for 40 hours @ £0·50 per hour | £20·00 |
| Time Piecework = (Output × Piece rate) × £0·50 per hour e.g. (20 × 48/60) × £0·50 = 16 hours @ £0·50 | £8·00 |
| Total Pay | £28·0 |

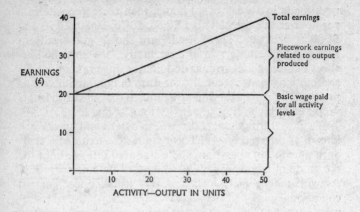

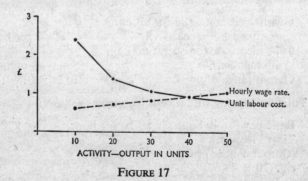

FIGURE 17

Taking the basic facts and assuming different output levels in the same number of hours we obtain:

| Attendance hours | 40 | 40 | 40 | 40 | 40 |
|---|---|---|---|---|---|
| Output units | 10 | 20 | 30 | 40 | 50 |
| Basic weekly wage | £20 | £20 | £20 | £20 | £20 |
| Time piecework at 48 minutes per unit | 4 | 8 | 12 | 16 | 20 |
| Total wages | £24 | £28 | £32 | £36 | £40 |
| Unit labour cost | £2·40 | £1·40 | £1·06 | £0·90 | £0·80 |

which gives the same answers as for the illustration of money piecework above; thus, Figure 17 would still apply.

It should be realised of course, that if lower levels of output are achieved in less than 40 hours the unit labour cost and the earned rate per hour will tend to go towards the results achieved for the output level of 50 units.

### 'Differential piecework'

In general, this system has gradations or steps which offer low reward for low effort but proportionally higher reward for increased effort. This stepped or differential system thus purports to encourage low-output workers to increase their productivity. However, it may also 'stop off' the high-output operatives if it appears to them that there is really no sense in extra hard work to achieve a proportionally smaller reward.

The setting of differential piece rates requires the crucial task of setting some norm or standard level of achievement. Once that point has been established, then for outputs of less than the standard task, lower piece rates would be offered. For outputs above the standard, proportionally higher piece rates would be offered.

If the same basic data is used as for the illustration for money piecework, differential piece rates might be established by calculations from the following information:

| Basic pay for hours clocked | £0·50 per hour |
| Standard output. Units per week | 50 units |
| Piece-rate for Operation 6 Component T72 | |
| At standard output per unit | £0·40 |
| At all other outputs | £0·008 (Output²) |

from which we could obtain the sliding scale or differential piecework rate per unit as follows:

| Output (units) | 10 | 20 | 30 | 40 | 50 | 60 | 70 |
|---|---|---|---|---|---|---|---|
| Output² | 100 | 400 | 900 | 1600 | 2500 | 3600 | 4900 |
| £0·008 (0²) | £0·80 | £3·20 | £7·20 | £12·80 | £20·00 | £28·80 | £39·20 |
| $\dfrac{£0·008\ (0²)}{\text{output}}$ = unit piece rate | £0·08 | £0·16 | £0·24 | £0·32 | £0·40 | £0·48 | £0·56 |

The factor—0·008—in the above illustration is but one example of the range of possibilities. It would clearly need an intensive work study before it could be established.

Thus the piece rate for work on this component would be stated in accordance with the last line of the schedule. That is, for every ten units of output increase, there would be an increase of eight pence in piece rate paid. The outcome of such a scheme could be illustrated graphically as in Figure 18.

The important point to note is that although the rate per hour continually increases, the unit labour cost decreases to the point of standard output and then begins to increase. Clearly, it is important to achieve standard outputs quickly and consistently in order to make the system beneficial to both parties. Whether some alternative scheme would then come into operation to continue to give decreasing, or at least constant, unit labour costs consistent with continued increased earnings per hour, may be a matter for further discussion.

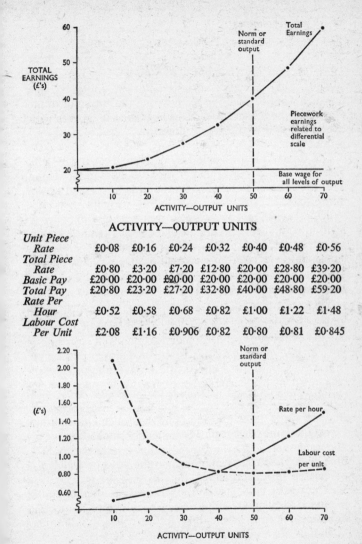

## ACTIVITY—OUTPUT UNITS

| | | | | | | | |
|---|---|---|---|---|---|---|---|
| Unit Piece Rate | £0·08 | £0·16 | £0·24 | £0·32 | £0·40 | £0·48 | £0·56 |
| Total Piece Rate | £0·80 | £3·20 | £7·20 | £12·80 | £20·00 | £28·80 | £39·20 |
| Basic Pay | £20·00 | £20·00 | £20·00 | £20·00 | £20·00 | £20·00 | £20·00 |
| Total Pay | £20·80 | £23·20 | £27·20 | £32·80 | £40·00 | £48·80 | £59·20 |
| Rate Per Hour | £0·52 | £0·58 | £0·68 | £0·82 | £1·00 | £1·22 | £1·48 |
| Labour Cost Per Unit | £2·08 | £1·16 | £0·906 | £0·82 | £0·80 | £0·81 | £0·845 |

FIGURE 18

## Results-based

These systems are generally described as Premium Bonus systems. They take as their basis a combination of the time in which work could be performed, and the output or results that could be achieved in that time. They thus attempt to overcome some of the disadvantages displayed by piecework systems.

The underlying principle of Premium Bonus or results-based systems is to give the operative a share in the saving, with the remainder accruing to the firm; the argument for doing so is that the increase in output is usually associated with increased effort by the operative together with improvement in equipment and organisation, which requires capital investment by the firm. Thus the firm is entitled to a share in any savings arising from increased outputs.

## Premium Bonus systems

Premium Bonus systems, although different in detail, all have two essential characteristics; firstly, a basic wage calculated by the product of attendance hours and basic hourly rate, and secondly, a bonus based on the relationship between the time allowed and the time taken and usually calculated on the operative's basic pay. Under such systems certain advantages are claimed:

1 Operatives' basic pay and bonus are calculated in hours on the same basic rate. The system of calculation is thus simple.
2 The method of sharing time and the basis on which it is calculated is acceptable.
3 Because of 1 and 2 above, operatives of different grades and skills who are employed on the same work are paid according to their standing. In other words, skill differentials are automatically made in the system.

4 There is a minimum wage. Thus, even with bad materials or excessive disorganisation there is no chance of operatives not receiving any wages at all.

5 There is a direct incentive to strive for higher outputs because the reward increases more than proportionally to the effort expended.

6 The operatives who work consistently at high productivity levels receive the most money.

We can observe from the foregoing comments that the specialism of work study plays an important role in determining the time to be allowed for achieving certain outputs.

We also observe from the foregoing discussion that results-based systems have the characteristic of shared time saving. The sharing may be done by two methods, 'direct' or 'proportional'.

The direct method uses an agreed and consistent percentage of time saved as the basis for bonus calculation. The most widely known of such systems is the 'Halsey'. This offers 50% of time saved as the bonus.

*Illustration*

| | |
|---|---|
| Time allowed (TA) for Job 123 | 10 hours |
| Time taken (TT) | 8 hours |
| Time saved (TA − TT) | 2 hours |
| Halsey bonus hours. 50% × Time saved | 1 hour |

The operative thus receives 9 hours' pay (Time Taken + Bonus hours) for 8 hours' work.

The proportional methods are based on an agreed relationship between the time allowed, time taken and time saved. The most widely known of such systems is the 'Rowan' system. This offers bonus hours equal to the proportion of time taken that time saved bears to time allowed. More formally:

$$\text{Bonus hours} = \frac{\text{Time saved}}{\text{Time allowed}} \times \text{Time taken}$$

### Illustration

| | |
|---|---:|
| Time allowed (TA) for Job 123 | 10 hours |
| Time taken (TT) | 8 hours |
| Time saved (TS) or (TT − TA) | 2 hours |
| Rowan Bonus hours = (TS/TA)TT | |
|          = (2/10)8 = | 1·6 hours |

The operative thus receives 9·6 hours' pay (Time taken + Bonus hours) for 8 hours' work.

It should be noted that although the Rowan system (indeed, like all proportional systems) yields a higher bonus for the smaller amounts of time saved than does the Halsey system, the latter offers greater gain to the operative, the greater the time saved.

The results of both systems over a varying range of time saved is shown in Figure 19.

The greater the opportunity taken by the operative to save time (consistent with good units produced) the more time is available for that operative to go on to other bonus work, and, thus, increase his total earnings.

This combination of increased activity with high earnings will show a benefit to the firm of decreasing or at least constant, unit labour cost.

We can demonstrate this effect by considering two operatives, both employed to work on consecutive batches of the same component. The time allowed is 1 hour per 100 units. Bonus is payable on all units which pass inspection. They both have a basic hourly rate of £1 per hour. The firm operates a Halsey system. The inputs and outcomes are shown in Figure 20.

The outcomes shown on Figure 20 show that if Jones had

| Time allowed | Time taken | Time saved | Bonus hours | % Bonus hours to time taken | Total paid hours | Comment |
|---|---|---|---|---|---|---|
| 10 | 10 | 0 | 0 | 0 | 10 | 10 Hrs. Pay for 10 Hrs. work |
| 10 | 9 | 1 | 0·5 | 5·5 | 9·5 | |
| 10 | 8 | 2 | 1·0 | 12·5 | 9 | |
| 10 | 7 | 3 | 1·5 | 21·4 | 8·5 | |
| 10 | 6 | 4 | 2·0 | 33·3 | 8 | |
| 10 | 5 | 5 | 2·5 | 50·0 | 7·5 | 7½ Hrs. Pay for 5 Hrs. work |
| 10 | 4 | 6 | 3·0 | 75·0 | 7 | |
| 10 | 3 | 7 | 3·5 | 116·6 | 6·5 | |
| 10 | 2 | 8 | 4·0 | 200·0 | 6 | |
| 10 | 1 | 9 | 4·5 | 450·0 | 5·5 | 5½ Hrs. Pay for 1 Hrs. work |

| Time allowed | Time taken | Time saved | Bonus hours | % Bonus hours to time taken | Total paid hours | Comment |
|---|---|---|---|---|---|---|
| 10 | 10 | 0 | 0 | 0 | 10 | 10 Hrs. Pay for 10 Hrs. work |
| 10 | 9 | 1 | 0·9 | 10 | 9·9 | |
| 10 | 8 | 2 | 1·6 | 20 | 9·6 | |
| 10 | 7 | 3 | 2·1 | 30 | 9·1 | |
| 10 | 6 | 4 | 2·4 | 40 | 8·4 | |
| 10 | 5 | 5 | 2·5 | 50 | 7·5 | 7½ Hrs. Pay for 5 Hrs. work |
| 10 | 4 | 6 | 2·4 | 60 | 6·4 | |
| 10 | 3 | 7 | 2·1 | 70 | 5·1 | |
| 10 | 2 | 8 | 1·6 | 80 | 3·6 | |
| 10 | 1 | 9 | 0·9 | 90 | 1·9 | 1·9 Hrs. Pay for 1 Hrs. work |

FIGURE 19

*Above:* the Halsey System; *below:* the Rowan System

continued his output performance for the same amount of hours as Smith, his total earnings would have amounted to £101·33.

From these simple examples may be drawn some conclusions as to the effectiveness or otherwise of Premium Bonus or incentive systems. Such systems offer rewards to operatives which are proportional to the time saved in per-

| Detail | Jones | | | Smith | | |
|---|---|---|---|---|---|---|
| Inputs: | | | Time taken hours | | | Time taken hours |
| Batch 1 — 1000 units | | | 7 | | | 9 |
| 2 — 2000 units | | | 12 | | | 21 |
| 3 — 1000 units | | | 6 | | | 10 |
| 4 — 4000 units | | | 23 | | | 36 |
| Total units 8000 | | | | | | |
| Total basic hours | | | 48 | | | 76 |
| Outcome Bonus hours: | | | | | | |
| Time allowed | 8000 × 1/100 | 80 | | 8000 × 1/100 | 80 | |
| Time taken | | 48 | | | 76 | |
| Time saved | | 32 | | | 4 | |
| Bonus hours @ 50% time saved | | | 16 | | | 2 |
| Total pay hours | | | 64 | | | 78 |
| Total pay @ £1 per hour | | | £64·00 | | | £78·00 |
| Effective hourly rate for hours taken: | £64/68 | | £1·33 | £78/76 | | £1·026 |
| Unit Labour Cost: | £64/8000 | | £0·008 | £78/8000 | | £0·00975 |

FIGURE 20

forming their work and consistent with an acceptable quality. The operative's reward is in the form of a higher effective hourly rate of pay. The outcome for the firm is constant or lower unit labour cost.

The combination of higher wages for the operative and low unit labour cost for the firm gives an economic advantage to both parties.

**Measured daywork**

The methods and systems so far discussed have assumed that the operative can control the speed at which he carries out his various tasks. Indeed, the individuality factor may be the very essence of incentive.

But, there are many situations where output is machine-dominated, where the individual's speed of working is largely governed by the speed of a machine, or group of machines.

For these situations the system of measured daywork has been developed, in order to combine the best characteristics of time or day rate systems with results-based incentive schemes.

In general terms the method allows for the payment of high basic time rates for attendance hours, against the expectation of standard performance at what would have been considered as bonus efficiency.

Such a system still requires that work measurement be used to determine some acceptable standard achievement. Statistical analysis of past performance is also needed to equate the bonus earned with outputs achieved. From these investigations a ratings schedule can be produced as demonstrated in Figure 21.

Let us assume that an operative with a basic rate of £0·70 per hour working on the components rated in Figure 21, regularly produces 55 components per week. His rate would be increased by £0·33 to £1·03 per hour. He would receive that high rate until the next review of measured daywork performance irrespective of his individual performance in the period up to the review date. If performance fell off, his rate would remain unchanged unless it was regularly below the expected output in which case both supervision and operative would attempt to discover the cause. If the operator achieves higher outputs during the review period, the high rate would be increased to the point on the scale consistent with his increased activity.

This system gives flexibility without the drawbacks of constant bonus calculations, disputes over output quantities and the resulting pay adjustments. The operative knows with reasonable certainty that he can earn a high rate for the hours attended provided he can achieve the agreed output.

| | MEASURED DAY WORK RATING SCHEDULE | | | | |
|---|---|---|---|---|---|
| Component _____ | | | Dept. _____ | | |
| Work Schedule _____ | | | Date _____ | | |
| Observed range units | Average bonus over observed range £ | Average hourly bonus £ | Rate range | | |
| | | | Units | Rate £ | |
| 30 | 5·67 | 0·27 ⎫ | 30–49 | 0·30 | |
| 40 | 7·84 | 0·28 ⎬ | | | |
| 50 | 10·54 | 0·30 ⎫ | 50–69 | 0·33 | |
| 60 | 13·86 | 0·33 ⎬ | | | |
| 70 | 18·13 | 0·37 ⎫ | 70–89 | 0·40 | |
| 80 | 20·72 | 0·37 ⎬ | | | |

FIGURE 21

*Group incentives*

In considering measured daywork we have started to move away from an incentive for the individual towards incentive for a group. Measured daywork can be, and is, readily adapted to a group situation, where group output can be easily measured. One example that may be used is the production of steel: in this situation we see the combined effect of say, six or eight men working in a team, each having an individual skill without which output would not be possible.

The advantages of such group or collective incentive schemes are:

1 The encouragement of team effort and the bringing together of various skills;
2 The encouragement of proficiency in each member, making the group more effective;
3 Such schemes are usually much simpler in terms of documentation and clerical effort.

There are, however, some disadvantages to be noted:

1 The absence of individual incentive may make the scheme less attractive in some work situations.
2 The considerable problem of dividing the group bonus among a group of operatives with different skills and different basic earnings.

## The non-production employee

Incentive schemes tend to be applied only to production employees, because only there are units produced by which output or activity can be easily measured. Such units of measurement are not usually available, or are extremely difficult to formulate, for supervisors, clerical staff, inspectors, managers, labourers and so forth. Indeed, we may even go so far as to say that it would not be in the best interests of the firm or the employee to have an incentive scheme; to do so could destroy an essential part of the quality of performance required by the application of a specific skill or occupation.

None the less, it must be accepted that without the back-up services provided by the non-production employee, the employee whose earnings are incentive-based would not enjoy the same opportunities to earn a bonus.

Many organisations have attempted to overcome this anomaly by setting aside a certain portion of bonuses earned by production employees to set up a pool from which distribution is made to non-production employees at predetermined intervals. The problems caused by such attempts are manifold. The most serious are:

1 The cut-back of production bonus creates ill-feeling amongst production operatives.
2 The difficulty of deciding the method of distribution of the pool among non-production employees of varying skills and rates of pay. All employees have individual expectations of how they have contributed personally to the effectiveness of the organisation.

The efforts of organisations to find a way round the problem in situations of non-measurable units of activity can be divided into three distinct approaches, the bases of which are (1) 'Flextime' working, (2) profit sharing, and (3) added value. We now consider each of these in turn.

*'Flextime' working*

This is a very recent innovation based upon the concept that:

1 An amount of work for an individual or a group may be predetermined in terms of the time needed to complete the task.
2 The individual or the group may perform that task within times to suit themselves.

For example, a particular task requires one clerical employee for 35 hours per week. Provided the task is performed within the span of one working week the employee may choose the hours of work in which he will perform that task —say, absent on Monday; ten hours per day on Tuesday, Wednesday and Thursday; five hours on Friday.

This scheme offers incentives to the employee in one of the biggest incentive areas, that of control over leisure time.

*Profit-sharing*

The concept is that every employee makes a direct contribution towards the profit-making capacity of an organisation.

These schemes have the advantages of:

1 giving employees a stronger personal interest;
2 consolidating that interest by the issue of shares in the business;
3 promoting longer service and thus continuity of action and effectiveness.

Some criticism has been made of such schemes:

1 Profit may be dependent on good management, good markets, good products and so forth, many of which are not controllable by the employee.
2 Profits are not certain; in a loss situation the employee will be concerned when no profit share comes his way.
3 Profit is a remote concept for the average employee. Its calculation may be beyond his comprehension and promote apathy rather than provide incentive.
4 Profits are declared annually, or, half-annually at best. The time-span of reward following effort is far too long to offer a real incentive.

*Added value*

Added value is the net output of an organisation and is the value added to materials and purchased services by the conversion of those materials and purchased services into saleable products. It represents the money available to the organisation to pay wages, salaries, expenses and interest and leave sufficient over as a surplus or profit.

It may be calculated as follows:

| | |
|---|---|
| Sales | £100 000 |
| *Less:* Raw materials bought out components sub-contracting or outside processing | £60 000 |
| Conversion cost *plus* profit | £40 000 |

Let us suppose that the £40 000 is made up as follows:

| | |
|---|---|
| Wages and salaries | £10 000 |
| Expenses | £15 000 |
| Profits | £15 000 |
| | £40 000 |

We see that the employees' share of conversion cost is represented by the sum of £10 000. That is to say that the organisation expects that for every £100 000 of sales, employees will add £10 000 of value.

The operation of an added value incentive scheme is now solely concerned with how much value employees will *actually* add with respect to labour cost. If it is greater than £10 000, there is no bonus payable. If it is less than £10 000 then the difference, or a substantial part of it, will be paid as a bonus.

For example:

| | |
|---|---|
| Agreed standard added value | £10 000 |
| Actual wages and salaries | £9 000 |
| Bonus payable | £1 000 |

Such a scheme is dependent on two major factors:

1   A high degree of confidence and trust between manage-

ment and employees in establishing the proportions of sales and profit attributable to each cost element;

2 The ability to discover some equitable means of sharing out the bonus between employees of varying skill, grade, and rate of pay.

Subject to satisfactory settlement of these important matters it is claimed that added value schemes:

1 Lead to an automatic payment to employees of their contribution towards conversion;
2 Overcome the problem of unsatisfactory payment systems;
3 Strengthen industrial relations and co-operation between management and employee;
4 Encourage employees to eliminate unnecessary actions and use of material, thus reducing scrap and economising on consumables.

## Job evaluation

We have seen from the discussions on wages and remuneration that one of the major problems is how to measure the efficiency and productivity of manpower. Over many, many years the technique of work measurement has been developed in an attempt to determine how work should be performed and how long it should take.

For almost as many years there has been a strong movement away from traditional piecework and Premium Bonus schemes which are now generally thought to be inappropriate to the current industrial environment. In their place, fixed wage systems based on job evaluation and measured daywork are being introduced. At the same time, some pay scales are being more scientifically evaluated, based on job evaluation, rather than arbitrary and subjective judgement.

It is universally accepted that an employee should be paid

a rate for the job and that the basic rate of an individual's occupation should be related to job value. This, then, is the purpose of job evaluation.

Job evaluation has been defined as:

> 'A ranking, grading and/or weighting of essential work characteristics of all job or job classes in some systematic manner such that the labour worth of each job or job class is relative to all other jobs or job classes.' (*Wage Incentive Methods*—Lytle)

Some of the work characteristics that may be important to include in an evaluation are education, qualifications, responsibility, working conditions, skill, mental effort and so forth.

A common method of evaluation is to use a points rating system, that is, to award point values on a scale of, say, 1 to 10 for each of the characteristics included in the evaluation system.

The points so awarded are totalled, and a wage rate based on either a value per point or ranges of values for ranges of points can then be formulated.

It is not an easy task even for a skilled assessor. In practice it is often carried out by a committee consisting of a skilled and experienced evaluator together with representatives of management at all levels and employees of all grades. The aim of such a committee should be to obtain impartial, or at least balanced, overall judgement that will resolve anomalies.

## Non-financial incentives

All the matters so far discussed have been concerned with monetary reward. There is no denying the fact that the incentive value of money is very strong. None the less, non-financial incentives can contribute a great deal towards the encouragement of increased activity, enthusiasm, loyalty and the decrease of labour turnover. By non-financial incentive we mean reward or encouragement other than by additional money in the pay packet.

Perhaps it would be incorrect to label job-satisfaction a non-financial incentive. It is certainly a factor to be considered in gauging the motivation of an employee and the quality of his work.

It is therefore important for an organisation to set up a working environment which encourages the employee. This can be accomplished by 'fringe benefits' such as:

1 Sports and social activities, especially if organised by a company club. It should cover such matters as dances, outings, entertainments and, probably, arrangements for staff discount.
2 Education and training facilities. These may take two forms:

   (*a*) *Internal*—Craft and skill training for technical apprentices, rotation of duties for clerical and managerial trainees;
   (*b*) *External*—day release to colleges, block release and sandwich courses, integrated courses at Universities, polytechnics and other colleges.

3 Canteen and welfare amenities. Subsidised meals, pension schemes, benevolent funds, protective clothing and so forth are a few benefits which are now quite common.
4 Health and medical facilities, covered by the provision of a fully-staffed aid centre and possibly a doctor, dentist or optician on an attendance or even full-time basis.

### The payment of wages

In carrying out this process we can confirm one of our other definitions of cost, that is, that cost is the expenditure necessary to obtain a good or service. In this case, wage payment may be equated with the idea of 'purchase of labour' from the employee. Thus the payroll can be regarded as the basic record which creates the necessary entries in the books of account. It will also be seen that it is the means of creating initial cost analysis.

The payment of wages is therefore considered in three distinct stages: payroll preparation and analysis, payment of wages to the employee and safeguards against malpractice, and cost analysis.

## Payroll preparation and analysis

The payroll is divided into three distinct elements: gross earnings, deductions and net payable wage. From the totals of these, plus the amount of Social Security payable by the employer, a payroll analysis is made which becomes the basis of the entry in the books of account.

The payroll form has many different rulings but generally is designed to give information as in the format shown in Figure 22.

The gross wages are determined from clock cards according to the time wages usually guaranteed to every employee and known as basic pay. This will have to be increased for bonus earnings calculated from a bonus ticket or activity or job card, and for holiday pay due to the employee during the payroll week in question. This section of the payroll can be redesigned to suit the firm, if necessary showing, quite separately, payments for overtime and overtime premium, shift allowances, long service payments and any other pay allowances that constitute total gross taxable pay. Thus any payments which are non-taxable, such as travelling expenses, must not be included in this section but shown in a separate column for addition to net taxed pay.

Deductions are of two types: the statutory deductions

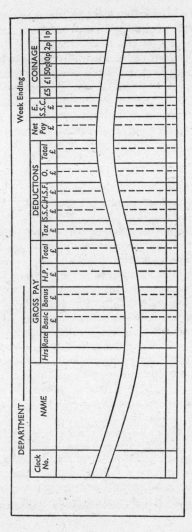

FIGURE 22

Abbreviations used are as follows:

H.P.       Holiday Pay
S.S.C.     Social Security Contribution
H.S.F.     Hospital Saturday Fund
O.         Other deductions
E.S.S.C.   Employers Social Security Contribution

for income tax, more popularly called PAYE, and Social Security contributions, previously known as the National Insurance Contribution.

The voluntary deductions are many and varied. We have included two columns in Figure 22 to allow for this process, which can only be carried out with the signed permission of the employee.

By taking total deductions from total gross pay we find the net sum due to the employee. There are three basic means by which this value may be transmitted to the employee:

1 By credit transfer from the firm's to the employee's bank account. This is a usual procedure adopted for monthly-paid employees.
2 By raising a cheque for the net sum. This system is now widely used especially for weekly-paid staff. It is often associated with an arrangement at a local bank for immediate encashment, instead of the employee paying the cheque into his or her own bank account. This clearly has the great advantage to the firm of not involving the carriage of large sums of money from the bank to the firm, with its attendant dangers. It also obviates the necessity of splitting large sums of money into individual amounts, placing those individual amounts in envelopes and handing the envelope to the employee.
3 Drawing the money from the bank and paying the employee the net sum due in hard cash.

*Payment of wages to the employee*

The examples used in the section above to illustrate the various points are, of necessity, simple. In practice there are many pages of payroll, sometimes for each department. It is therefore vitally necessary to have a well-ordered but simple routine for making up the many individual pay packets from the large sum of money drawn from the bank.

One of the most important aspects of this routine is concerned with advising the employee how much pay is contained in his pay packet. Two basic methods exist for doing this:

1 Printing the front of the pay envelope in such a way that details of gross pay, deductions and net amount may be copied on to it from the payroll.
2 Backing the payroll sheet with carbon paper and a duplicate payroll. The duplicate will be perforated at each line so that after the payroll is completed the copy may be divided at the perforations thus allowing every employee to have an exact copy of his line of entry on the payroll enclosed in his pay packet. This saves the additional copying work necessitated by method 1 above.

The next step is to divide the total money drawn from the bank among individual payroll sheets.

After establishing that the cash drawn is correctly inserted into individual pay packets, those packets are then sealed and the process of distribution to employees can be made. Pay clerks are appointed specifically for this task.

At the pay station or pay point each employee comes forward in 'clock number' sequence and in exchange for his clock card receives his pay packet. The supervisor or foreman of the department is thus able to assist the pay clerk in the ready identification of the person receiving the money.

It is clear that the clock card may be used for two purposes: firstly, as a means of informing the employee as to the amount of wages to be received at the next pay day. Secondly, as a means of obtaining the signature of the employee in acceptance of the calculation of the amount and as a receipt for the pay packet.

## Safeguards against malpractice

It must be accepted that however stringent are the checks and re-checks in the system, there still exists the possibility of fraud or malpractice. This will usually be of two basic forms: firstly, dummy employees on the payroll, and secondly, additional or unauthorised documentation.

The following precautions are offered as deterrents against malpractice:

1  The payroll section should be adequately staffed. Understaffing leads to poor checking.
2  A payroll sheet should not be completed by one pay clerk only. Ideally the functions of gross pay, deductions and net pay should be done by three separate clerks.
3  The clerks involved should have rotation of duties. This has a two-fold effect: a checking process between duties, and staff development of duties.
4  The pay packets should be 'cashed up' by clerks not concerned with payroll preparation.
5  The distribution of pay packets at the pay point should be carried out by employees not concerned with payroll preparation or pay packet encashment.
6  The collection of one employee's packet by another employee must be strictly prohibited. Any unclaimed pay packets should be carefully investigated.
7  Strict supervision of clock cards and job cards must be carried out. The checking of hours is thus an important aspect in this deterrent system. Any payment to be made outside of this system must be duly authorised.
8  Periodic but irregular checks by physical inspection of employees against records should be carried out.

There is much to be said for carrying out irregular or erratically spaced checks throughout the entire wage payment system. It should be remembered that while these measures do not make malpractice impossible, they make it highly impracticable without the aid or assistance of a senior employee. Therefore every point of the system requires a checkpoint, and every suspicious document requires investigation, irrespective of the level of its operation or origin.

## Cost analysis

This is really the reason for everything that has been expounded so far in this chapter. We have examined the manner in which people will be employed, the systems of payment and reward and the manner in which that reward will be transferred to them in the form of cash. However, we should remember that cost ascertainment implies analysis. So far we are only in possession of the fact that a certain sum of money drawn from the bank has been paid to employees. We now need to discover, in total terms, just how that sum of money is to be distributed in the following terms:

1  into direct or indirect wages;
2  into departmental or section or cost centre charges;
3  into product or service charges;
4  into trade or craft or skill charges.

This list is indicative but by no means complete. Other headings will become apparent as we examine in greater detail the methods of cost ascertainment.

The analysis is usually carried out by means of a wage analysis sheet as illustrated in the two forms in Figure 23.

It will be seen from both forms that the question of total labour cost is emphasised. That is the sum of gross pay and the employer's Social Security contribution. Any labour analysis must always take both factors into account, since these provide the true total cost of the purchase of labour.

One of these forms shows analysis by employee into direct

WAGES ANALYSIS

DEPARTMENT_____                                    Week ending____

| Clock No. | Name | Gross Pay | E. S.S.C. | Total | Direct Labour | Ind. Lab. | Indirect Labour Analysis | | | | |
|---|---|---|---|---|---|---|---|---|---|---|---|
| | | | | | | | | | | | |

FIGURE 23 (a)

WAGES ANALYSIS

Week ending____

| Department | Gross Pay | E. S.S.C. | Total | Product Labour Cost | | | | Indirect Labour Cost | | | |
|---|---|---|---|---|---|---|---|---|---|---|---|
| | | | | | | | | | | | |

FIGURE 23 (b)

and indirect labour and makes provision for the further analysis of indirect labour under such headings as 'waiting for materials', 'tool changes', 'repairs' and so forth.

The other form indicates analysis by department of the direct labour associated with individual products or models and the analysis of indirect labour under such headings as are mentioned above.

The manner in which this analysis will be carried out is dependent on the industry, the firm and the method of cost ascertainment being employed. It is clear that by re-arrangement of certain procedures associated with payroll analysis, clock cards, job cards and other documents in the wage

payment system, it may be possible to carry out analysis
directly on the payroll itself.

We should not infer that Figure 23 is the definitive version
but should see it rather as the necessary adjunct to the accurate ascertainment of labour cost.

*Accounting entries*

We should realise that the payroll and wages analysis will
form the basis on which entries are made in the books of
account. The manner in which those ledgers are kept will
depend on whether an interlocked or integrated accounting
system is used. We also need to understand the methods of
cost ascertainment before we examine the bookkeeping
system. For these reasons we shall deal with the accounting
entries at that time rather than now.

**Exercises**

1 (*a*) Using the data shown below, calculate the remuneration of each employee, as determined by
each of the following methods:

  (i) Hourly rate
  (ii) Basic piece rate
  (iii) Individual bonus scheme, where the employee
  receives a bonus in proportion of the time
  saved to the time allowed

*Data*

| Name of employee | Salmon | Roach | Pike |
|---|---|---|---|
| Units produced | 270 | 200 | 220 |
| Time allowed per unit minutes | 10 | 15 | 12 |
| Time taken (hours) | 40 | 38 | 36 |
| Rate per hour | £1·25 | £1·05 | £1·20 |
| Rate per unit | £0·20 | £0·25 | £0·24 |

(*b*) Comment briefly on the effectiveness of method (iii).
(ICMA)

2   GI Engineering Company Ltd operates a group incentive
scheme in Department 6. A minimum hourly rate is
guaranteed to each of the six employees in the group if
actual output for the week is less than standard output.
If actual output is greater than standard output, the
hourly rate of each employee is increased by 4 % for each
additional 300 units of output produced. The standard
output for the group is 6000 units for a 40-hour week.
During the week ending May 4, each employee in the
group works 40 hours; actual output and minimum
hourly rates were as follows:

| Employee | Actual output in units | Minimum hourly rate |
|---|---|---|
| Crow I | 1250 | 0·70 |
| Finch B | 1350 | 0·75 |
| Gull C | 1200 | 0·60 |
| Hawk S | 1250 | 0·70 |
| Jay A | 1230 | 0·60 |
| Sparrow C | 1220 | 0·65 |

You are required to:

(a) calculate the earnings of each employee;
(b) appraise the effectiveness to the company of this
group incentive scheme;
(c) suggest briefly the advantages and disadvantages
which may accrue from an effective group incentive
scheme.                                            (ICMA)

3   The managing director of a manufacturing company is
considering the introduction of a group incentive scheme
into one of its production departments. As cost accountant you are required to present a report to him, in which
you should discuss briefly the following:

(a) The advantages of this scheme, compared with
those of an individual incentive scheme;

(b) two schemes which are classified as group incentive schemes;

(c) the safeguards which should be incorporated into the group incentive scheme in order to minimise any possible disadvantages. (ICMA)

4 The chairman of W Limited, a medium-sized company in the engineering industry, has recently attended a conference on 'Piecework Abandoned', and decided that the company should discontinue payment by piecework. As cost accountant to the company, you are required to present to the chairman a report on profit-sharing and co-partnership schemes. Your report should describe such schemes generally and then discuss briefly:

(a) how you would propose such a scheme should be introduced;

(b) the benefits to be obtained by implementing such a scheme;

(c) the possible defects of such a scheme. (ICMA)

5 (a) Amongst the many schemes of incentive remuneration which have evolved over the last one hundred years, two of the better known are the Halsey or Halsey–Weir bonus scheme and the Rowan bonus scheme. Briefly give your views on why these two schemes are not more widely used in industry.

(b) The details given below relate to an employee on job number 27. You are required to calculate his remuneration on this job based on the Halsey 50% scheme and the Rowan scheme.

*Data*

| | |
|---|---|
| Direct wages per hour | £0·80 |
| Time allowed | 40 hours |
| Time taken | 32 hours |

(ICMA)

6  S Manufacturing Limited operates a day-rate system of
   employee remuneration at the factory at Newtown. The
   managing director proposes to introduce a differential
   piece rate system and has asked you, as cost accountant,
   to prepare a report on whether or not you consider his
   proposal would be of economic benefit to the factory.

   Your report should be based on the information given
   below and should contain a statement showing the
   present and proposed situations to support your view.
   You should also enumerate briefly the disadvantages
   and advantages of operating a differential piece rate
   system.

   Under the present system, employees are paid £6·00
   for an eight-hour day and on average, each employee
   produces fifteen units of good output. Production overheads are consistently incurred and absorbed at a rate of
   £1·50 per direct labour hour. Under the proposed system
   an increase in good output will lead to increased remuneration according to the following scale:

   | Production in units of good output | Remuneration per unit |
   |---|---|
   | 16 | £0·42 |
   | 17 | £0·44 |
   | 18 | £0·46 |
   | 19 | £0·48 |
   | 20 | £0·50 |

   (ICMA)

7  The Langham Engineering Company Ltd has a number
   of factories, one of which is situated in a busy industrial
   region. The managing director is concerned to hear of the
   apparently high rate of labour turnover in this factory
   and has asked you, as cost accountant, to prepare a
   report to help him to understand and improve the situation.

You are required to prepare a formal report to the managing director and in it to:

(*a*) show how labour turnover is calculated;
(*b*) explain the influences it can have on costs;
(*c*) suggest steps that could be taken in an attempt to reduce the rate of labour turnover. (ICMA)

8  In the wood machining shop of X Limited a group bonus scheme operates. Under this scheme time saved is shared among the members of the group *pro rata* to the time worked and is paid at agreed percentages of the hourly basic rates. Bonuses are calculated weekly and for a given week, using the following information, you are required to calculate and present in the form of a schedule:

(*a*) time allowed, taken and saved for each of the three work groups;
(*b*) for each employee:

    (i) bonus hours and bonus earnings
   (ii) time wage including overtime premium
  (iii) gross wage.

| | *Work Groups* | | |
| | Cabinets | Bunks | Kitchens |
|---|---|---|---|
| Actual hours in progress | | | |
|   at the beginning of the week | 70 | 47 | 66 |
|   at the end of the week | 76 | 54 | 63 |
| Actual hours worked during the | | | |
|   week | 48 | 60 | 42 |
| Output completed during the week | | | |
|   (in sets) | 15 | 18 | 12 |
| Bonus time allowances per set | | | |
|   completed i n hours | $4\frac{1}{3}$ | $3\frac{2}{3}$ | $5\frac{1}{6}$ |

Of this production there was rejected work, not paid for, of:

| Sub assemblies | 40 | 60 | 55 |
| With bonus time allowance | | | |
| per sub assembly — in minutes | 15 | 6 | 12 |

In addition there was rectification work completed (from production of previous weeks), also qualifying for bonus of:

| Units | 120 | 108 | 140 |
| With bonus time allowance | | | |
| per unit, in minutes | 4 | 5 | 3 |

The following workers were employed on the above:

| Name | Hours worked | Base rate per hour | Bonus % of base rate |
|------|------|------|------|
| A.H. | 60 | £0·45 | 66⅔ |
| D.E. | 50 | £0·40 | 50 |
| O.S. | 40 | £0·35 | 45 |

Overtime is paid for at time and a quarter for the first eight hours in excess of 40; time and a half for hours in excess of 48. (ICMA)

# 5

# Overhead

## Introduction

Overhead is the third element of cost and is defined as 'the aggregate of indirect materials cost, indirect labour cost and indirect expense cost'. Unlike direct material cost and direct labour cost, overhead costs are those costs which cannot be associated with a particular product or individual cost unit.

It is reasonably easy to look at a product, for example, a wooden table, and be able to identify physically all the direct material costs as represented by the timber. It is reasonably difficult if not altogether impossible to identify how much of the managing director's salary is included in that same product. From this we see that there are problems in arriving at a charge to product to cover overheads. We are also aware that cost has the characteristic of variability; that is, some costs change as activity changes, others remain fixed irrespective of activity. This is no less true of overhead costs.

Figure 24 sets out in the form of a table some of the more usual overhead expenditures in terms of character and function. It should be noted that some items, for example, rates, appear against more than one functional area and in both character columns.

The approach to an overall solution is to consider the problem in four steps: collection, classification, apportionment and absorption.

| Character \ Function | Variable | Fixed |
|---|---|---|
| PRODUCTION | Indirect Material<br>   ,,   Labour<br>Small Tools<br>Oil and Grease<br>Lighting<br>Power | Depreciation<br>Salaries<br>Rates<br>Insurance<br>Lighting<br>Power |
| ADMINISTRATION | <br><br><br><br>Office Supplies<br>Lighting<br>Power | Depreciation<br>Salaries<br>Rates<br>Insurance<br>Office Supplies<br>Lighting<br>Power |
| SELLING | Sales Commission<br>Royalties<br>Discounts<br>Bad Debts<br>Office Supplies<br>Lighting<br>Power | Depreciation<br>Salaries<br>Rates<br>Insurance<br>Office Supplies<br>Lighting<br>Power |
| DISTRIBUTION | Petrol and Oil<br>Repairs<br>Warehouse Labour<br>Packing Materials<br>Lighting<br>Power | Depreciation<br>Salaries<br>Rates<br>Insurance<br>Lighting<br>Power |

FIGURE 24

## Collection

Overhead costs arise as a result of the overall operation of a business, and the expenditures can be traced from one or more of the following five sources:

1 Issues from stores of consumable items such as oil, grease, rag and so forth; small tools, materials to be used on repair work, stationery, and so on.
2 Expenditure contained on the payroll and not associated directly with production. This would include the wage payments made to all non-productive staff such as managers, supervisors, clerks, labourers, storekeepers, inspectors and so forth.
3 Invoices received, covering goods and services other than production raw materials. Rates, telephone, electricity, stationery, are a few examples.
4 A smaller group of expenditures may also be gathered from the cash book and petty cash book covering items such as postage stamps, travelling expenses and many of the day-to-day expenses requiring immediate cash.
5 An important group of expenditures will also arise from the use of the journal.

## Classification

We have discovered from our studies of materials and labour that it is necessary to distinguish one material or component from another, one grade of employee from another and one employer from another. From what has already been said about overhead expenditure it is clear that the need for classification is vital.

The alternatives that must be considered are those of subjective and objective classification. By subjective classification we mean analysis according to the expenditure base, i.e.

all indirect wages, irrespective of functional location will be chargeable to the indirect wages account. By objective classification we mean analysis according to responsibility or function, i.e. indirect wages will be charged to the department or function responsible for the expenditure.

| Account Number | Account Title | Function | Department or Cost Centre |
|---|---|---|---|
| 071 | REPAIRS AND RENEWALS | 1. PRODUCTION | 1. Mills<br>2. Drills<br>3. Assembly |
| | | 2. ADMINISTRATION | 1. Accounts<br>2. Personnel<br>3. Canteen |
| | | 3. SELLING | 1. Salesmen<br>2. Sales Office<br>3. Area Office A<br>4. Area Office B |
| | | 4. DISTRIBUTION | 1. Warehouse<br>2. Depot X<br>3. Depot Y |
| 316 | SUPERVISOR AND MANAGEMENT SALARIES | 1. PRODUCTION | 1. Mills<br>2. Drills<br>3. Assembly |
| | | 2. ADMINISTRATION | 1. Accounts<br>2. Personnel<br>3. Canteen |
| | | 3. SELLING | 1. Sales<br>2. Sales Office<br>3. Area Office A<br>4. Area Office B |
| | | 4. DISTRIBUTION | 1. Warehouse<br>2. Depot X<br>3. Depot Y |

FIGURE 25

It is usual to find that in the financial accounts expenditures are classified subjectively, in other words as 'rates account', 'electricity account', 'depreciation account' and so on. In cost accounting, overhead expenditures should be classified objectively, and located according to responsibility or function.

The problem arises when financial records and cost account records follow different methods of recording overheads; the solution is a proper system of classifying accounts which will list the subjective financial accounts numerically, in such a way that the objective analysis can be obtained for the cost accounts. An example of such a system is found in Figure 25.

It can be seen from this illustration that entries would be made in the financial accounts against Account 071 (repairs and renewals), and Account 316 (supervision and management salaries).

For cost accounting purposes, all the source documents would be functionally coded, and in issuing a stores requisition for repair materials, the authorising manager would be required to ensure that his locational code appeared on the document. Thus, if the warehouse manager was authorising a requisition for some repair materials to be sent to Depot Y, he would ensure that the classification 07143 appeared on that document: 071 signifying repair and renewal expense, 4 to signify distribution function and 3 to signify Depot Y within that function.

## Collection and classification—'standing orders'

Any system of coding or numbering used for cost classification must be properly integrated with the system in use for financial accounting.

We have seen that it is possible to build up a product or unit or service cost by direct material and direct labour.

We can assume that departmental managers will want to see what is being charged in the way of direct materials, direct labour and overheads attributable to their functions.

A dichotomy exists: we may be building up the prime cost (direct material and direct labour) on a product or unit basis,

FUNCTION __Production__          STANDING ORDER No. __071·1__

| DATE 19— | REFERENCE Repairs and renewals | TOTAL | SUB FUNCTION | | |
|---|---|---|---|---|---|
| | | | 1 Mills | 2 Drills | 3 Assy |
| Jan. 10 | Stores Req'n 76 | 7 42 | | 7 42 | |
| 14 | Labourer's Payroll | 290 00 | 106 16 | 72 14 | 111 70 |
| | | | | | |
| | | | | | |
| | | | | | |

FUNCTION __Administration__          STANDING ORDER No. __316·2__

| DATE 19— | REFERENCE Supervision and Management Sales | TOTAL | SUB FUNCTION | | |
|---|---|---|---|---|---|
| | | | 1 Accounts | 2 Personnel | 3 Canteen |
| Jan. 14 | Payroll | 1784 87 | 980 50 | 740 21 | 64 16 |
| | | | | | |
| | | | | | |
| | | | | | |

FUNCTION __Sales__          STANDING ORDER No. __071·4__

| DATE 19— | REFERENCE Repairs and renewals | TOTAL | SUB FUNCTION | | | |
|---|---|---|---|---|---|---|
| | | | 1 Sales | 2 Sales Office | 3 Area A | 4 Area B |
| Feb. 16 | Stores Req'n 161 | 16 26 | | | 16 26 | |
| | | | | | | |
| | | | | | | |
| | | | | | | |

FIGURE 26

yet building up overhead cost on a functional or cost centre basis. The usual way to overcome some of the difficulties of overhead cost ascertainment and control is to use a system known as 'standing orders'.

Figure 26 shows an example of the layout with entries for these analyses. It will be seen that the standing order takes its number from a combination of an accounting system for classifying expenditure and the functional classification shown in the example in Figure 25.

As documents flow through the cost accounts department they are entered on a standing order by reference to the classification number appearing on the document. There will therefore be an analysis by function and sub-function for every main overhead expenditure account held in the accounts ledgers.

From this it is clear that any system of classification for analysis by the standing order system must be simple, easily understood and flexible, although it may be extensive in a large organisation. It must suit the conditions and environment of the business and the needs and aims of the cost accounting system.

The examples and illustrations shown are necessarily simple so as to indicate the possibilities. It should be clearly understood that there are very many variations in use.

## Apportionment

In examining the procedure for the collection and classification of overhead costs we have assumed that all overhead expenditures can be charged to a specific cost centre. That is only true under certain conditions.

Suppose the accounts department needed some more ledger sheets—an indirect material. The chief accountant, in authorising the purchase requisition, would ensure that the correct accounts classification appears on that document, in accordance with the idea advanced in our discussion of classification.

An invoice will be received from the supplier and will be coded in accordance with the classification number appearing on the purchase order. This charge will appear on the stationery account in the accounts ledgers and also be charged to the accounts department by standing order.

On the other hand, at frequent intervals the organisation will receive other invoices. These will cover such expenses as rates, electricity, rent, insurance and so on. For this type of expenditure there is no individual location or function that can be charged, since all functions, all sections, all managers, will have to bear a small part of the total, which will be divided up on some equitable basis.

Expenditures that can be directly charged to the functional cost centre are referred to as 'directly allocatable' overhead costs.

Expenditures such as rates, electricity, insurance, which cannot be directly charged to a functional cost centre, are referred to as 'common' or non-allocatable overhead costs. It is with this latter group, the common overhead costs, that the process of apportionment is concerned.

## Methods of apportionment

In apportioning common costs, the basis used must be as realistic as possible so as to minimise the possibilities of inaccuracy and subjective assessment. A concept that should be observed is that 'The basis of apportionment should be related to the basis of the expenditure.' The following methods of apportionment are generally in use, and have given good results when correctly applied:

1　Apportionment by numbers employed. This basis would be suitable for such expenditures as the subsidy required for a canteen; the expenditure on personnel, wages and welfare departments; for distributing supervisory and managerial salaries over several cost centres. It should never be used as a general method but only for those costs which are related to the employment of people.

2 Apportionment by floor area or cubic capacity. Some overhead expenditures are related to these measurements, particularly the 'building occupation' costs of rent, rates, building maintenance and security services. It has also been used as a general method when it has been felt that no other means were available or suitable. Notably this method is used for expenditures such as lighting and heating. Generally it is not to be recommended except in the last resort.

3 Apportionment by asset value. There are a number of expenditures whose level and value is directly related to asset value; depreciation and fire insurance are two. Because we know where a particular building or piece of equipment is located, the two expenditures mentioned are more likely to be directly allocatable rather than common overhead costs, and thus may not be subject to apportionment. Equally, where common costs do exist, and where the expenditure is directly related to asset value, then the method is of great value. Stock insurance and fire prevention costs are examples.

4 Apportionment by direct wages. The only expenditures which really vary with wages are insurance premiums covering employers' liability. This method is generally unsatisfactory for other costs because of the variations to be found in wage rates between departments. It does not therefore meet the standard of equitability that is necessary for apportionment.

5 Apportionment by direct labour hours or production machine hours. Some expenditures such as works office costs, internal transport, materials handling, inspection and timekeeping costs can be related to work or machine hours. That is, some costs may be output- or activity-related. One should be extremely careful in the application of this method and remember that the number of hours can vary in different functional or cost centres.

6 Apportionment by technical estimate. This must be re-

| | | | | | | |
|---|---|---|---|---|---|---|
| | | | TECHNICAL ESTIMATE | | | |

Expenditure _Electricity_  
Basis: _Watt/Hours_

Accounts Code _342_  
Total Cost _£1600_  
Invoice/other reference _B789 Elec. Board_

| Function | Ref. | Basis | | | Per cent function basis to total | Apportion cost £ |
|---|---|---|---|---|---|---|
| | | Watts (1000's) | Hours (1000's) | Watt/ Hours | | |
| Production | 1·1 | 2·0 | 10 | 20·0 | 26·4 | 423 00 |
| | 0·2 | 1·0 | 10 | 10·0 | 13·3 | 211 00 |
| | 0·3 | 0·4 | 8 | 3·2 | 4·2 | 68 00 |
| Admin. | 2·1 | 0·4 | 7 | 2·8 | 3·7 | 59 00 |
| | 0·2 | 0·5 | 5 | 2·5 | 3·3 | 53 00 |
| | 0·3 | 1·5 | 2 | 3·0 | 4·0 | 63 00 |
| Sales | 3·1 | — | — | | | |
| | 0·2 | 0·6 | 7 | 4·2 | 5·5 | 89 00 |
| | 0·3 | — | — | | | |
| | 0·4 | — | — | | | |
| Distribution | 4·1 | 3·0 | 10 | 30·0 | 39·6 | 634 00 |
| | 0·2 | — | — | | | |
| | 0·3 | — | — | | | |
| | | | | 75·7 | 100·00 | £1600 00 |
| | | | | 75·7 | 100·00 | £1600 00 |

FIGURE 27

garded as the most satisfactory method of achieving equal distribution. It requires the gathering of technical data as the basis for apportioning such expenditures as lighting, power and heating. An example is shown in Figure 27. It will be seen that we are using the product of the wattage of all light sources and the hours that these will be in use in each of the functional cost centres.

7 Direct measurement. This is not so much a method of apportionment as a desirable goal. It depends on the location of meters in functional or cost centres through which electricity, gas, water, steam and so on are fed. The existence of such devices removes the need for apportionment and converts the distribution of this form of expenditure into a directly allocatable cost. It is the most satisfactory method of dealing equitably with the cost of services, but tends to be expensive.

*The apportionment and treatment of two overhead expenditure items of special interest*

1 Interest payable. Opinions differ as to whether interest payable is an expenditure to be dealt with in cost accounting, except where its inclusion is justified by special circumstances. The argument for and against may be briefly summarised as follows:

*Against:*

(a) Cost accounting should be concerned with operational matters. Interest payable is usually a matter of financial management.

(b) To assess the amount of capital relevant to operational matters is often a complex matter. It increases the difficulty of presenting costing information and cost accounts promptly.

(*c*) The need to pay interest may arise out of the necessity to raise short-term capital to overcome a situation beyond the control of the firm. This is not related to the ability of the organisation to operate effectively and should not be regarded as a cost.

*For:*

(*a*) Interest is the cost of money. Any funds requiring to be serviced by interest payments are a legitimate part of the operation, and the interest payable on these funds is a legitimate cost.

(*b*) The running of an organisation is a total concept. To attempt to divorce financial management from the flow of information produced by a cost accounting system may create dangers.

(*c*) Overall cost cannot be properly ascertained unless all items of cost are included.

If interest payable is regarded as an overhead cost, the question of equitable distribution will arise.

2 Depreciation and obsolescence. Depreciation is defined as a diminution in the value of a fixed asset caused by use and/or the passage of time. It represents the loss in value of an asset due to two main causes:

(*a*) Natural wear and tear through using the asset; for example, the wear on bearings in a piece of production equipment.

(*b*) Simple physical deterioration; for example, the erosion of brickwork by pollution or the corrosion of the metal parts of a motor vehicle. This occurs even when the asset is not in use.

Obsolescence is the diminution in the value of a fixed asset due to its being superseded by one which is technologically superior, or due to a fall in demand for it, resulting from a change in the programme of production.

The major problem associated with depreciation is to obtain a reasonably accurate estimate of its cost. The three relevant factors are:

1 the original cost of the asset;
2 the estimated life of the asset;
3 a residual or scrap value of the asset at the end of its estimated life.

The first factor is known with certainty since it is the value of the asset when installed. The difficulty comes in attempt-

PLANT REGISTER

Asset No. _____

Description _____     Location _____

Supplier _____     Cost £ _____

Installed by _____     Cost £ _____

Effective life _____ Depreciation Rate _____

Residual Value     £ _____

| Date | Ref. | Details | Original Cost | Dep'n | Dep'n to Date | Book Value Year End |
|------|------|---------|---------------|-------|---------------|---------------------|
|      |      |         |               |       |               |                     |
|      |      |         |               |       |               |                     |

FIGURE 28

ing to evaluate the second and third factors. It is not our purpose to discuss here all the various methods available.

In any event there should be a plant register comprising forms similar to that shown in Figure 28. Such records provide a basis for the direct allocation of depreciation to functional or cost centres. Without such records, apportionment of depreciation costs must lean heavily on the rather more imprecise asset value method.

## Overhead distribution analysis

The collection, classification and apportionment processes so far discussed will enable us to marshal the overheads under the functional headings of Production, Administration, Selling and Distribution, and to have additional information as to the further analysis over cost centres within those functions. We now need to gather these facts and calculations together before we can finalise an apportionment process. This is usually done by an overhead distribution analysis as illustrated in Figure 29. The account number, reference, and title describe a particular subjective account in the books of account. The basis of apportionment is the manner in which the subjective total has been apportioned objectively over functional and cost centres. This may involve transferring information from the records maintained under a standing order system.

To demonstrate the process and provide some information for the consideration of a secondary apportionment we now look at a simple example.

Assume that the following information is available for a small manufacturing firm which is organised into three production departments and two ancillary or non-productive departments: general administration and sales and service.

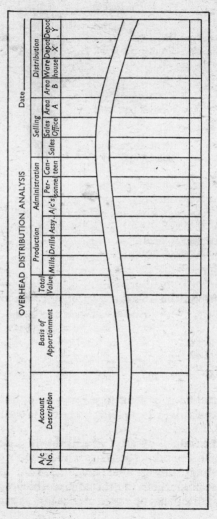

FIGURE 29

*Illustration*

## TWIGS LTD

| *Overhead Expenditure Summary* | | £ | *Period 4* |
|---|---|---|---|
| Consumable Stores — Production Dept. 1 | | 400 | £ |
| 2 | | 600 | |
| 3 | | 900 | |
| | | — | |
| | | | 1900 |
| Maintenance — Production Dept. 1 | | 360 | |
| 2 | | 200 | |
| 3 | | 240 | |
| General Admin. | | 150 | |
| Sales and Service | | 50 | |
| | | — | |
| | | | 1 000 |
| Depreciation | | | 7 000 |
| Rates | | | 4 000 |
| Electricity | | | 1 200 |
| Fire Insurance | | | 800 |
| General Management Salaries | | | 3 000 |
| Employees Liability Insurance | | | 1 500 |
| | | | ——— |
| | | | £20 400 |

The following information is also available for each department:

| | Production Depts. | | | General Admin. | Sales and Service |
|---|---|---|---|---|---|
| | 1 | 2 | 3 | | |
| Asset values (£000's) | 5 | 7 | 4 | 3 | 1 |
| Floor area (000's sq. ft.) | 20 | 10 | 30 | 15 | 25 |
| Kilowatt Hours | 144 | 252 | 180 | 108 | 36 |
| Total Employees | 100 | 100 | 400 | 200 | 200 |

This information is brought together in an overhead distribution analysis as in Figure 30, using the procedures so far discussed.

To give an example: we are told that the total electricity charge is £1200. The proportions of each function's kilowatt hours to the total kilowatt hours are 20: 35: 25: 15: 5. By applying those proportions to the charge of £1200 we obtain the individual functional or cost centre charge as shown.

TWIGS LTD.  OVERHEAD DISTRIBUTION ANALYSIS  PERIOD———

| Account | Basis of Apportionment | Total | Production Depts. | | | General Admin. | Sales and Service |
|---|---|---|---|---|---|---|---|
| | | | 1 | 2 | 3 | | |
| Consumable Stores | Direct Allocation | 1 900 | 400 | 600 | 900 | — | — |
| Maintenance | Direct Allocation | 1 000 | 360 | 200 | 240 | 150 | 50 |
| Depreciation | Asset Value | 7 000 | 1 750 | 2 450 | 1 400 | 1 050 | 350 |
| Rates | Floor Area | 4 000 | 800 | 400 | 1 200 | 600 | 1 000 |
| Electricity | Kilo Watt Hours | 1 200 | 240 | 420 | 300 | 180 | 60 |
| Fire Insurance | Asset Value | 800 | 200 | 280 | 160 | 120 | 40 |
| General Management Salaries | Total Employees | 3 000 | 300 | 300 | 1 200 | 600 | 600 |
| Employees Liability Insurance | Total Employees | 1 500 | 150 | 150 | 600 | 300 | 300 |
| | | £20 400 | £4 200 | £4 800 | £6 000 | £3 000 | £2 400 |

FIGURE 30

It cannot be emphasised too strongly that this is a simple example used for the purposes of demonstration. In practice, this procedure is complex; to produce an analysis more in keeping with Figure 30, an intensive clerical effort is required. This, in turn, is a simplified version of a practical approach.

## Secondary apportionment

In carrying out the process of apportionment we have attempted to be fair and equitable in the distribution of overhead costs. Even so, we have still built up overhead charges for the non-productive or ancillary functions such as accounting, sales, maintenance and so forth.

It follows that as the ancillary functions or cost centres are not part of the production cycle, we must now re-apportion the overhead costs of those cost centres over the production functions in order to establish the basis of recovery.

This is known as a secondary apportionment. It is sometimes thought that as a general rule of thumb we should apply one of the two following concepts:

1　Re-apportion over all other departments the overhead costs of the ancillary department giving the most service; then the department giving the next most service, and so on.
2　Alternatively, re-apportion over all other departments the overhead costs of the ancillary department giving the least service. Then the department giving the next least, finishing with the ancillary department giving the most service.

We see that both these concepts require us to make some subjective assessment as to who gives what to whom.

It may be said that we could have avoided the necessity for secondary apportionment at the original or primary stage, for example, in apportioning rates by square area. By simply leaving out the area occupied by ancillary cost centres we automatically increase the rates charge to production cost centres. In general terms, this would indeed have been done. But it still does not overcome the problem of, say, the wages and salaries charged to the accounts department.

There are three methods commonly in use for carrying out secondary apportionment: elimination, repeated distribution and simultaneous equations.

## *Elimination*

This is the basis used in applying one or other of the rule of thumb concepts outlined above.

Each ancillary cost centre is re-apportioned in turn amongst all other cost centres. Once the ancillary cost centre has been apportioned, it is eliminated from any subsequent re-apportionments from any other ancillary cost centre.

To illustrate, we use the totals from Figure 30 in conjunction with the first and more usually applied rule of thumb. That is, take first the ancillary cost centre serving the greatest number of other cost centres.

We also need to assume some *pro rata* basis in order to carry out the re-apportionment. Let us therefore assume the following information:

|  | Production Depts. | | | General Admin. | Sales and Service |
|---|---|---|---|---|---|
|  | 1 | 2 | 3 | | |
| Percentage service given by general administration to all other departments | 40 | 30 | 20 | — | 10 |
| Percentage service given by sales and service to all other departments | 30 | 40 | 30 | — | — |

By applying the percentages to the total overhead costs shown in Figure 30, we will be able firstly to eliminate the general administration department total of £3000 in the proportions 40 : 30 : 20 : 10. This will build up the sales and service department total from £2400 to £2700 which will then be spread over the production departments only in the proportions 30 : 40 : 30. A table showing the full result is given in Figure 31(*a*).

| | Total | Production Depts. | | | Gen. Admin. | Sales and Service |
|---|---|---|---|---|---|---|
| | | 1 | 2 | 3 | | |
| Totals b/f from Figure 30 | 20 400 | 4 200 | 4 800 | 6 000 | 3 000 | 2 400 |
| General Admin. re-apportioned to all other cost centres | | 1 200 | 900 | 600 | (3 000) | 300 |
| Sales and Service re-apportioned to other cost centres | | 810 | 1 080 | 810 | — | (2 700) |
| *New overhead total costs* | £20 400 | £6 210 | £6 780 | £7 410 | — | — |

FIGURE 31 (a)

| | Total | Production Depts. | | | Gen. Admin. | Sales and Service |
|---|---|---|---|---|---|---|
| | | 1 | 2 | 3 | | |
| Totals b/f from Figure 30 | 20 400 | 4 200 | 4 800 | 6 000 | 3 000 | 2 400 |
| General Admin. re-apportioned | | 1 200 | 900 | 600 | (3 000) | 300 |
| Sales and Service re-apportioned | | 675 | 945 | 675 | 405 | (2 700) |
| General Admin. re-apportioned | | 162 | 122 | 81 | (405) | 40 |
| Sales and Service re-apportioned | | 10 | 14 | 10 | 6 | (40) |
| General Admin. re-apportioned | | 2 | 2 | 2 | (6) | |
| *New overhead total costs* | £20 400 | £6 249 | £6 783 | £7 368 | — | — |

FIGURE 31 (b)

| | Total | Production Depts. | | | Gen. Admin. | Sales and Service |
|---|---|---|---|---|---|---|
| | | 1 | 2 | 3 | | |
| Totals b/f from Figure 30 | 20 400 | 4 200 | 4 800 | 6 000 | 3 000 | 2 400 |
| General Admin. re-apportioned | | 1 364 | 1 024 | 683 | (3 411) | 341 |
| Sales and Service re-apportioned | | 685 | 959 | 685 | — | (2 741) |
| *New overhead total costs* | £20 400 | £6 249 | £6 783 | £7 368 | — | — |

FIGURE 31 (c)

## Repeated distribution

Under this method we continuously re-apportion any balances left under ancillary cost centre headings over all other cost centres, until none remains. We need to amend slightly the assumptions used under the elimination method as follows:

| | Production Depts. | | | General Admin. | Sales and Service |
|---|---|---|---|---|---|
| | *1* | *2* | *3* | | |
| Percentage service given by general administration to all other departments | 40 | 30 | 20 | — | 10 |
| Percentage service given by sales and service to all other departments | 25 | 35 | 25 | 15 | — |

We note that the last line has been changed so as to incorporate the general administration cost centre into the re-apportionment of sales and service overheads.

The method obtains its title for the following reason: the general administration overhead cost of £3000 shown in Figure 30 is re-apportioned over all other cost centres in the proportions 40 : 30 : 20 : 10. This will mean charging £300 to sales and service, thus increasing the total to £2700. This value is then distributed over all cost centres in the proportions 25 : 35 : 25 : 15. This will have the effect of charging another £405 to general administration. Therefore the distribution will have to be repeated to re-apportion the £405 over all other cost centres. This results in another charge to sales and service of £40. A table showing the full result is given in Figure 31(*b*).

## Simultaneous equations

These are a means of shortcutting the repeated distribution method by algebra. The accuracy or reliability of this method depends on judging the amount of service given by each ancillary cost centre to all other cost centres.

Assuming the information given under repeated distribution and the values from Figure 30, we proceed as follows:

1  General administration total overheads will be the £3000 already charged, plus 15% of the total overheads of Sales and Service.

2   Sales and Service total overheads will be the £2400 already charged plus 10% of the total overheads of General Administration.

These facts can now be assembled in notation form as follows:

Let $x$ = General administration total overhead
Let $y$ = Sales and service total overhead

|  |  |  |
|---|---|---|
|  | $x = £3\,000 + 15/100y$ | (1) |
|  | $y = £2\,400 + 10/100x$ | (2) |
| Multiply (1) by 100 | $100x = 300\,000 + 15y$ | (3) |
| Multiply (2) by 1000 | $1000y = 2\,400\,000 + 100x$ | (4) |
| Rearrange (3)    $100x$ | $- 15y = \quad 300\,000$ | (5) |
| Rearrange (4)    $- 100x$ | $+ 1000y = 2\,400\,000$ | (6) |
| Add (5) and (6) | $985y = 2\,700\,000$ |  |
| Therefore: | $y = £2\,741 \text{ (approx)}$ |  |
| Substitute $y$ in (1) | $x = £3\,000 + 15/100y$ |  |
|  | $x = 3\,000 + 411$ |  |
|  | $= £3411 \text{ (approx)}$ |  |

The appropriate values are now distributed over other cost centres by means of the distribution percentages, as demonstrated in Figure 31 (c).

## Absorption

This is the fourth and final step. It is the allotment of overhead to job, product, process or unit, that is, the recovery of overhead by the product. In order to cover the matter fully we need to consider the process in three distinct stages: the calculation of an absorption rate, the application of that rate to the base, and lastly a comparison to ensure that stages one and two are reconciled.

### The calculation of an absorption rate

Having collected, classified, allocated, apportioned and re-apportioned overhead costs, it would be foolish to calculate one rate only for the absorption of overhead for the firm as a whole. But this procedure is adopted by many organisations. It may be that they have good reason to use a 'blanket rate', as it is termed. It is more likely that there are at least three production departments who between them are manufacturing three or four different products. Some of those departments will be highly mechanised. Others will be largely manual. Others will have a combination of both machinery and operatives.

To use a blanket rate of absorption under those conditions is dangerous, since it can produce a total cost figure that may be misleading.

Even so, not all firms are blessed with organised and effective cost accounting departments or trained staff. Under these circumstances a blanket rate is better than nothing, provided the dangers are recognised.

There is no entirely suitable method of overhead absorption. Also, no one method is entirely suitable for any particular firm or type of industry.

The methods to be discussed are bases that can be amended or developed to suit the circumstances encountered.

All the methods call for predetermination and estimation of the numerator and denominator shown in the calculations.

There are three areas of calculation:

1  Percentage rates on direct labour cost, direct material cost and prime cost
2  Cost unit rates
3  Time rates: machine hour rates, direct labour hour rates and departmental hour rates.

*Percentage on direct labour cost*

Calculated by the following:

$$\frac{\text{Estimated overhead cost to be absorbed}}{\text{Estimated direct labour cost}} \times \frac{100}{1}$$

For example:

> *Production Dept 1.*
>
> >  Estimated overhead cost      £24 000
> >  Estimated direct labour cost   £20 000
>
> Overhead absorption rate:
>
> $$\frac{£24\,000}{£20\,000} \times \frac{100}{1} = 120\%$$

This method is simple and easy to work and has a universal appeal. It gives a reasonably satisfactory result where the overhead is low in relation to direct wages, and where relatively little machinery is being used. Some serious short-comings are that:

(a) owing to variations in the speed of operation and operator skill, overhead charges on the same or similar work could be incorrect.

(b) many overhead expenditures are time-related. Wage payments may be results-related.

*Percentage on direct material cost*

This is calculated as follows:

$$\frac{\text{Estimated overhead cost to be absorbed}}{\text{Estimated direct material cost}} \times \frac{100}{1}$$

For example:

> *Production Dept 1.*
>
> >  Estimated overhead cost      £24 000
> >  Estimated direct material cost   £10 800
>
> Overhead absorption rate:
>
> $$\frac{£24\,000}{£10\,800} \times \frac{100}{1} = 45\%$$

This is not usually regarded as a sound or practical method because few overhead expenditures vary directly with the value, quality or quantity of the material used. Consider the following situation: a component takes ten minutes to manufacture; it may be made of sheet steel or sheet gold. Manufacturing from the latter material would mean that the product would be charged with high time-related expenses.

*Percentage on prime cost*

This is calculated as follows:

$$\frac{\text{Estimated overhead cost to be absorbed}}{\text{Estimated prime cost}} \times \frac{100}{1}$$

For example:

*Production Dept 1.*

| | |
|---|---|
| Estimated overhead cost | £24 000 |
| Estimated prime cost | £30 800 |

Overhead absorption rate:

$$\frac{£24\,000}{£30\,800} \times \frac{100}{1} = 78\%$$

We note that the prime cost of £30 800 in the example above is the sum of estimated direct labour cost and estimated direct material cost from the previous examples.

Generally, the prime cost method is only suitable where the products of a firm are always made in the same manufacturing mix and always have the same direct labour/direct material proportion to prime cost. There can be very few circumstances that meet those fairly stringent conditions.

*Cost unit rate*

This is calculated as follows:

$$\frac{\text{Estimated overhead cost to be absorbed}}{\text{Estimated units of production}}$$

For example:

Estimated overhead cost       £24 000
Estimated production       160 000 units

Overhead absorption rate:

$$\frac{£24\,000}{160\,000} = £0{\cdot}15 \text{ per unit}$$

This method is only suitable for use in firms or cost centres producing uniform or homogeneous units.

If used in any other situation there is a great danger that costs will be over- or under-loaded for overhead absorption.

*Machine hour rate*

This is calculated as follows:

$$\frac{\text{Estimated overhead cost to be absorbed}}{\text{Estimated machine hours}}$$

For example:

*Production Dept 1.*

Estimated overhead costs       £24 000
Estimated machine hours       32 000

Overhead absorption rate:

$$\frac{£24\,000}{32\,000} = £0{\cdot}75 \text{ per machine hour}$$

Where the firm or production cost centre is predominantly

capital-intensive, this is undoubtedly an accurate method of overhead absorption provided estimates are correct.

Much clerical and investigation work is necessary before a machine hour rate can be calculated. One must first decide whether a machine or group of machines will be used as the basis, and this may require a reappraisal of the apportionment procedure being used for a particular functional cost centre.

Secondly, we face the difficulty of the machine hours factor. The important step is to calculate net machine hours, that is, machine hours exclusive of idle time or machine breakdown and so forth. The labour cost for these non-

| MACHINE HOUR RATE | | REVIEW PERIOD |
| --- | --- | --- |
| Department | | Department No. |
| Machine group | | Machine Group no. |
| Direct operatives per M/C | | Total machines |
| Normal operator hours per week | | Total H.P. |
| Normal set-up time per week | | Total annual depreciation |
| Allowed personal time per op. | | Total machine hours |

| Detail of expense | Basis of Apportionment | Total | Machine Value | M/c Hour Rate |
| --- | --- | --- | --- | --- |
| | | | | |
| | | | £ | £ |

MACHINE HOUR RATE

| Prepared by | Date |
| --- | --- |
| Checked by | Date |
| In use from | Next review date |

FIGURE 32

productive hours will be part of the overhead cost chargeable to the department. By including indirect costs in the overhead but excluding non-productive hours from net machine hours, the machine hour rate can be made a realistic basis for absorption.

The machine hour rate method requires constant attention, and review. The use of machines can be irregular or erratic, for causes outside the general control of individual managers. Machine running hours may vary considerably from the estimate from period to period. This could cause repercussions in the recovery of overheads. Figure 32 gives a general view of the type of machine hour rate computation that is required.

## *The direct labour hour rate method*

This is calculated as follows:

$$\frac{\text{Estimated overhead cost to be absorbed}}{\text{Estimated direct labour hours}}$$

For example:

*Production Dept 1.*

| | |
|---|---|
| Estimated overhead cost | £24 000 |
| Estimated direct labour hours | 40 000 |

Overhead absorption rate:

$$\frac{£24\,000}{40\,000} = £0\!\cdot\!60 \text{ per direct labour hour}$$

In the case of a department or cost centre which is predominantly labour-intensive, with little or no expensive equipment, this method has much to recommend it in terms of simplicity and accuracy.

It is emphasised that the direct labour hours used in the

calculation must be net of lost time and personal allowances. That is, it must be the real estimated productive time.

## The departmental hour rate

This is calculated by the following:

$$\frac{\text{Estimated overhead cost to be absorbed}}{\text{Estimated departmental labour hours}}$$

For example:

*Production Dept 1.*

| | |
|---|---|
| Estimated overheads | £24 000 |
| Estimated departmental labour hours | 24 000 |

Overhead absorption rate:

$$\frac{£24\ 000}{24\ 000} = £1{\cdot}00 \text{ per departmental labour hour}$$

This is a variation on the machine hour rate, but it takes as its basis a group of people working as a team, rather than a group of similar machines being used in the productive process. There are some group manufacturing situations in which the individual members perform an individual skill. There is no advantage in regarding operatives as individuals in this case but every advantage to be gained by considering their blend of skills as a team.

## An example of the calculations

Let us take the example of Figure 30. By referring back it will be seen that this formed the basis of secondary apportionment which we summarised in Figure 31.

We take the values shown in Figure 31 (*b*) for each of the production departments. These contain the re-apportioned overhead costs of all the ancillary cost centres. The production department total overhead costs are now:

| Production Dept 1 | £6 249 |
| 2 | 6 783 |
| 3 | 7 368 |
| | £20 400 |

We assume that, after investigation, a decision has been reached to calculate overhead absorption rates on the following bases:

Production Dept 1: machine hour rate
Production Dept 2: direct labour hours
Production Dept 3: percentage on direct labour cost

The following information is available:

| | | Production Depts. | | |
| | Total | 1 | 2 | 3 |
| --- | --- | --- | --- | --- |
| Direct labour costs | £20 578 | £4 166 | £9 044 | £7 368 |
| Machine hours | | 8 680 | | |
| Direct labour hours | | | 13 044 | |

We can now calculate overhead absorption rates for the three production departments:

| | Production Depts. | | |
| | 1 | 2 | 3 |
| --- | --- | --- | --- |
| Total overhead costs | £6 249 | £6 783 | £7 368 |
| Machine hours | 8 680 | | |
| Direct labour hours | | 13 044 | |
| Direct labour cost | | | £7 368 |
| Absorption rate | £0·72 | £0·52 | 100% |
| | *per machine hour* | *per labour hour* | *on direct labour cost* |

*The application of the rate to the base*

We now have all the information to be able to carry out overhead absorption, that is, the recovery of overhead by the product.

To do this we shall consider part of a manufactured product—Component 936.

The direct material cost as recorded on stores requisitions and established, in accordance with one of the methods discussed in Chapter 3, was £2·00.

The direct labour cost as recorded and paid in accordance with the procedures discussed in Chapter 4 was:

| Production Dept | Direct Labour Cost | Machine Hours | Direct Labour Hours |
|---|---|---|---|
| 1 | £10·00 | 21 | |
| 2 | 5·00 | | 7·25 |
| 3 | 3·00 | | |

Using this data, we can make up the cost of production as follows:

*Component 936*

| | | | |
|---|---|---|---|
| Direct materials | | | £2·00 |
| Direct labour: *Dept 1* | | £10·00 | |
| 2 | | £5·00 | |
| 3 | | £3·00 | £18·00 |
| | | | |
| Overheads absorbed: | | | |
| *Dept 1* 21 machine hours @ £0·72 | | £15·12 | |
| 2 7·25 labour hours @ £0·52 | | £3·77 | |
| 3 100% on direct lab. £3·00 | | £3·00 | £21·89 |
| | | | |
| Total cost of component | | | £41·89 |

Thus we are able to build up the total cost of manufacture from the three elements of cost. If Component 936 were a saleable item whose general market price were, say, £60, the organisation could continue to manufacture, knowing that its cost was £41·89. If the market price was, say, £40, then there is a clear warning to the firm that it cannot enter the market at current cost price; alternatively it could continue to manufacture but would have to look at the cost structure to see if it can discover where cost reductions could be made.

## *Absorption of administration, selling and distribution overheads*

We have apportioned administration, selling and distribution overheads on the assumption that the same sort of relationship exists as for production overheads. But is this a practical assumption?

Works or production overheads can be related to some reasonably realistic unit of measurement such as the machine hour or direct labour cost. To make the same assumptions for non-production overheads may encourage hit or miss absorption. It is quite usual to have a totally separate basis for the major areas of administration, selling and distribution overhead absorption. The methods most widely used are:

(a) As a percentage of works cost—a popular method because of its simplicity, and quite suitable where the overhead cost of the non-productive department is small relative to total cost.

(b) As a percentage of conversion cost, where conversion cost is calculated as selling price less direct material costs and profit. This method disposes of the anomalies which arise from differing material costs and material types.

(c) As a percentage of selling price. An easy and popular method especially if administration, selling and distribution overheads tend to be fixed rather than variable. Where the products are sold at standard or catalogue prices, this method can give quite accurate results.

(d) At a rate per article sold. This method presents difficulties where a wide variety of dissimilar articles is manufactured and sold, unless separate rates can be established for each major group of goods. Where the organisation makes a narrow range of similar goods or is a single-product company, this method can be reasonably accurate.

*Comparison to ensure that calculation and application are reconcilable*

This is the third aspect of the absorption process that will need attention, since overheads may be over- or under-absorbed.

How will the over- or under-absorbed balance arise? The following matters need to be considered:

1 In calculating the absorption rate, estimates were necessary to predetermine the rate.
2 If the actual overhead is at a higher level than the estimated overhead, then, other matters remaining constant, overheads will be under-recovered. For example:

| | |
|---|---|
| Estimated overheads | £1 000 |
| Estimated direct labour costs | £1 000 |
| Overhead absorption rate | 100% |
| Actual overheads | £1 200 |
| Actual direct labour cost | £1 000 |
| Overheads recovered at 100% on direct labour | £1 000 |

*Under-recovery:*

| | |
|---|---|
| Actual recovery *less* actual expenditure | £200 |

The reverse is true if actual overheads are lower than estimated overheads; there will then be an over-recovery of overheads.

3 If the actual costs or units are higher than estimated, with actual and estimated overhead costs the same, there will be an over-recovery of overheads. For example:

| | |
|---|---:|
| Estimated overheads costs | £1000 |
| Estimate direct labour cost | £1000 |
| Overhead absorption rate | 100% |
| Actual overhead cost | £1000 |
| Actual direct labour cost | £1200 |
| Overheads recovered at 100% on direct labour | £1200 |

*Over-recovery:*
Actual recovery *less* actual expenditure   £200

The reverse is true if actual costs or units are lower than estimated. There will then be an under-recovery.

4 More serious problems arise when both the numerator and the denominator in the calculation have changed. In this case establishing under- or over-recovery becomes more difficult. For example:

| | | |
|---|---|---:|
| (*a*) | Estimated overhead costs | £1000 |
| | Estimated direct labour costs | £1000 |
| | Overhead absorption rate | 100% |
| | Actual overhead cost | £800 |
| | Actual direct labour | £1200 |
| | Overheads recovered at 100% on direct labour | £1200 |

    *Over-recovery:*
    Actual recovery *less* actual expenditure   £400

or

| | | |
|---|---|---:|
| (*b*) | Actual overhead cost | £1100 |
| | Actual direct labour | £900 |
| | Overheads recovered at 100% on direct labour | £900 |

    *Under-recovery:*
    Actual recovery *less* actual expenditure   £200

If the actual expenditures rise or fall in the same relationship there will be neither over- or under-recovery.

Observation of under- and over-recovery is a necessary part of control and an important part of the cost ascertainment system. Each case of under- and over-recovery must be investigated so that action can be taken if necessary.

In cost accounting these differences are dealt with in one of two ways:

1 By transferring them to a costing profit and loss account after each costing period.
2 By allowing the differences to accumulate in an overhead control account and hopefully cancel out. Any balance remaining at the end of the year must be transferred to the profit and loss account.

Large interim differences are generally caused by some abnormal factor. If it is known that there will be no repetition it is best to adopt Method 1 above. If the differences are large but are covered by known and anticipated abnormal conditions, it is best to adopt Method 2 above and wait for things to even out. There is no purpose to be served by constantly adjusting absorption rates to make up for minor differences: to do so would produce inconsistent cost comparisons.

### Exercises

1 From the following information you are required to prepare a report recommending (with brief supporting reasons) which of the following types of overhead absorption rate the XY Company Limited should use for its factory, which consists of eight production departments.

  (a) A rate for the factory as a whole or a rate for each department;
  (b) An actual rate or a pre-determined rate;

    (c) A rate based on any one or combination of the following;

        (i)   direct wages
        (ii)  direct labour hours
        (iii) prime cost
        (iv) machine hours

The following information about the company is given:

(a) The company makes a wide range of products.
(b) Although 15–20 products account for about 30% of sales each year, sales of the remainder vary considerably from year to year.
(c) Direct material costs of individual products vary from about 10% to 60% of their selling prices.
(d) Total sales volume can vary considerably from year to year.
(e) Because of the company's stock policy, about 70% of total manufacturing is carried out in the second half of the year.
(f) Throughout the factory, direct wage rates vary from £0·65 to £1·80 per hour, but within any individual department, the differences between the highest and the lowest rates do not exceed 5%.
(g) Every product passes through each department but does not spend a proportionately equal amount of time in each.
(h) In two departments which are heavily mechanised, the ratios of overhead to direct labour are 3·5 and 4·0 to 1 respectively. In the other departments, this ratio ranges from about 2·0 to 1, to 0·5 to 1. (ICMA)

2 The overhead allocated to the three production cost centres and two service cost centres of the manufacturing division of a company were:

| Production cost centre | 1 | £20 000 |
|---|---|---|
| | 2 | 24 000 |
| | 3 | 36 000 |
| Service cost centre | S | 13 500 |
| | T | 9 500 |

After a study it is decided that the costs of the service cost centres should be apportioned as follows:

| | | Production cost centres | | | Service cost centres | |
|---|---|---|---|---|---|---|
| | | 1 % | 2 % | 3 % | S % | T % |
| Service cost centre: | S | Nil | 55 | 35 | — | 10 |
| | T | 45 | 35 | 15 | 5 | — |

You are required to calculate the total overhead chargeable to each production cost centre by each of the following methods:

(a) ignoring the service that each of the two service cost centres gives to the other;

(b) using a 'two-step' method of apportionment, whereby costs of the service cost centre that serves most cost centres is apportioned first, and the other cost centre is then apportioned to the production cost centres;

(c) using the 'repeated distribution' or 'continuous allotment' method of apportioning the costs of service cost centres among the production and the two service cost centres.           (ICMA)

3  As a cost consultant you have been given the periodic profit statements and the product cost sheets of a number of companies in the same line of business. List five important overhead topics on which you would expect to find similarity of costing treatment before you could make any direct comparisons between the figures. For

each topic give a simple example of how differences might arise in the make-up of the relevant figures.

(ICMA)

4   The Super Filing Cabinet Company has three production departments, Machining, Assembling and Spraying, and, two service departments, Internal Transport and Production Control. During 1971 the company plans to produce 5000 filing cabinets. The estimated costs being:

| | | |
|---|---|---|
| *Material* | Direct | £75 000 |
| | Internal transport | 5 000 |
| *Labour* | Machining: | |
| | 20 000 hours at £0·60 | |
| | 5 000 hours at £0·50 | |
| | Assembling: | |
| | 10 000 hours at £0·60 | |
| | 10 000 hours at £0·50 | |
| | 10 000 hours at £0·40 | |
| | Spraying: | |
| | 8 000 hours at £0·50 | |
| | 2 000 hours at £0·40 | |
| | Internal Transport | 3 000 |
| | Production Control | 6 000 |
| *Other allocated costs:* | | |
| | Machine shop | 11 000 |
| | Assembly shop | 9 360 |
| | Spray shop | 4 020 |
| | Internal Transport | 2 000 |
| | Production Control | 2 000 |

On the basis of the estimated benefit received, the service departments' costs are apportioned as follows:

*Internal Transport:*

Machine shop 60%, Assembly shop 30%, Spray shop 10%

*Production Control:*

Machine shop 30%, Assembly shop 30%, Spray shop 30%, Internal Transport 10%

You are required to:

(*a*)  prepare a statement showing the overhead to be absorbed by each of the three production departments;

(*b*)  briefly describe three methods by which overhead can be absorbed;

(*c*)  using the method you consider most appropriate, calculate the rate to be used for absorbing the machine shop overhead.  (ICMA)

# Part II

## Cost Ascertainment

# 6

# Introduction to Cost Ascertainment

In the first five chapters we have laid the groundwork for the remainder of this book.

We now need to define, discuss and examine cost ascertainment, that is, to look at the various methods used in practice to arrive at the costs of jobs, products, processes and services.

It will be appreciated that the same ascertainment system would not be used to determine the cost of a new multi-million pound hospital, a typewriter, a packet of biscuits or flying a scheduled service aircraft between London and New York. We shall see that the cost unit differs for each of those products. The cost unit is important in determining which method of ascertainment will produce the desired result. It may be necessary to have more than one method in an organisation owing to diversity of production.

## The need for cost ascertainments

It is said that accountants only deal with facts and that facts can only be substantiated because they are yesterday's events. It is true that the ascertainment systems we shall look at are concerned with recording past events. For that reason cost ascertainment has become known as 'historical costing'.

Because of this 'compilation in arrears', many critics take the view that cost ascertainment, as we shall discuss it, is an outmoded concept with little relevance to the competitive economic climate of today. The information it produces is so out of date as to be useless for making the decisions of tomorrow.

Excessive time-lag is usually due to poor organisation; a well-organised cost ascertainment system produces historical data so close to the event that effective action for the future *can* be taken. The first reason for having a cost ascertainment system is cost control; the counterpart to cost control is fast, accurate cost reporting.

The second reason concerns selling price and the state of the market. However much the critics take historical costing to task, when decisions are being made about selling prices and product markets, there is no substitute for fast, accurate cost reporting. Without the recording of the cost data connected with manufacture of a particular product, the organisation is blind. A firm without a cost reporting system could, for instance, make a range of products and sell them at what seems to them to be the relevant price; at the end of the year when all the expenditures are added up and the total is found to be greater than the sales revenue, there is nothing to explain the how and why of the loss.

A third reason follows from the previous two. It centres around the need to measure profit and hence profitability. The term 'profit' is expressed as an absolute sum of money and can be measured as the difference between revenue and cost; but we still need to define 'what revenue?' and 'what cost' in order to justify the magnitude of profit. The term 'profitability' is a relationship, expressed in percentage terms, or as a ratio, between the absolute sum of profit and some other absolute money sum such as sales or capital employed.

It may be an extremely difficult and time-consuming operation to arrive at figures of this nature in a multi-product organisation which does not have a cost ascertainment system.

A fourth reason for having a cost ascertainment system is to enable the firm to discover what should *not* happen— that is, to discover something about the characteristics of cost which we defined as 'normality' and 'controllability'. If something is happening other than is normally expected, action must be taken to control that deviation.

For example, let us suppose that a scrap or wastage level is established at 10% of the cost of direct material inputs. In the actual event, calculation shows scrap levels at 12%. Immediate management action to discover the cause and avoid a repetition could be taken if a cost reporting system brought the fact to light. This type of information is a highly desirable asset in effective management control. It would be difficult to produce such information without an effective ascertainment and reporting system.

## The main methods

We have established that, in relating costs to job, product, process or service, the nature of the cost unit concerned will determine the recording and analysis system required. We can identify two major areas of recording and analysis, one concerned with the cost of the job, the other concerned with the cost of the unit.

### Systems concerned with the cost of the job

These involve relating costs to an individual job or batch of production or contract. The order to proceed may be customer-originated or internally-originated.

The method is employed:

1 When each job or batch or contract is different from every other job or batch or contract either by reason of the physical dimensions, by reason of numbers produced, or by method of production.

2 When, although a job or batch or contract does not differ by reason of size or numbers, it is desirable to identify and segregate cost for each job, batch or contract.

## Systems concerned with the cost of the unit

This is another way of describing the methods used to ascertain an 'average unit cost' over a given period of time for a known or calculated number of homogeneous units. The units in question might be as follows:

1 The number of passengers carried over a particular route—passenger/miles.
2 The amount of coal or sand or ballast extracted—tons.
3 The output of a brewery—gallons.
4 The products of a food factory—cartons or gross of tins.

These examples are not exhaustive but they indicate the variety of ways in which unit description may be employed to measure output. Under these circumstances we are concerned with unit costing in one of two major forms:

1 Process costing—where the output is almost continuous, as in food and drink production.
2 Operating costing—where the output is measured by the service produced. For example, where the units are passenger miles.

## Non-manufacturing and commercial operations

It may appear that we are overly concerned with manufacture and production, to the exclusion of all other forms of enterprise. This is not really so. It may be true that in discussing cost accounting, greater emphasis is given to trade than to commerce. This is due, in the main, to the fact that manufacturing and production industries gave rise to and nurtured the process of cost accounting because of their intrinsic need and desire to control day-to-day operations. This may not apply in the same sense to banks, insurance companies, estate agents and so forth, but even so, there is evidence to indicate that these commercial functions, together with central and local government, do generally subscribe to the tenets advanced within the general understanding of cost accounting. The fund of knowledge and expertise in commercial and public services with respect to control and decision theory is as authoritative as in any other sphere. The method of cost ascertainment is more likely to be concerned with unit than job.

## What cost?

The methods outlined will be explained in detail in subsequent chapters. Meanwhile, note that we are discussing the matter of recording or ascertaining the *actual* costs of job, product, process or service on a historical cost basis. At a later point we shall discuss the computation of costs on a standard cost basis in an attempt to formulate more effective information for management control.

Remember, no one system of costing can be regarded as common to all organisations. A system must be tailor-made to suit an organisation, its products and the method of manufacture.

## Exercises

1  What are the requirements of a good information system? Discuss the function of cost ascertainment within that system.

2  A principal point in connection with the creation of a cost system is a knowledge of the company's plant,

methods, layout and flow of work. With this knowledge the accountant possesses the essential background information to develop cost ascertainment procedures. Explain how the accountant would use this knowledge.

3 Every firm and industry is different and requires to be studied before we decide which ascertainment will be most suitable. Attempt in a general way to decide which method would be best for each of the following organisations and industries:

| | |
|---|---|
| Cardboard boxes | Office equipment |
| Breakfast cereals | Man-made fibres |
| Toys and games | Baby foods |
| Steel | Paint |
| Meat | Wallpaper |
| Leather goods | Motor cars |

You are now required to justify your choice with respect to your answer for 'Breakfast cereals', 'Office equipment' and 'Motor cars'. You should make as full an explanation as possible.

4 One of the prime functions of the management accountant is to prepare data on which management can base their decisions. Outline the reasons why, in preparing such data, the accountant should relate this information to a system of 'responsibility' accounting. (ICMA)

5 'The accounting system is intertwined with operating management. Business operations would be a hopeless tangle without the paperwork that is so often regarded with disdain.' Do you agree? Explain, giving examples.

# 7

# Job and Batch Costing

## Job costing

The Concise Oxford Dictionary gives two possible definitions of 'job',

Job (*Noun*): Piece of work, especially one done for hire or profit;
Job (*Verb*): Do jobs, hire for definite time or job, let out on hire.

It is implicit that 'the piece of work' or 'doing the job' would not be done without specific instructions to that effect.

In the manufacturing field we find a great array of diverse operations being performed on a jobbing basis by organisations who are selling their skill, expertise and factory capacity in order to produce a job to order.

We should not assume that the job is only a single item; it could be for hundreds.

The features of jobbing within which a system of job costing will operate may thus be as follows:

1  Every job order may be different.
2  Every job order is to *customer* specification.
3  Every job is subject to estimation before acceptance.
4  Every job is subject to the receipt of a firm order before proceeding.
5  A job is not necessarily for one item only.

6 A jobbing organisation has no product but sells skill, expertise, experience and capacity.

As a corollary to these general features there are usually other features affecting the operation of the jobbing organisation. They are as follows:

1 Because each job is different, the firm may need to have greater mobility of operatives. That is, the degree of skill in the work force will need to be at a higher level than in many other manufacturing situations.

2 Because each job is different the firm will have to adopt a unique stock holding and control policy. This will be necessary due to the fact that specific orders require specific materials, the specifications and quantities for which will not be the subject of a firm purchase order until the customer gives the go-ahead. However, if an organisation has a known skill in, say, fabricating stainless steel, it will almost certainly have some stocks of stainless steel sheets and nuts and bolts. But the problems of control are vastly different from the organisation which knows future production commitments with reasonable certainty.

3 Due to the two features mentioned above, the most important requirements are a reliable system of production control, and an up-to-date, accurate system of cost ascertainment, analysis and reporting.

Job costing is therefore a method devised to provide separate actual cost information for each individual job or order, to ascertain whether the job has been profitable, and as some form of check on the estimating procedure.

## Job identification

If a jobbing organisation is carrying out a wide range of work on numerous orders for a wide range of customers, identification of each job, both physically and with documents, is essential.

The usual practise in a jobbing organisation is to issue a job number as each order is received. This number then becomes a very useful means of identification because:

1  Material can be ordered against that number.
2  Material destined for use on the order can be physically tagged or labelled.
3  Job cards for operatives can be prepared, quoting that number.
4  All documents, drawings and specifications together with the original estimate can be identified.
5  A cost ascertainment system can be devised around the fact that each customer order going round the production floor has a number against which all facts can be gathered.

The principles of classification can be used to advantage in devising a job number system which will be informative, flexible, expandable—perhaps along the following lines:

*1st digit*—indicating year the customer placed the order.
*2nd and 3rd digits*—the month in which the order was received.
*4th and 5th digits*—the number of the order in that month.

For example:

> *Job number 51092*
> —received in 1975                                         —5
> —during the month of October   —10
> —was the 92nd order received
>     in October                                              —92

By reference to the original documents, the estimated delivery time can be established and a simple control system evolved.

## Job planning and estimating

Factories that undertake jobbing work need very careful and detailed planning to ensure that production facilities are used effectively.

Every job is different although it may have a share of standard components, or even be a repeat order.

The production planning department is usually responsible for drawing up material and labour schedules for each job and fitting them into some form of overall master plan.

These schedules must be based on some clear statement of the customer's requirements as interpreted by the organisation and agreed by the customer. The responsibility for this rests with the estimating department.

An estimate is a predetermined cost, calculated by considering all the aspects of the material to be used and its availability, the grade, skill and availability of the labour to be used, the capacity and availability of machines. These facts are then evaluated in monetary terms with some addition for the recovery of overheads, and for profit. The skill of the estimator and the manner in which he can be supported by the cost ascertainment system are very important to a production planning department and to their confidence in scheduling customers' orders. A feedback system of cost reporting is of vital importance in this situation.

## Job cost procedure

The principal function of a job costing procedure is the accurate assignment of actual cost to the individual job.

To do this it is usual to have a job cost card for each individual job on which to record all the details of cost.

Because the number of entries against any one job tend to be small it is usual to find full details entered on the face of the card together with the estimate for comparison purposes. Where experience shows that numerous entries are usual for each job, the card could be redesigned to accommodate details on the reverse, the totals of costs being transferred to the face of the card at the end of the job for comparison with the estimate.

A typical job cost card of the 'few entries' type mentioned above is shown in Figure 33. We see that this is a

| | JOB COST CARD | | | | | Job No._____ | | |
|---|---|---|---|---|---|---|---|---|
| Customer_____ | | | | | | Order No._____ | | |
| Job Description_____ | | | | | | Date_____ | | |
| _____ | | | | | | Delivery by _____ | | |

| MATERIALS | | | | | | TOTAL COST | | |
|---|---|---|---|---|---|---|---|---|
| Date | Reference | Details | Qty. | Rate | Value | Actual | Estimate | Diff. |
| | | | | | | | | |
| | | | | | | | | |
| | | | | | | | | |
| | | | | | | | | |
| **LABOUR** | | | | | | | | |
| Date | Cost Centre | Operative | Hrs. | Rate | Value | | | |
| | | | | | | | | |
| | | | | | | | | |
| | | | | | | | | |
| | | | | | | | | |
| **OVERHEADS** | | | | | | | | |
| Date | Cost Centre | Basis | Base | Rate | Value | | | |
| | | | | | | | | |
| | | | | | | | | |
| | | | | | | | | |
| | | | | | | | | |
| Total Factory Cost | | | | | | | | |
| Administration Overhead | | | | | | | | |
| Selling and Distribution Overhead | | | | | | | | |
| *TOTAL COST* | | | | | | | | |
| *PROFIT* | | | | | | | | |
| *SELLING PRICE* | | | | | | £ | £ | £ |
| Costs prepared by_____ | | | | | | Date____ | | |
| Sales Invoice No. _____ | | | | | | Date____ | | |

FIGURE 33

complete record of actual cost with reference back to source, together with the estimated cost, and a column to record differences between actual and estimated costs.

Not only is this a record of final actual costs, but it may also be used as the basis for the production of interim reports whilst the job is still in progress on the shop floor.

## The source of entries

Let us remind ourselves of the origin of the elements of expenditure: direct materials will be charged by

(a) Stores requisition, where standard or stock material is withdrawn from stores;
(b) Purchase invoices for special material bought in for that specific job;
(c) Transfer notes, to transfer stock or standard material issued to one job but now required for a different job.

Direct labour will be charged through the time- and job-booking process in use. One normally finds an extensive job card system in jobbing industries, in conjunction with some form of incentive payment. Clearly it is in the best interests of the organisation to maintain a smooth flow of work, not only to meet the customer's delivery time, but also to allow the capacity to be made available for the next order. High levels of activity may be encouraged by good incentive systems, and the result can be high quality with low unit labour cost.

Overhead cost will be absorbed in the manner described in Chapter 5, on predetermined rates probably based on direct labour cost or direct labour hours. Where the unit is man- rather than machine-power, it is usually difficult in jobbing to evolve any other basis. It was mentioned that jobbing is usually found to have a high degree of labour mobility, that is, employees capable of operating a wide range of equipment and having a wide number of skills. Thus, direct labour cost or hours may be the most reasonable basis for absorption.

## Completed jobs

The remaining point for discussion arises after the job has been completed, the work delivered to the customer and the sales invoice raised. A control procedure must include some system by which the cost accounts department is notified that a job is completed. Such a procedure could simply mean a document being used to transfer the work from the shop floor to the despatch department. Alternatively a despatch note might be raised to accompany the goods on delivery.

A copy of either document sent to the cost accounts department would be a sufficient signal to close down the job cost card and finalise the figures.

Finalisation is usually carried out, after adding and checking actual cost figures, by inserting any necessary calculations for administration, selling and distribution overheads, where allowance has not been made for them within the overhead being applied in the main body of costs.

Cards for finished jobs can then be summarised in a schedule, for the purpose of completing the accounting entries and as a basis for reporting to management.

## Accounting and recording entries

These are shown in Figure 34, where each block represents a ledger account.

Lines numbered 1, 2 and 3 represent the initial inputs to stock, wages and overheads; those numbered 4, 5 and 6 show the transfer of materials, wages and overhead to work in progress, whilst lines numbered 7 and 8 show the output

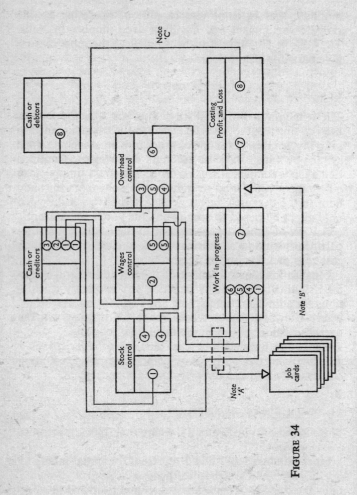

FIGURE 34

of completed work to finished goods and thence to customers.

Note 'A' indicates the point at which the collection of costs is made to individual job cards; note 'B' indicates the point at which the final total cost of completed jobs can be extracted as the basis for making entry 7; and note 'C' indicates the point at which the total sales value of completed and delivered jobs may be entered from sales invoices as a comparison with final job cost, in order to establish profit. This block diagram should be studied in conjunction with a separate text on accountancy and the later chapter on cost accounting bookkeeping, to establish the more formal debit and credit entries.

## Batch costing

This is a method of cost ascertainment which uses all the features of a job costing system and, at the same time, has the basic feature of a unit costing system, in that orders of similar amounts which have a distinct relationship to each other are arranged in batches. Each batch is described as a batch or 'works order'. At the end of the batch the costs are totalled, divided by the numbers of units produced on that batch, to give the unit or average cost.

The circumstances under which this method of cost ascertainment would be used are twofold:

1 By the smaller business which has its own recognisable and saleable products, but which, because of the limited market for those products, cannot adopt the more intensive methods of production used by large organisations. Such organisations might be found among producers of hardware and electrical equipment.
2 By the larger business with a multi-product range. Such organisations may be found in the consumer goods and

consumer durables markets such as household and garden equipment, furniture and so forth.

Essentially, batch costing is a factory job costing system within which the order is created internally for the manufacture of a quantity of identical components or parts, usually for stock. It is usual to find that in an organisation using batch production, the batch order is referred to as a 'stock order'; on completion, the finished parts are delivered to a specific store, known as a 'parts' or 'component' store, for future issue. It is essential in such a system to have well-organised production control and cost accounting documentation.

## Batch size

With this method the size of the batch to be produced is highly critical in ensuring a 'least cost' operation. The general principles that were discussed with respect to an Economic Order Quantity apply equally to the batch size of productions.

The same constraints or limitations apply: to carry too much stock by increasing batch size and decreasing the number of batches, will increase stock costs; but to decrease batch size, and increase the number of batches, will increase the set-up costs of preparing a machine or piece of equipment for production. Set-up usually involves fixing specific tools or jigs in a particular manner to a machine. It requires either a highly-skilled setter, if the machine is to be operated by a semi-skilled operative, or a skilled setter/operator. In neither case can set-up time be regarded as a direct labour cost to production.

### Batch costing procedure and classification

The comments made with respect to job planning, estimating and procedure for a job costing system, apply here almost without exception, right down to the job card displayed in Figure 33. The only real differences are those of title; rather than refer to 'job planning', 'job cards', 'job number' and so forth, one refers to 'batch planning', 'batch card', and 'batch number'. There are, however, some essential differences in the procedure on the production floor, and on completion of the job. These differences occur because the customer is not a third party outside the firm, but an internal customer for stores, partly finished stores, component stores and other batch numbers or assembly sections. For this reason a well-thought-out and well-designed part number, component, sub-assembly and assembly classification system is a critical feature of batch production and control.

It is outside the scope of this work to discuss the manner in which a parts and component numbering system can be organised. There are many excellent texts on production control in which reference is made to flexible coding.

### Accounting and recording entries

These are shown in Figure 35, where each block represents a ledger account and follows the general pattern established in Figure 34.

We observe that Figure 35 is really an extension of the 'work-in-progress' and 'completed work' sections of Figure 34, with batch cards replacing job cards and notes 'A', 'B', 'C' and 'D' indicating the point at which values of completed parts, components, sub-assemblies and finished goods are established for transfer to their respective stocks.

This block diagram should be studied in conjunction with

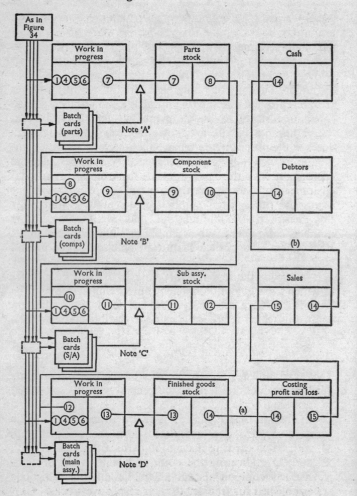

FIGURE 35

a separate text on accountancy and the later chapter on cost accounting bookkeeping, to establish the more formal debit and credit entries.

## Exercises

1 XY Constructors Ltd manufactures special purpose machines to customers' specifications, the average production time being three months. Quotations to customers are based on carefully prepared estimates of costs. Describe a system which will enable the management to be made aware of excess material usage and operatives' times and comment briefly upon the way in which information should be given. (ACCA)

2 An automatic lathe is loaded, tended and unloaded by a machinist. Different parts, requiring resetting of the lathe, are made in batches of 500. A skilled setter is employed and his cost works out at £7 per setting. Rejects average five per run. The additional cost of rectifying a reject is £0·2 each.

The foreman suggests to the production manager that the machinist would do his own setting if he received an extra allowance of £3 per run. The foreman appreciates that less skill would be employed, but from unofficial tests he estimates the outcome of runs would be as follows:

> 70% of runs would have   5 rejects
> 10% of runs would have  25 rejects
> 10% of runs would have  75 rejects
> 10% of runs would have 125 rejects

You are required to advise the production manager whether this suggestion merits further consideration and quantify any advantage. (ICA)

3  A jobbing factory requires a costing system to show works cost and gross profit on each job and against estimate. You are required to describe briefly the important factors in such a system and design a suitable job cost card for use in the system.

4  Jobbers Ltd are general engineers with machine – tool capacity. Job No. T64 has now been completed after incurring the following costs:

| | |
|---|---|
| *Direct Material* | 2 tons 13 cwt at £1·75 per cwt |
| *Direct Wages:* | |
| Machining 1 | 38 hours at £0·78 per hour |
| Machining 2 | 70 hours at £1·07 per hour |

Overhead recovery for jobs is calculated from the following basis:

| | *Estimated annual overheads* | *Estimated annual hours* |
|---|---|---|
| Machining 1 | £25 200 | 70 000 |
| Machining 2 | £35 840 | 56 000 |

The fixed overheads are recovered on a basis of 'per week job'. The current rate is £2 per T64, which has been running for 15 weeks.

You are required to:

(a)  design a suitable record card
(b)  enter the above information to ascertain the job cost.

# 8

# Contract Costing

Contract costing is job costing as applied to the building and civil engineering industry and certain types of heavy engineering firms.

In the main, the work is performed out of doors, the jobs in question being hospitals, motorways, oil tankers, bridges and so on. Although the elements of cost do not change their characteristics, direct costs represent a more significant portion of total costs. The general features of job costing are present; in other words, costs are charged against the contract and when compared with the agreed contract price or value, profit or loss is ascertained.

Perhaps the most fundamental difference between contracting and any other form of business venture is in the relationship between the parties. The customer, more formally referred to as the contractee, is usually a person or organisation having little or no experience of the skills and expertise required to carry out the work he wants performed. To overcome what might prove to be a problem, a third party, an architect, is employed. He will design and lay out the project and, as part of the operation, employ another specialist, a quantity surveyor, to indicate the quantities of materials specified in those plans.

The next stage is that the contract will be put out to tender. That is to say, a number of firms will be selected. They will be sent the full plans together with the specifications and quantities of materials, and requested to indicate in detail the price at which they would be prepared to perform the work.

The successful firm, the contractor, will be required to sign a fairly extensive legal contract detailing all matters of importance to all the parties concerned. Hence the name—contract costing.

## The elements of cost

In contract costing direct costs are a significant portion of total costs.

### Materials

These will, in the large majority of cases, be ordered specifically for a particular contract and delivered directly to the site of operations. Thus actual costs will be charged direct to the contract. There will be little evidence of stocks of materials as we have encountered them under other systems, since it is unlikely that a building contractor will have vast stocks of bricks, sand, window frames and so forth, other than on site.

We therefore have none of the physical or pricing problems associated with stock control in the sense of Minimum and Maximum Levels, Re-order Quantities, L.I.F.O., F.I.F.O. and so forth.

### Labour

We have seen that any labour which could be specifically identified with a job, product, process or service is classed as direct.

If this is applied in contracting, all labour used on the site or having any direct relationship with the contract must be regarded as direct labour, and charged direct to the contract.

A general labourer employed on the site is as much direct labour as a bricklayer or carpenter. On large contracts it is usual to have a resident cost accountant and staff on site. Their wages would also be chargeable as direct labour.

The reason is that there is no difficulty in deciding the actual job on which the labourer or cost accountant is working. All the wages of *everyone* engaged on a specific contract are chargeable to that contract.

The problems of allocation and apportionment experienced with job or batch costing largely disappear. They are, however, replaced by other problems peculiar to contract control. These problems are associated with individual elements of the contract; for example, it may be necessary to distinguish between the inputs and outputs of the various tradesmen in an effort to check against the price agreed in the tender. The clock card and job card systems may not be appropriate: instead it is more usual to use a well-organised time office and time sheet system as the basis of cost analysis.

## Expenses

It would be slightly incorrect to use the term 'overheads' for the third element of cost.

A site must have its own services if it is to operate effectively and efficiently. Telephones, gas, water and electricity must be connected on a temporary basis. The paper and pencils it uses will probably be purchased locally rather than sent from head office. Repairs and maintenance will be carried out by site labour using site materials.

All expenses incurred by the site are directly charged to the contract in the same way as materials and labour.

*Overheads*

However small the contracting firm, there is usually some location referred to as the head office. It will incur expenditures on paper, telephones, rates, supervisory, clerical, managerial salaries and a host of other things. It is usual to group them together under the collective term of 'administration or head office charges' and to charge them to contracts on a percentage basis.

The difficulty arises in determining how the percentage is to be calculated. Contracting is a notoriously volatile industry: one moment it has more work than it can cope with, and the next moment it is in the doldrums.

It would seem that a reasonably stable basis on which overhead absorption rates could be based is the direct labour cost value of the nucleus of staff. This is not an unusual practice, but reflection suggests that the inferred stability could be incorrect; absorption rates so calculated could produce unbalanced results.

## Other matters peculiar to contracting

These are four; subcontracting, depreciation, payment methods and profits on uncompleted contracts.

## Subcontracting

A contractor may find that the nature and amount of work he gets does not justify keeping staff of a particular trade. Alternatively, he may be asked to tender for a contract which will require him to be involved in carrying out work in an area in which he has no specific skill. The contractor would then enter into a separate contract with a firm specialising in that skill to carry out that part of the contract for him. This is termed *subcontracting* and the agreed value of the subcontract would be included in the main contract value at the tender or estimating stage. Many firms regard subcontracting expenditures as a fourth element of cost.

## Depreciation

The treatment of plant depreciation in the contracting industry requires different treatment for, very often, special plant must be obtained to carry out the work effectively. The term 'depreciation' takes on a somewhat different aspect, for although we must still take into account the diminution of asset value over time, the time scale and plant usage are not the same. For these reasons two main methods of dealing with contract plant are in general use:

1 Where plant is expected to be used for a lengthy period on one contract, new plant is charged at cost to the contract for which it was purchased. Old or second-hand plant is charged to the contract at its book or second-hand value. Plant which is returned or transferred to another contract will be taken out of the contract at its second-hand value as of the date of removal. The contract is thus automatically charged with the depreciation on what is called a 'revaluation' basis.

2 Where the plant is to be used for a comparatively short time on any contract, it is customary to make a charge to that contract on a time basis.

## Payment methods

Under normal commercial trading conditions the money due from the customer passes to the manufacturer almost as soon as the goods change hands. Contracting does not conform to this general concept. The contract may extend over a period of years and be for exceedingly large sums of money. It is doubtful whether the financial stability of contractors could stand the impact of such conditions.

The contract generally provides for payments to be made periodically as certain stages are reached and the work certified. The certification is carried out jointly by representatives of the contractor and contractee and is formally covered in a document signed by the contractee's representative.

Upon presentation of the certificate the contractee makes payment to the contractor. This sum is referred to as a *progress payment*.

Another section of the contract will provide for retention: this means that the contractee will retain an agreed proportion of the certified sum due. This is done to give the contractee some monetary cover in the event of faulty work or of penalties arising from the failure of the contractor to comply with conditions of the contract.

Retention money is a form of guarantee against default by the contractor. The balance of such sums of money will be held in the contractee's ledger account in the contractor's books of account, until the time after contract completion specified in the contract has elapsed. The balance is then paid to the contractor either in full, where no default has occurred, or less sums to cover the costs of default, where default has occurred.

## Profits on uncompleted contracts

A fundamental principle of accounting practice is that no profit should be taken into account until actually earned, and that all known or anticipated losses should be provided for.

In contracting, it is usual to calculate the proportion of profit earned on the completed part of the contract. The amount so calculated must be reasonable, and must take

into account the extent of the work completed in relation to
the total value of the contract.

The profit on incomplete contracts may be arrived at in
one of two ways:

1  When the contract is nearing completion, it is usually
   possible to estimate the costs necessary to complete the
   contract and thus the total contract cost. Comparison
   with contract value will then give contract profit which
   can be apportioned on a time basis between the period
   already taken and the time to complete the contract.

*Illustration*

| | | |
|---|---:|---:|
| Contract value | | £100 000 |
| Cost to date | £60 000 | |
| Estimated costs to | | |
| complete contract | £20 000 | £80 000 |
| Anticipated contract profit | | £20 000 |
| Contract time | 2 years | |
| Time taken to date | 1½ years | |
| Profits taken: 1½/2 × £20 000 | = | £15 000 |

It is usual to reduce this amount by some proportion—
normally one-third—to allow for errors of estimation
and the risk of unforeseen contingencies. Profit eventually incorporated into the accounts would then be:

$$\tfrac{2}{3} \text{ of } £15\,000 = £10\,000$$

2  When the contract is in its early stages or is nowhere
   near completion, it is usual to apply a formula. An
   accepted method of calculating the profit on an uncom-
   plete contract is:

$$\text{Notional profit} \times \tfrac{2}{3} \times \frac{\text{Cash received to date}}{\text{Amount certified to date}}$$

Where a contract is nearing completion it is usual to drop the fraction of two-thirds from the calculation.

*Illustration*

| | |
|---|---:|
| Contract value | £500 000 |
| Contract time | 3 years |
| Work certified to date | £80 000 |
| Cash received to date | £64 000 |
| Net costs incurred to date | £68 420 |

| | |
|---|---:|
| *Thus*: Work certified to date | £80 000 |
| Net cost incurred to date | £68 420 |
| | |
| Notional profit | £11 580 |

Using the formula given above we obtain:
£11 580 × $\frac{2}{3}$ × £64 000/£80 000 = £6 176

Thus, the sum of £6176 would be incorporated into the accounts for the profit to date on the uncompleted contract.


## 'Work done not yet certified'

In the example we have assumed that the certification of work has taken place *exactly* at the end of the accounting period. Although this situation may arise, the chances of its doing so for every contract at the end of every year are quite remote.

Thus, certification is almost bound to occur at some point before the end of the accounting period, and it would create an anomaly if some attempt were not made to cover the gap by some form of valuation. To overcome this problem it is usual for the contractor to evaluate the work done between the date of certification and the end of the accounting period, at cost. This valuation, referred to as 'work done not yet certified', should be pessimistic rather than optimistic, to avoid anticipating or overstating contract profit.

## The contract ledger

One of the features of contracting is the relatively small number of contracts on which work is being done at any one point in time. For this reason the recording of work in

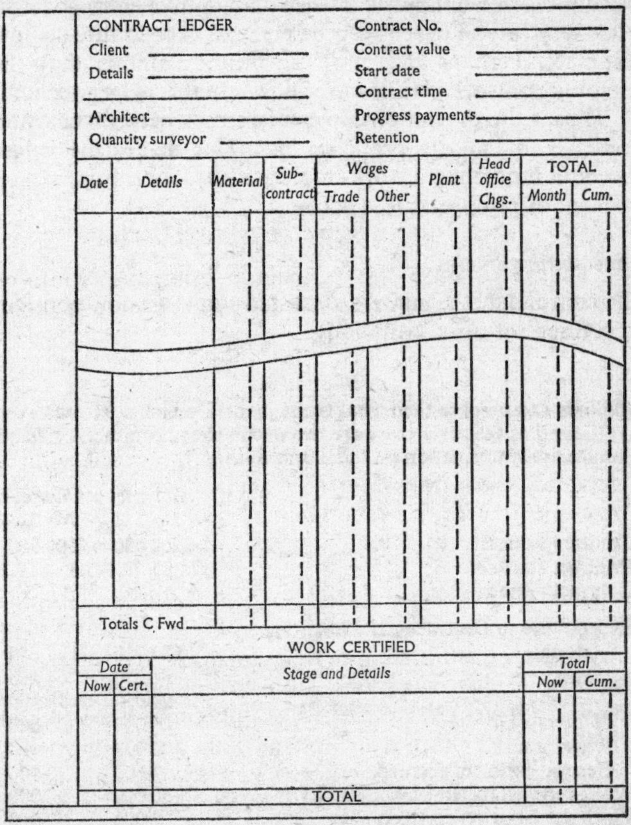

| | | | | Wages | | | Head office Chgs. | TOTAL | |
|---|---|---|---|---|---|---|---|---|---|
| Date | Details | Material | Sub-contract | Trade | Other | Plant | | Month | Cum. |

CONTRACT LEDGER  
Client  
Details  

Architect  
Quantity surveyor  

Contract No.  
Contract value  
Start date  
Contract time  
Progress payments  
Retention  

Totals C. Fwd

WORK CERTIFIED

| Date | | Stage and Details | Total | |
|---|---|---|---|---|
| Now | Cert. | | Now | Cum. |

TOTAL

FIGURE 36

progress is usually organised on the basis of a separate ledger account for each contract.

Figure 36 illustrates one way in which the contract account in the contract ledger may be designed. Note that the heading of the ledger sheet is informative, that the body of the account is in a columnar, rather than double entry style, so that very careful checks can be made of expenditure against estimate. Perhaps the most significant point is that the amounts of work certified are shown on this ledger account.

Thus, a direct relationship can be struck between cost and revenue to indicate profit or loss. This makes the ledger account more than a work-in-progress account. It is, in fact, a form of profit and loss account.

*Accounting entries*

To consolidate the matters discussed above we now consider a stylised set of information:

*Illustration*

Builders Ltd prepare their final accounts on December 31 each year. At the end of year 19.1 there are two uncompleted contracts on hand. Summarised information on them is as follows:

|  | Contract No 183 | Contract No 202 |
|---|---|---|
| Contract value | £250 000 | £500 000 |
| Contract start date | Jan 1 19.1 | July 1 19.1 |
| Contract period | *2 years* | *3 years* |
| Expenditure to December 31 19.1: |  |  |
| Materials | £34 700 | £27 650 |
| Wages | 61 250 | 54 160 |
| General expenses | 29 050 | 18 190 |
| Plant value at site | 20 000 | 20 000 |
| Wages accrued | 2 400 | 1 600 |
| General expenses accrued | 1 600 | 2 400 |
| Work certified to November 30 19.1 | 130 000 | 90 000 |
| Work done not yet certified | 2 000 | 2 000 |
| Value of materials on site December 31 19.1 | 6 000 | 10 000 |

Plant is charged to site at cost and depreciated at 10% per annum.
Cash has been received in respect of 80% work certified.

We are required to prepare statements of accounts to show the profit
or loss on each contract, together with the entries to appear on Builders
Ltd balance sheet as at December 31 19.1.

Figure 37 demonstrates the normal ledger account form of
recording the summarised information given in the illustration for Contract 183. It also shows the basis on which this
period profit and profit provision are calculated.

From this account and the notes appearing in the illustration we would proceed to evaluate the basis of work in progress to be shown on the balance sheet.

The procedure for Contract 202 will follow the same pattern and when its work in progress balance has been calculated, it will be aggregated with Contract 183 and all
other contracts, in a total sum to be shown on the balance
sheet.

There are two methods of calculating the work in progress
figure for inclusion in the balance sheet:

| | | | |
|---|---|---|---|
| 1. | Work done not yet certified | 2 000 | |
| | Contractee's balance: | | |
| | (£130 000 — £104 000) | 26 000 | |
| | | 28 000 | |
| | *Less:* profits provision | 3 267 | |
| | | | £24 733 |
| 2. | Cost incurred | 125 000 | |
| | Profit taken | 3 733 | |
| | | 128 733 | |
| | *Less:* cash received to date | 104 000 | |
| | | | £24 733 |

The balance sheet will include this figure together with all
the other items to be carried forward from the closure of the

CONTRACT LEDGER

Client _____

Details _____

_____

Architect_____

Quantity Surveyor _____

Contract No._____ 183

Contract Value ___ £250 000

Start Date_____ 1 Jan. 19

Contract Time ___ 2 yrs.

Progress Payments_ Mthly

Retention_____ 20%

*Account for the period to December 31 19.1.*

| | | | | |
|---|---|---|---|---|
| Materials | 34 700 | | Work certified to | |
| *Less* Materials on site | 6 000 | | 30 November 19.1 | |
| | | 28 700 | (Cash received £104 000) | 130 000 |
| Wages | 61 250 | | Work done not yet certified | 2 000 |
| *Plus* Accruals | 2 400 | | | |
| | | 63 650 | | |
| General Expenses | 29 050 | | | |
| *Plus* Accruals | 1 600 | | | |
| | | 30 650 | | |
| Plant at site | 20 000 | | | |
| Depreciation at 10% p.a. | | 2 000 | | |
| Total costs | | 125 000 | | |
| Profit this period | 3 733 | | | |
| Balance being profit provision c/fwd | 3 267 | | | |
| Notional profit | | 7 000 | | |
| | | £132 000 | | £132 000 |

*Profit calculation*

Notional profit $\times \frac{2}{3} \times \dfrac{\text{Cash received}}{\text{Amount certified}}$

$= \quad 7\,000 \quad \times \frac{2}{3} \times \dfrac{104\,000}{130\,000}$

$= \quad 7\,000 \quad \times \frac{2}{3} \times \dfrac{80}{100}$

$= \quad \dfrac{11\,200}{3} \; = \; £3\,733 \;=\;$ Profit to be taken into account this period

FIGURE 37

accounting period. The following extract shows the general idea:

BALANCE SHEET

BUILDERS LTD.                    *as at December 31 19.1*

|  |  |  | *Fixed Assets* |  |  |  |
|---|---|---|---|---|---|---|
| Capital |  |  | Plant |  |  |  |
| Reserves |  |  | Vehicles |  |  |  |
| Profit and Loss | 3 733 |  | Equipment |  |  |  |
|  |  | £ |  |  |  | £ |
| *Current Liabilities* |  |  | *Current Assets* |  |  |  |
| Creditors |  |  | Stock | 6 000 |  |  |
| Accruals | 4 000 |  | W.I.P. | 24 733 |  |  |
|  |  |  | Debtors |  |  |  |
|  |  |  | Cash |  |  |  |
|  |  | £ |  |  |  | £ |

## Accounting and recording entries

These are shown in Figure 38, where each block represents a ledger account with the contract account in the central prominent position.

The inputs to the contract account from the various control accounts are shown by line 1. Lines 2, 3 and 6 trace the basis of entries between the contract account, profit and loss account and the balance sheet. Lines 4 and 5 show the relationship between the contractee and contractor. Lines 7 and 8 represent the entries necessary to establish the monetary transfers that take place between the contractee and contractor.

This block diagram should be studied in conjunction with a separate text on accountancy and the later chapter on cost accounting bookkeeping, to establish the more formal debit and credit entries.

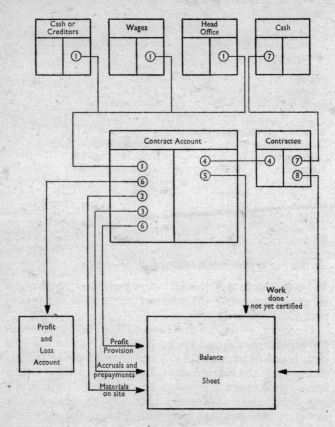

FIGURE 38

## Exercises

1 A construction company works on two contracts during the year ended December 31 19.1. Relevant information relating to these contracts is given below:

| Date started | Contract No. 271<br>January 1 19.1<br>£ | Contract No. 272<br>April 1 19.1<br>£ |
|---|---|---|
| Contract value | 300 000 | 150 000 |
| Work certified as at December 31 19.1 | 150 000 | 100 000 |
| Materials delivered by supplier to site | 50 000 | 70 000 |
| Returns to suppliers | 2 000 | 1 000 |
| Wages | 40 000 | 30 000 |
| Other direct expenses | 2 000 | 4 000 |
| Materials delivered from Company's central stores | 7 000 | 5 000 |
| Plant at cost | 10 000 | — |
| Plant hire | — | 3 000 |
| Work completed, but not yet certified as at December 31 19.1 | 9 000 | 2 000 |
| Materials on site as at December 31 19.1 | 3 000 | 1 000 |
| Value of plant on site | 6 000 | — |

The company's administrative overhead amounted to £28 000 for the year; it is to be apportioned to the contracts in proportion to the calendar months each contract has been in progress. The company has received cash from their client for each contract in respect of the work certified as at December 31 19.1, subject to a retention of 20% by the client on Contract 271 and 10% on Contract 272.

It is the company's practice to reserve one third of its profit on any contract against contingencies, after allowing for the amount retained by the client.

You are required to:
(*a*) prepare a statement of the profit or loss on each contract, showing the amount to be taken into the company's profit and loss account for the year ending December 31 19.1;
(*b*) state the value of each contract as it would appear on the company's balance sheet as at December 31 19.1, showing how you have arrived at those figures.

(ICMA adapted)

2   Builders Limited have three uncompleted contracts in hand at the end of their financial year, December 31, 19.1. Details of these contracts are as follows:

|  | Contract | | |
|---|---|---|---|
|  | *1* | *2* | *3* |
|  | £ | £ | £ |
| Contract price | 150 000 | 470 000 | 198 000 |
| Materials to site | 16 000 | 45 000 | 35 000 |
| Wages paid | 18 000 | 81 000 | 31 000 |
| General expenses | 4 500 | 25 000 | 7 000 |
| Plant sent to site | 6 000 | 7 000 | 5 000 |
| Materials stock on site | 2 000 | 4 000 | 3 000 |
| Accruals for wages | 1 000 | 2 000 | 2 000 |
| Accruals for general expenses | 1 500 | 1 000 | 1 000 |
| Cash received from clients | 36 000 | 117 000 | 72 000 |
| Cost of work done but not yet certified | 5 000 | 19 000 | 4 000 |
| Contract starting date | 1.7.19.1 | 1.4.19.0 | 1.11.19.0 |
| Estimated contract time | 2 years | 3 years | 3 years |

Plant depreciates at the rate of 10% per annum

You are required to show in columnar form the contract accounts for the three contracts shown. You are also required to calculate the profit to be taken into the current end-of-year accounts and the provision to be carried forward. The balance sheet value for work in progress is to be added as a footnote to your presentation.

(ACCA adapted)

3  The data given below refers to Contract M101 for the construction of a section of a motorway. The contract was commenced on April 1 19.1 at an agreed price of £20 million, and was expected to take four years to complete. Retention money was agreed at 10% of work certified. Details of the contract during the first year are as follows:

|  |  | £000's |
|---|---|---|
| Direct Materials: | *received on site* | 2560 |
|  | *returned from site* | 25 |
|  | *lost from site but insured* | 30 |
|  | *on site March 31 19.2* | 335 |
| Direct Wages paid: |  | 1320 |
|  | *accrued at March 31 19.2* | 30 |
| Direct expenses paid: |  | 240 |
|  | *accrued at March 31 19.2* | 10 |
| Plant in use on site at cost: |  | 2000 |
|  | *Valuation at March 31 19.2* | 1500 |
| Site overhead |  | 370 |
| Allocated head office charges |  | 180 |
| Cash received in respect of work certified |  | 4500 |
| Cost of work completed but not certified |  | 700 |

You are required to:

(a)  prepare the account of the contract;
(b)  evaluate the work in progress as at March 31 19.2.

Your evaluation of the account should include an indication of the profit to be taken in the year up to March 31 19.2.                                    (ICMA)

# 9

# Process Costing

Two features characterise the process industries, firstly, that the manufacturing process is continuous, and, secondly, that the units of production are homogeneous. Under these circumstances the identity of the individual order is lost, and the cost of a unit of output can only be obtained by establishing some relationship between period costs, period inputs and period outputs. This means that we are calculating the average cost per unit for a definite period of time.

Process costing methods are used in industries producing food and drink, petrol and oil, chemicals, textiles, and some building materials. We also find process manufacture in organisations whose outputs have grown beyond the batch production stage, and in the utilities industries of electricity and gas.

Process costing is used when products are manufactured under a continuous or mass-production system, in which the homogeneity of product can be determined at any one point.

Two points are clear: first, the need for job or batch identification disappears, for now we are concerned with a departmentalised cost, identifiable with a particular process, for an entire processing operation; second, production data is needed, if confident, reasonably accurate costs are to be obtained.

This will need to be expressed in appropriate units of

measurement for the direct material and labour inputs to the process, the output emerging from the process, the by-products, the scrap and waste and so forth. We should remember also the change in unit that often occurs between

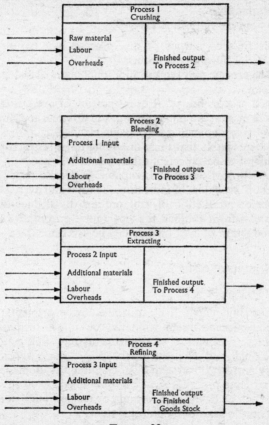

FIGURE 39

input and output; for example, solid material *in*puts may result in gaseous or liquid *out*puts.

Consider a simple example. A product is produced by going through four distinct processes: crushing, blending, extracting and refining. Figure 39 indicates relevant input and output flows.

We note the following features:

1 The finished output of one process is a basic input material for the next process.
2 Each process may require additional material and labour input.
3 Each process bears a relevant portion of overheads.
4 Each process is a miniature work in progress account and will have an opening and closing balance.
5 It is inevitable that there are going to be losses, some of which will be expected, others which will not.
6 Each process account is capable, if precise production data is available, of indicating the total and average unit cost of production of that process. By deducting one process from another, the total and average unit cost of production of *each* process can be ascertained.

## The elements of cost

### Material

In processing, materials are consumed by departments; thus the requisitioning system will either be simpler or quite unnecessary. The number of departments requiring materials will be small, and the range of materials required will usually be very narrow. If a system of stockholding is adopted, control and issue procedures may be simplified. The issue procedure will be based on a formula or recipe which, in itself, could be the basis of a control system.

Alternatively, the organisation may adopt a system of

delivery of materials direct to the point of usage. This would involve setting up a series of sub-stores, rather than having one central stores.

## Labour

This element presents little difficulty where the work is continuous and those employed are always engaged on the same work in the same process or department. The gross wages earned will be the total labour cost of the process. This applies to both production and non-production employees. A cleaner or inspector wholly employed in a process area, is seen as a charge directly allocatable to the process.

Where a group of employees is engaged on more than one process, the gross wages earned must be divided between the processes upon some equitable basis. This will necessitate some form of time allocation or time analysis by supervisors.

## Overheads

In a process costing system the problems discussed with respect to apportionment and absorption tend to diminish. With the exception of some common overheads such as rates, the matter of charging overheads to process or departments is nearly always on a directly allocatable basis. But there remains the question of service or ancillary departments, for which some basis of apportionment will need to be established. There are also certain conditions which are needed to make the concept acceptable. They are as follows:

1 Production should be stable.
2 Overheads, especially fixed overheads, should not be a significant part of cost.
3 There should not be a multi-product situation in any process.

As to the matter of absorption, the need for such a procedure diminishes in a process costing system as we have outlined it. However, where one or more products are being manufactured in one process area it will be necessary to have some means of charging each product with its relevant portion of the overheads of that process. As time is usually the constraining factor, it would be appropriate to calculate overhead absorption on the basis of direct labour cost, direct labour hours, or machine hours.

We bring the foregoing discussion together by considering a simple example.

An organisation operates three processes to produce a single end product—'Mix'. Process 1—Mixing; Process 2—Refining, and Process 3—Finishing and packing. The following particulars are extracted from the records for a week in March. We are required to show how these particulars would appear in the process accounts. We are to calculate the total cost and cost per ton at each process and in total.

|  | Process | | |
|  | 1 | 2 | 3 |
|  | Mixing | Refining | Finishing |
|  | £ | £ | £ |
| Material input—250 tons | 10 000 | | |
| Additional materials | | 850 | |
| Labour | 2 000 | 3 500 | 4 000 |
| Power | 140 | 300 | 1 000 |
| Overheads | 500 | 1 750 | 500 |
| Steam | | 200 | |
| Packing Materials | | | 2 000 |
| Residue scrap sold—14 tons | 40 | | |
| Process loss—Mixing—25 tons | — | | |
| Evaporation loss—18 tons | | — | |
| Finishing loss sold—6 tons | | | 102 |

The process accounts to show this information are given in Figure 40. In this demonstration the facts are marshalled

### PROCESS 1
### MIXING

|  | Tons | £ |  | Tons | £ |
|---|---|---|---|---|---|
| Raw material | 250 | 10 000 | Residue scrap sold | 15 | 40 |
| Labour |  | 2 000 | Process loss | 25 | — |
| Power |  | 140 | Transfer to Process 2 | 210 | 12 600 |
| Overheads |  | 500 |  |  |  |
|  | 250 | 12 640 |  | 250 | 12 640 |

Cost per ton £60

### PROCESS 2
### REFINING

|  | Tons | £ |  | Tons | £ |
|---|---|---|---|---|---|
| Transfer from Process 1 | 210 | 12 600 | Evaporation loss | 18 | — |
| Additional material |  | 850 | Transfer to Process 3 | 192 | 19 200 |
| Labour |  | 3 500 |  |  |  |
| Power |  | 300 |  |  |  |
| Steam |  | 200 |  |  |  |
| Overheads |  | 1 750 |  |  |  |
|  | 210 | 19 200 |  | 210 | 19 200 |

Cost per ton £100
Process cost per ton £40

### PROCESS 3
### FINISHING AND PACKING

|  | Tons | £ |  | Tons | £ |
|---|---|---|---|---|---|
| Transfers from Process 2 | 192 | 19 200 | Finishing loss sold | 6 | 102 |
| Packing materials |  | 2 000 | Transfer to Finished Goods | 186 | 26 598 |
| Labour |  | 4 000 |  |  |  |
| Power |  | 1 000 |  |  |  |
| Overheads |  | 500 |  |  |  |
|  | 192 | 26 700 |  | 192 | 26 700 |

Cost per ton £143
Process cost per ton £43

FIGURE 40

into their respective accounts so that the cost per ton can be calculated. In Process 1 the relevant calculation is

$$\frac{£12\ 600}{210} = £60 \text{ per ton}$$

In Process 2 the relevant figures are:

$$\frac{£19\ 200}{192} = £100 \text{ per ton}$$

The difference between this sum and that obtained for Process 1 will give the Process 2 cost per ton of £40.

Some salient questions arise from this illustration which we list as follows:

1 Is the price of transfer always the actual cost?
2 Do single input materials always produce single outputs?
3 How are losses evaluated?
4 How do opening and closing stocks of partially completed products affect evaluation?

These four matters constitute the bulk of the problems in process costing and are examined in the remainder of this chapter.

### The price of transfer and inter-process profits

The system considered so far involves charging expenditures on production, including overheads, and passing on this production at cost to the next process. The total cost of one process becomes the raw material input cost for the next. This is a simple system of transfer based on the assumption that the finished product must bear all the relevant costs. It does not, however, allow of any method of measuring the effectiveness of production at any one process stage. Various methods have been evolved in an attempt to set up a means of control over each process, the basic ideas of which are given below:

1 Transfer at actual cost. Already discussed above. Passes all costs of production from one process to the next. Inefficiencies of one process are thus passed on to the next. No effective control.

2 Transfer at some target or predetermined or standard price.

3 Transfer at some price which allows for variability. That is to say, only the actual variable costs will be charged to production, transfers to the next process being made on the same actual basis.

4 Transfer at some price based on actual, standard or marginal value but with the addition of a process profit. The profits so ascertained are transferred to the general profit and loss account. The problem is that if there is any work in progress part of its value will consist of profit. In such cases a profit provision must be calculated for unrealised profits. This must be set against the profits on processes, if one is to arrive at a profit in a way which conforms with the general axiom of 'never anticipate profits, always write off a loss'.

*Illustration*

Toffee Bars Ltd. manufacture sticky lollipops through the medium of three processes. The production of Process 1 is passed to Process 2 at a price which shows 10% profit on transfer price. Process 2 passes on its total production to Process 3 at a price which shows 25% profit on transfer price. The following information is known for March. We are required to produce the three process accounts and the profit and loss account after making provision for unrealised profits. To save rewriting common descriptions a

tabular presentation may be adopted. Calculations may be
made to the nearest £1.

|  | Process | | |
|---|---|---|---|
|  | *1* | *2* | *3* |
|  | £ | £ | £ |
| Opening stock | — | 500 | — |
| Raw material | 2000 | 300 | — |
| Direct labour | 1500 | 2000 | 800 |
| Supervision | 300 | 300 | 300 |
| Overheads | 700 | 800 | 900 |
| Closing stock | — | 800 | — |

There is a stock provision for the previous period of £100.
Four-fifths of final production is sold for £13 000. Administration and other expenses amounted to £1000.

Figure 41 demonstrates a practical approach to the problem by using three separate columns for cost, profit and
total. It will be seen that by using this method it is relatively
easy to segregate those figures which contain a profit element
from those which do not. Thus, the closing stock of Process 2
contains unrealised profits of £54. The transfer from Process
3 to finished goods stock contains a profit element of £3246.
If only four-fifths of the transfer is sold, the remaining one-
fifth must be the closing stock of finished goods. Therefore
the figure of £3246 must include an element of unrealised
profit equivalent to one-fifth, or £649.

## By-products and joint products

Many process organisations are faced with the difficult and
complex problem of assigning cost to a by-product and/or
joint product.

*By-products* can be defined as the *output* of saleable
products which are obtained from the manufacturing process of the main product. Any residue, scrap or waste which
has saleable value may be regarded as a by-product. We may

| Details | Process 1 Cost | Profit | Total | Process 2 Cost | Profit | Total | Process 3 Cost | Profit | Total |
|---|---|---|---|---|---|---|---|---|---|
| **(a)** | | | | | | | | | |
| Opening stock | — | — | — | 400 | 100 | 500 | — | — | — |
| Transfer from last process | — | — | — | 4 500 | 500 | 5 000 | 7 554 | 3 246 | 10 800 |
| Raw material | 2 000 | — | 2 000 | 300 | — | 300 | — | — | — |
| Direct labour | 1 500 | — | 1 500 | 2 000 | — | 2 000 | 800 | — | 800 |
| Supervision | 300 | — | 300 | 300 | — | 300 | 300 | — | 300 |
| Overheads | 700 | — | 700 | 800 | — | 800 | 900 | — | 900 |
| | 4 500 | — | 4 500 | 8 300 | 600 | 8 900 | 9 554 | 3 246 | 12 800 |
| **(b)** *Less Closing Stock* | — | — | — | 746 | 54 | 800 | — | — | — |
| Net Costs | 4 500 | — | 4 500 | 7 554 | 546 | 8 100 | 9 554 | 3 246 | 12 800 |
| Transfer Profit | — | 500 | 500 | — | 2 700 | 2 700 | — | — | — |
| **(c)** Transfer price to next Process | 4 500 | 500 | 5 000 | 7 554 | 3 246 | 10 800 | 9 554 | 3 246 | 12 800 |

(a) Opening Stock, *Process 2*—£500. Split to show £100 profit provision in previous period.

(b) Closing Stock, *Process 2*—£800, *Process 3*—£800. Split to show profit in the same proportions as the costs for period before deducting stock:

i.e. 600 : 8900 as $x$ : 800 where $x$ is profit in closing stock.

$$\therefore \frac{600}{8\,900} \times \frac{x}{800} = 8\,900x = 480\,000 \quad \therefore x = 53{\cdot}9325 = £54.$$

(c) Transfer profit is taken as a percentage on Transfer price.

i.e. 10% or 1/10th of Transfer Price = 1/9th of Net Cost.
25% or 1/4 of Transfer Price = 1/3rd of Net Cost.

$\therefore$ Process 1 = 1/9th of £4 500 = £500. 10% of £5 000 = £500.
Process 2 = 1/3rd of £8 100 = £2 700. 25% of £10 800 = £2 700.

**FIGURE 41**

find that the by-product is of the same value as the main product. Where this occurs there is very often reference to 'joint product output'.

*Joint products* may be defined as the saleable products arising from a common *input*. The problem that arises is in the assignment of the cost of the joint input over the processing of the several outputs.

The term 'By-product' denotes that one or more products of relatively small value are produced simultaneously with a product of relatively higher value, the latter being usually referred to as the main product.

These incidental products may be divided, according to their probable sales value, at the point where the by-products become separated from the main product, into

1 those which are saleable without further processing;
2 those which require further processing to make them saleable.

This is illustrated in Figure 42. Any accounting treatment must be based on a thorough understanding of the method of manufacture and the technical factors involved. Information is required to enable decisions to be made concerning stock valuations, and product profitability.

Acceptable methods of by-product costing fall into the following two main categories:

1 Specific costs are not reassigned, any income arising from the sales of by-products being added to income from the main product.
2 Some portion of input costs are assigned as input costs to the by-product process.

The first category avoids the cost reassignment problem but does not produce any effective management control in-

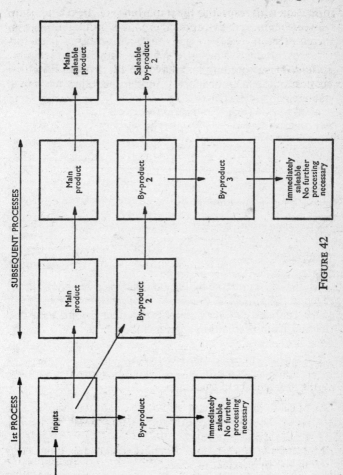

FIGURE 42

formation with respect to the importance of the relationship between main and by-product mix and profitability. It is therefore more usual to find this method being used for those by-products which are saleable without further processing. This procedure may have the effect of reducing the net cost of the main product. Consider the following simple statement.

*Illustration*

| | | | |
|---|---|---:|---:|
| Sales of main product | 18 000 units at £2·50 each | | £45 000 |
| Input production cost | 20 000 units | £40 000 | |
| *Less:* closing stock | 2 000 units | 4 000 | |
| Cost of units produced | 18 000 | | 36 000 |
| Operating profit | | | 9 000 |
| *Less:* other costs and expenses | | | 5 000 |
| Net operating profit | | | 4 000 |
| *Add:* Income from by-products | | | 1 000 |
| Total profit | | | £5 000 |

This method shows the by-product income as an addition to revenue.

Alternatively, we may show by-product income as a deduction from production costs as follows:

*Illustration*

| | | | |
|---|---|---:|---:|
| Sales of main product | 18 000 units at £2·50 each | | £45 000 |
| Input production costs | 20 000 units | £40 000 | |
| *Less:* closing stocks | 2 000 units | 4 000 | |
| Cost of units produced | 18 000 | 36 000 | |
| *Less:* by-product income | | 1 000 | |
| | | | 35 000 |
| Operating profit | | | 10 000 |
| *Less:* other costs and expenses | | | 5 000 |
| Total profit | | | £5 000 |

The overall profit remains unchanged but the production costs have decreased.

Where the by-product requires additional processing, the point at which the by-product separates from the main product must be ascertained, and the total expenditures up to that point apportioned between the main and by-product on some inevitably arbitrary basis. When the calculation has been done, a transfer from the main to the by-product processing account may be completed. The effectiveness of such information is founded on an ability to produce a basis for the apportionment of cost between main and by-product.

The term 'Joint products' denotes two or more equally important products linked together by a physical relationship and requiring simultaneous production. In such a process there may still be the added complication of by-products. Figure 43 shows a schematic possibility. From this diagram we can realise the problem that organisations face when attempting to assign or apportion costs.

Up to the point of separation, that is, to the point where the several products emerge as individual products, the costs have been incurred as a whole. A good illustration of joint product manufacture is found in an oil refinery where, from the input of crude oil, a resultant production of lubricants, distillates and petroleum is obtained. Thus, the total cost of production includes the joint cost up to the point of separation, together with the cost of production after the point of separation. The latter are readily identifiable with individual products, but the former present problems.

## Apportioning or reassigning joint costs

There are four basic methods of assigning costs: by sales value, by quantitative or physical units, by average unit cost, or finally, by weighted average based on some evaluation.

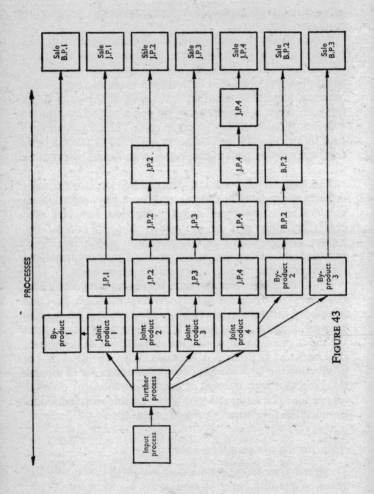

FIGURE 43

*The sales value method*

This is popular for two reasons: firstly, because of its simplicity; and secondly, the analogy that selling price is relative to production cost—that is, if one product sells for more than another, it is because more expenditure was needed to produce it. Therefore, it would seem reasonable to apportion joint cost on the basis of selling price. The calculation may be based on a simple or weighted average calculation.

The simple average method uses the unit sales price of the products as follows:

*Illustration*

|  | Products | | | |
| --- | --- | --- | --- | --- |
|  | *1* | *2* | *3* | *4* |
| Unit sales price | £2 | £5 | £4 | £9 |
| Joint costs to the point of separation | | | | £30 000 |
| Apportioned to product on the basis of unit sales price | £3 000 | £7 500 | £6 000 | £13 500 |

This type of calculation overlooks the possibility of unequal production quantities, which would result in an unfair reassignment. Consider the possibility that only ten units of Product 1 but one thousand of Product 4 were produced. Each product one would have to bear a tenth of the apportioned joint cost of £3000. There is no profit to be made in selling that product at £2.

For this reason we consider the weighted average to be less contentious:

*Illustration*

| Product | Unit sales price | production units | Total sales value | percent. product to total | Apportionment of joint cost |
| --- | --- | --- | --- | --- | --- |
| 1 | £2 | 30 000 | £60 000 | 10·0 | £3 000 |
| 2 | 5 | 19 000 | 95 000 | 15·8 | 4 740 |
| 3 | 4 | 100 000 | 400 000 | 66·7 | 20 010 |
| 4 | 9 | 5 000 | 45 000 | 7·5 | 2 250 |
| | | | £600 000 | 100·0 | £30 000 |

There may still be some disagreement over the use of such a method since processing after separation may not occur at the same rate and in the same proportion for each product. After separation, we may find that one product needs only to be bottled whilst another product requires several more intensive processes before it becomes saleable. Thus, it seems, some modification to the sales value method will be necessary. The average calculation can be modified to include the costs after separation as follows:

| | | | | *Illustration* | | | | |
|---|---|---|---|---|---|---|---|---|
| Product | Unit Sales price | Production units | Total sales value | Costs after separation | Net value | Percent product to total | Apportionment of joint cost |
| 1 | £2 | 30 000 | £60 000 | £3 000 | £57 000 | 11·4 | £3 420 |
| 2 | 5 | 19 000 | 95 000 | 60 000 | 35 000 | 7·0 | 2 100 |
| 3 | 4 | 100 000 | 400 000 | 20 000 | 380 000 | 76·0 | 22 800 |
| 4 | 9 | 5 000 | 45 000 | 17 000 | 28 000 | 5·6 | 1 680 |
| | | | £600 000 | £100 000 | £500 000 | 100·0 | £30 000 |

## The quantitative or physical unit method

This is a relatively simple method based on the output quantities of each joint product at the point of separation. The joint products must be measured in the same basic unit, such as gallons or tons, and if this is not possible the joint product units must be converted to some common denominator covering all units produced. The assumption is that each product has the same unit cost at the point of separation. In organisations where the input unit changes for output, for example, a solid material input in tons producing a liquid output in gallons, this system may not be so applicable.

Given that this physical problem can be solved, the cost apportionment can be carried out in the following manner:

*Illustration*

(*Assuming input costs of £82 per ton before separation*)

| Product | yield per ton of input | Technical ton rate factor | yield lbs per ton | % product to total | Joint cost per ton apportionment |
|---------|------------------------|---------------------------|-------------------|--------------------|----------------------------------|
| A | 100 gallons | 2·80 | 280 | 13·5 | £11·07 |
| B | 1500 lb | 0·94 | 1410 | 67·8 | 55·60 |
| C | 20 cubic metres | 10·50 | 210 | 10·0 | 8·20 |
| D | 200 lb | 0·90 | 180 | 8·7 | 7·13 |
| | | | 2080 | 100·0 | £82·00 |

It will be noted that the technical ton rate factor used has automatically allowed for a normal loss or wastage factor, as evidenced by the figure of 2080. There are, as we know, 2240 lbs to the ton. Thus the apportioned joint input ton rate is inclusive of normal losses. We also see that for every hundred gallons of Product A transferred to its individual manufacturing processes, a charge of £11·07 will be made to cover joint costs up to the point of separation. Though more acceptable than those discussed so far, this method leans heavily on the ability to discover and evaluate the conversion factors.

*Average unit method*

This is a method which apportions joint costs to the various products on the basis of units produced. Provided that all units produced are measurable in the same form, that is, tons or gallons, and do not differ greatly in a physical sense, the method can be used without too much difficulty. Where those conditions do not exist the method is unsuitable.

Organisations using this basis justify its use by saying that all products manufactured by the same process should share the total costs in proportion to units produced. Our previous comments apply equally to this method: unless there is reasonable, if not precise homogeneity, the method can produce unreasonable, inequitable answers.

### Illustration

| Product | Production units | % product to total | Joint cost apportionment |
|---|---|---|---|
| 1 | 30 000 | 19·5 | £5 850 |
| 2 | 19 000 | 12·3 | £3 690 |
| 3 | 100 000 | 65·0 | £19 500 |
| 4 | 5 000 | 3·2 | 960 |
| | 154 000 | 100·0 | £30 000 |

*Weighted average based on some evaluation*

This method is sometimes referred to as the *technical factors* basis, and is probably the most complicated of the methods. It attempts to gather up all the best and reject all the worst aspects of the other methods in general use, by considering all the factors likely to indicate some responsibility for cost and then apportioning joint cost on that basis. Thus, sales value, costs after separation, difficulty of production, amount of sales capability needed, technical acceptance in the market, may be just some of the more important factors incorporated in the method.

### Illustration

| Product | 1 | 2 | 3 | 4 |
|---|---|---|---|---|
| Unit sales price | £2 | £5 | £4 | £9 |
| Unit cost after separation | £0·10 | £3·18 | £0·20 | £3·40 |
| Technical difficulty factor | 2 | 9 | 4 | 5 |
| Advertising factor | 5 | 1 | 8 | 6 |
| Costs before separation £30 000 | | | | |

Where similar products are being produced, we regard one product as the standard and evaluate the other products from that standard, noting the four factors enumerated above, and the units produced. This is a matter of some arbitrary judgement, which may have the effect of producing a cost bias against a particular product. For the purposes of demonstration we regard Product 2 as the standard and assign the base 100 to it. If Products 1, 3 and 4 were weighted relative to this, their factors could be, say, 40, 70 and 120 respectively. Applied to the joint product costs of £30 000 an apportionment would result as follows:

| Product | Production Unit | Evaluation Factor | Factor × Units | % of total | Apportionment |
|---|---|---|---|---|---|
| 1 | 30 000 | 40 | 1 000 000 | 11·21 | £3 363 |
| 2 | 19 000 | 100 | 1 900 000 | 17·76 | £5 328 |
| 3 | 100 000 | 70 | 7 000 000 | 65·42 | £19 626 |
| 4 | 5 000 | 120 | 600 000 | 5·61 | £1 683 |
| | | | 10 700 000 | 100·00 | £30 000 |

Where dissimilar products are being produced, a full factor analysis would be used to arrive at the basis of apportionment for joint costs. The method is illustrated in Figure 44.

The method of factor evaluation may not be any more scientific than the other three methods we have examined, and unless great care is taken when selecting and evaluating the relevant factors, the results may be as inaccurate as any other method; but provided the problem is approached logically, with a reasonable knowledge of the pertinent facts, there is no reason to suppose that factor evaluation will not provide the most accurate apportionment.

## A digression

There are some facts which are known with certainty, for example, production labour used on subsequent processes after separation. It follows from this that a cost reporting system could distinguish between known facts and doubtful issues such as input costs before separation.

| Product | Sales Price | | Unit Cost | | Technical difficulty | | Advertising | | Total factor % | Prod'n units | Production units × factor % | % To total | Joint cost appl't |
|---|---|---|---|---|---|---|---|---|---|---|---|---|---|
| | Factor | % | Factor | % | Factor | % | Factor | % | | | | | |
| A | £2 | 10 | £0·10 | 1·45 | 2 | 10 | 5 | 25 | 46·25 | 30 000 | 1 387 500 | 10·65 | 3 195 |
| B | 5 | 25 | 3·18 | 46·22 | 9 | 45 | 1 | 5 | 121·22 | 19 000 | 2 303 180 | 17·68 | 5 304 |
| C | 4 | 20 | 0·20 | 2·91 | 4 | 20 | 8 | 40 | 82·91 | 100 000 | 8 591 000 | 65·94 | 19 782 |
| D | 9 | 45 | 3·40 | 49·42 | 5 | 25 | 6 | 30 | 149·42 | 5 000 | 747 100 | 5·73 | 1 719 |
| | 20 | 100·0 | 6·88 | 100·0 | 20 | 100·0 | 20 | 100·0 | 400·0 | | 13 028 780 | 100·0 | £30 000 |

FACTOR EVALUATION

FIGURE 44

| Product | Unit sales price | Additional cost per unit after separation | Differ-ence | Sales units | Sales units × Difference |
|---------|------------------|-------------------------------------------|-------------|-------------|--------------------------|
| A | £3·00 | £1·70 | £1·30 | 25 000 | £32 500 |
| B | 10·00 | 3·80 | 6·20 | 20 000 | 124 000 |
| C | 0·50 | 0·37 | 0·13 | 100 000 | 13 000 |
| D | 25·00 | 23·50 | 1·50 | 5 000 | 7 500 |

| | |
|---|---|
| Total difference | £177 000 |
| *Less* Unallocatable joint costs before separation | £95 000 |
| Net operation profit | £82 000 |
| *Less* Other administrative and selling expenses | £40 000 |
| Net profit | £42 000 |

FIGURE 45

A report of this kind is shown in Figure 45. Notice that no attempt has been made to apportion joint costs. The method used is based on the characteristic of variability, and allows for the fact that costs after separation are related to the individual product, whilst costs before separation are fixed irrespective of the final product. In other words, an oil refinery has to start with crude oil whether it produces petrol, oils and distillates, or only one of these products.

We may well question the need to apportion costs if this system of reporting is found satisfactory.

## The evaluation of process losses

It is in the nature of things that losses occur in processing methods of manufacture. This is not to say that they do not occur in other forms of production, but merely that they are more common in this particular type of industry.

We have already raised the question of normality—of whether a situation can be understood or anticipated from past experience or technical knowledge; this feature applies equally to losses: changes which occur beyond what was normally expected can be regarded as abnormal and can be either losses or gains.

To illustrate the treatment of loss, consider the following information:

*Illustration*

Input units to production cost £2·25 per unit
Losses can be sold as scrap for £0·10 per unit

**Period 1**

| | | | |
|---|---|---|---|
| Input | 10 000 units at £2·25 | | £22 500 |
| *Less:* normal loss at 10% | 1 000 | ,, | — |
| Normal yield | 9 000 | ,, at £2·50 | 22 500 |
| *Less:* abnormal loss | 100 | ,, at £2·50 | 250 |
| Actual yield | 8 900 | ,, at £2·50 | £22 250 |
| Scrap sales—residue | 1 100 units at £0·10 | | £110 |

**Period 2**

| | | | |
|---|---|---|---|
| Input | 10 000 units at £2·25 | | £22 500 |
| *Less:* normal loss at 10% | 1 000 | ,, | — |
| Normal yield | 9 000 units at £2·50 | | £22 500 |
| *Plus:* abnormal gain | 200 | ,, at £2·50 | 500 |
| Actual yield | 9 200 | ,, at £2·50 | £23 000 |
| Scrap sales—residue | 800 units at £0·10 | | £80 |

Abnormal gain and loss account

| Period 1: | loss | £250 | |
|---|---|---|---|
| | *less:* scrap sales | 110 | |
| | | | £140 |
| Period 2: | gain | 500 | |
| | *plus:* scrap sales | 80 | |
| | | | £580 |
| Overall gain | | | £440 |

These workings are shown in formal accounting manner in Figure 46. It should be noted that the net effect in unit terms on the abnormal gain and loss account is always the actual loss figure.

PROCESS ACCOUNT

| | Units | Rate | £ | | Units | Rate | £ |
|---|---|---|---|---|---|---|---|
| *Period 1*<br>Input | 10 000 | 2·25 | 22 500 | Output<br>Normal loss<br>Abnormal loss | 8 900<br>1 000<br>100 | 2·50<br>—<br>2·50 | 22 250<br>—<br>250 |
| | 10 000 | | £22 500 | | 10 000 | | £22 500 |
| *Period 2*<br>Input<br>Abnormal gain | 10 000<br>200 | 2·25<br>2·50 | 22 500<br>500 | Output<br>Normal loss | 9 200<br>1 000 | 2·50<br>— | 23 000<br>— |
| | 10 200 | | £23 000 | | 10 200 | | £23 000 |

ABNORMAL GAIN AND LOSS ACCOUNT

| | Units | Rate | £ | | Units | Rate | £ |
|---|---|---|---|---|---|---|---|
| *Period 1*<br>Process loss | 100 | 2·50 | £250 | Scrap sales | 1 100 | 0·10 | 110 |
| *Period 2* | | | | Process gain<br>Scrap sales | 200<br>800 | 2·50<br>0·10 | 500<br>80 |

FIGURE 46

This simple calculation shows how all output except the normal loss shares the value of the normal loss in proportion. To take an extreme example:

| Input units | 1000 | @ | £2·70 each | £2700 |
|---|---|---|---|---|
| Normal loss 10% | 100 | @ | — | — |
| Normal yield | 900 | @ | £3·00 each | £2700 |
| Actual yield | 100 | @ | £3·00 each | £300 |
| Abnormal loss | 800 | @ | £3·00 each | £2400 |

Then the normal loss of 100 is spread over actual yield and abnormal loss in the ratio 1:9 and 8:9. On the other hand, to deduct abnormal units at, say, input value, would have the following effect:

| Input units | 1000 | @ | £2·70 each | £2700 |
|---|---|---|---|---|
| *Less* normal loss 10% | 100 | | — | — |
| Normal yield | 900 | @ | £3·00 | £2700 |
| *Less* abnormal loss | 800 | @ | £2·70 | £2160 |
| Actual yield | 100 | @ | £5·40 | £540 |

Thus actual good production transferred to the next process would be valued at £5·40 per unit, and therefore overstated.

The last step is to consider where the loss may occur. The three general possibilities are at the very beginning of the process, during the course of production, or at the very end of the process.

In the first possibility the normal/abnormal approach is applied and the normality must increase or inflate the unit costs of the *inputs*. The abnormality will be taken out of the process in the manner described above. In the second and third possibilities, any calculations will affect the *output* or transfer price from one process to the next, or from one process to the abnormal gain and loss account.

## The evaluation of equivalent units

This is the last of the four matters for discussion. It introduces the further complication of partly-processed units at the end of a particular period represented by what are known as *process stocks* or work in progress. It will therefore be necessary to evaluate how much of the process costs relate to this partially-completed work.

This is achieved by expressing partly-completed work in terms of equivalent units. Thus, 100 units which are three-quarters complete are said to be equivalent to 75 completed units.

*Illustration*

| | | |
|---|---|---|
| *Inputs:* | Materials—1000 units at £2·00 each | £2000 |
| | Labour | 1012 |
| | Overhead | 1312 |
| | | £4324 |

*Output:* 700 completed units to next process
*Work in progress:* 300 units whose degree of completion is:

Materials—100%
Labour— 60%
Overhead— 40%

We are required to calculate the cost per unit and total cost of the transfer and the total value of work in progress.

The process account and its evaluation are shown in Figure 47. The equivalent units are calculated for closing work in progress: if 300 units of the input are only 60% complete with respect to labour, then the equivalent is to say that 180 are fully complete:

300 units at 60% complete $\equiv$ 180 units 100% complete

EVALUATION STATEMENT

| Stage reached | No. of equivalent units | | | |
|---|---|---|---|---|
| | Total | Material | Labour | Overhead |
| Complete units | 700 | 700 | 700 | 700 |
| Work in progress | 300 | | | |
| Degree of completion: | | | | |
| Material 100% | | 300 | | |
| Labour 60% | | | 180 | |
| Overhead 40% | | | | 120 |
| *Total equivalent units* | 1000 | 1000 | 880 | ·820 |
| *Added costs* | £4324 | £2000 | £1012 | £1312 |
| *Cost per unit* | £4·75 | £2·00 | £1·15 | £1·60 |
| *Cost of Transfer* | | | | |
| 700 units at £4·75 | £3325 | | | |
| *Cost of W.I.P.* | ·999 | | | |
| 300 units of Material | | ·600 | | |
| 180 units of labour | | | 207 | |
| 120 units of overhead | | | | 192 |
| | £4324 | | | |

PROCESS ACCOUNT

| | Units | £ | | Units | £ |
|---|---|---|---|---|---|
| Material | 1000 | 2000 | Transfer of | | |
| Labour | | 1012 | complete units | 700 | 3325 |
| Overhead | | 1312 | Closing W.I.P. | 300 | 999 |
| | 1000 | £4324 | | 1000 | £4324 |

FIGURE 47

This is an important concept which allows us to calculate the
unit costs on an equitable equivalent basis.

We now introduce the matter of process loss, by taking
note of the following modified information to the above
example:

> *Output*—700 units completed but only 600 passed inspection
> for transfer to the next process
> *Normal loss*—10% of completed units

Reject units were partially completed as follows:

|  |  |
|---|---|
| Material | 100% |
| Labour | 70% |
| Overhead | 50% |

From this additional information we calculate the loss as follows:

| | |
|---|---|
| *Total completed production* | 700 |
| *Normal loss @ 10%* | 70 |
| *Normal yield* | 630 |
| *Actual yield* | 600 |
| *Abnormal loss* | 30 |

In accordance with our previous discussions we spread the cost of the normal loss over all the units transferred, the units of work in progress and the units of abnormal loss.

The modified evaluation is shown in Figure 48. We note that the unit cost structure has increased for work in progress by reason of the inclusion of the relevant share of normal loss. The abnormal loss is valued on the basis already discussed.

So far we have only taken the closing state of work in progress into account. We must now allow for the fact that an 'opening work in progress' will exist.

In order to evaluate a current period, we will need to take into account not what *has* been done, but *what still needs to be done*.

*Illustration*

| | | |
|---|---|---|
| Opening work in progress | 800 units | £1376 |
| Degree of completion—Material | | 80% |
| Labour | | 60% |
| Overhead | | 30% |

EVALUATION STATEMENT

| Stage reached | No. of equivalent units | | | |
|---|---|---|---|---|
| | Total | Material | Labour | Overhead |
| Complete units transferred | 600 | 600 | 600 | 600 |
| Normal loss (10% of 700) | 70 | — | — | — |
| Abnormal loss (700 — 670) | 30 | | | |
| Degree of completion: | | | | |
| Material    100% | | 30 | | |
| Labour       70% | | | 21 | |
| Overhead    50% | | | | 15 |
| Work in progress | 300 | | | |
| Degree of completion: | | | | |
| Material    100% | | 300 | | |
| Labour       60% | | | 180 | |
| Overhead    40% | | | | 120 |
| | | | | |
| Total equivalent units | 1000 | 930 | 801 | 735 |
| Added costs | £4324 | £2000 | £1012 | £1312 |
| Cost per unit | £5·198 | £2·150 | £1·263 | £1·785 |
| | | | | |
| Cost of transfer: | | | | |
| 600 units @ £5·198 | 3119 | | | |
| | | | | |
| Abnormal loss | 119 | | | |
| 30 units of material | | 66 | | |
| 21 units of labour | | | 26 | |
| 15 units of overhead | | | | 27 |
| | | | | |
| Work in progress | 1086 | | | |
| 300 units of material | | 645 | | |
| 180 units of labour | | | 227 | |
| 120 units of overhead | | | | 214 |
| | | | | |
| | £4324 | | | |

PROCESS ACCOUNT

| | Units | £ | | Units | £ |
|---|---|---|---|---|---|
| Material | 1000 | 2000 | Transfer of | 600 | 3119 |
| Labour | | 1012 | complete units | | |
| Overhead | | 1312 | Normal loss | 70 | — |
| | | | Abnormal loss | 30 | 119 |
| | | | Work in progress | 300 | 1086 |
| | 1000 | £4324 | | 1000 | £4324 |

FIGURE 48

This is information about the end of the *previous period*. What we are concerned with in the *current period* will be how much of the input costs will be required to complete the opening work in progress, that is,

> Material 20% additional issue
> Labour 40% additional work
> Overhead 70% additional recovery

which will complete the 800 units for transfer to the next stage of manufacture. Let us consider this in the following example:

*Illustration*

| | | |
|---|---|---|
| Opening Work in Progress | 800 units | £1376 |
| Degree of completion at end of previous period: | | |
| Material 80% | | |
| Labour 60% | | |
| Overhead 30% | | |
| Inputs: Material | 5000 units | £5488 |
| Labour | | £2106 |
| Overhead | | £4784 |
| Closing Work in Progress | 1000 units | |
| Degree of completion | | |
| Material 40% | | |
| Labour 50% | | |
| Overhead 80% | | |
| Units scrapped | 800 units | |
| Degree of completion | | |
| Material 50% | | |
| Labour 60% | | |
| Overhead 70% | | |
| Transfer to next process | 4000 units | |

There is a normal loss of 10% calculated on total period production. We are required to calculate the costs of output, loss and work in progress, and to complete the process account.

Two matters need to be considered first:

1 What is the abnormal gain or loss? This is calculated from the number of units in total production, as follows:

|  |  |
|---|---|
| Opening work in progress | 800 units |
| Input units | 5000 |
|  | 5800 |
| *Less* closing work in progress | 1000 |
| Total production | 4800 |
| Normal loss 10% | 480 |
| Actual loss | 800 |
| Abnormal loss | 320 units |

2 How many units were completed entirely within this period? This is calculated from the relationship between opening work in progress and the number of units transferred:

|  |  |
|---|---|
| Units transferred | 4000 |
| *Less* opening work in progress | 800 |
| Units completed within period | 3200 |

We can deduce that a 100% input has resulted in a 100% output only for those units completed within the period.

The full evaluation and process account is shown in Figure 49.

This seems to indicate a F.I.F.O. approach to valuation and an assumption that costs do not fluctuate from one period to another. Where costs do fluctuate from period to period a change of approach will be needed in order to avoid the need for increased clerical effort.

| Stage reached | No. of units | | | |
| --- | --- | --- | --- | --- |
| | Total | Material | Labour | Overhead |
| Complete units this period (transfer less opening W.I.P.) | 3 200 | 3 200 | 3 200 | 3 200 |
| Opening work in progress | 800 | | | |
| Degree of completion needed: | | | | |
| Material 20% | | 160 | | |
| Labour 40% | | | 320 | |
| Overhead 70% | | | | 560 |
| Normal loss—10% | 480 | — | — | — |
| Abnormal loss | 320 | | | |
| Degree of completion: | | | | |
| Material 50% | | 160 | | |
| Labour 60% | | | 192 | |
| Overhead 70% | | | | 224 |
| Closing work in progress | 1 000 | | | |
| Degree of completion: | | | | |
| Material 40% | | 400 | | |
| Labour 50% | | | 500 | |
| Overhead 80% | | | | 800 |
| *Total equivalent units* | 5 800 | 3 920 | 4 212 | 4 784 |
| *Added costs* | £12 378 | £5 488 | £2 106 | £4 784 |
| *Cost per unit* | £2·90 | £1·40 | £0·50 | £1·00 |
| *Cost of transfer* 4 000 units at £2·90 | 11 600 | | | |
| *Abnormal loss* | 544 | | | |
| 160 units of material | | 224 | | |
| 192 units of labour | | | 96 | |
| 224 units of overhead | | | | 224 |
| *Closing work in progress* | 1 610 | | | |
| 400 units of material | | 560 | | |
| 500 units of labour | | | 250 | |
| 800 units of overhead | | | | 800 |
| | £13 754 | | | |

PROCESS ACCOUNT

| | Units | £ | | Units | £ |
| --- | --- | --- | --- | --- | --- |
| Opening work in progress | 800 | 1 376 | Transfer to next process | 4 000 | 11 600 |
| Material | 5 000 | 5 488 | Normal loss | 480 | — |
| Labour | | 2 106 | Abnormal loss | 320 | 544 |
| Overhead | | 4 784 | Closing work in progress | 1 000 | 1 610 |
| | 5 800 | £13 754 | | 5 800 | £13 754 |

FIGURE 49

In this demonstration some of the assumptions and bases have been slightly modified but the basic concept and approach are still the same.

*Illustration*

The following information is abstracted for Process 2
for the month of March

|  | Units | £ |
|---|---|---|
| Opening Work in Progress | 1 400 |  |
|   Materials |  | 598 |
|   Labour |  | 341 |
|   Overhead |  | 766 |
| Inputs: Material | 14 800 | 8 000 |
|       Labour |  | 4 000 |
|       Overhead |  | 8 000 |
| Transfers to next process | 14 000 |  |
| Closing Work in Progress | 1 200 |  |
| Degree of completion: |  |  |
|   Material  40% |  |  |
|   Labour    60% |  |  |
|   Overhead 80% |  |  |
| Units scrapped | 1 000 |  |
| Degree of completion: |  |  |
|   Material  30% |  |  |
|   Labour    50% |  |  |
|   Overhead 70% |  |  |

Normal loss is 10% of production.
Scrap units can be sold for £50 per 100 units

The valuation of unit cost and the entries in the process account and abnormal gain and loss account are shown in detail in Figure 50.

This approach shows the different ways of evaluating unit cost. The relationship between opening work in progress units and transferred units, previously used to ascertain units completed totally within this period, has now been dropped. In its place we use the units transferred. The reason

## EVALUATION STATEMENT

| Stage reached | No. of equivalent units | | | |
|---|---|---|---|---|
| | Total | Material | Labour | Overhead |
| *Units* | | | | |
| Transfer to next process | 14 000 | 14 000 | 14 000 | 14 000 |
| Normal loss | 1 500 | — | — | — |
| Abnormal gain | (500) | | | |
| Degree of completion: | | | | |
| Materials 30% | | (150) | | |
| Labour 50% | | | (250) | |
| Overhead 70% | | | | (350) |
| Closing work in progress | 1 200 | | | |
| Degree of completion: | | | | |
| Materials 40% | | 480 | | |
| Labour 60% | | | 720 | |
| Overhead 70% | | | | 960 |
| *Total equivalent units* | 16 200 | 14 330 | 14 470 | 14 610 |
| *Costs* | | | | |
| Opening work in progress | 1 705 | 598 | 341 | 766 |
| Inputs | 20 000 | 8 000 | 4 000 | 8 000 |
| *Total Costs* | | £8 598 | £4 341 | £8 766 |
| *Cost per unit* | £1·50 | £0·60 | £0·30 | £0·60 |
| *Cost of transfer* | | | | |
| 14 000 units @ £1·50 | £21 000 | | | |
| *Closing work in progress* | 1 080 | | | |
| 480 units of material | | 288 | | |
| 720 units of labour | | | 216 | |
| 960 units of overhead | | | | 576 |
| *Abnormal gain* | (375) | | | |
| (150) units of material | | (90) | | |
| (250) units of labour | | | (75) | |
| (350) units of overhead | | | | (210) |

## PROCESS ACCOUNT

| | Units | £ | | Units | £ |
|---|---|---|---|---|---|
| Opening work in progress | 1 400 | 1 705 | Transfer to next process | 14 000 | 21 000 |
| Material | 14 800 | 8 000 | Normal loss | 1 500 | — |
| Labour | | 4 000 | Closing work in progress | 1 200 | 1 080 |
| Overhead | | 8 000 | | | |
| Abnormal gain | 500 | 375 | | | |
| | 16 700 | £22 080 | | 16 700 | £22 080 |

## ABNORMAL GAIN AND LOSS ACCOUNT

| | |
|---|---|
| Gain from process | 375 |
| Scrap sales | |
| 1000 units @ £50/1000 | 50 |

FIGURE 50

is that opening work in progress is not, in this case, on a
F.I.F.O. basis, but on an *average* basis.

Thus, costs rather than units are more important; this is
reflected in the cost section, where the balances brought forward for the opening work in progress are included in the
calculations for obtaining the average unit element cost.

The other matter for special note concerns the treatment
of the scrap value of losses. It was indicated earlier that sums
received from the sale of scrap should not be allowed to influence unduly the cost structure of the process account. If
this policy is not followed, the evaluated unit cost decreases.

If the scrap value of £50 had been shown as a deduction in
the material cost column, the effect would be to reduce the
sum of £8598 to £8548, and the cost per unit would then be
£0·596 (£8548/14 330). This may appear to be a trifling
difference, but in other circumstances, where the gains or
losses are greater or smaller or scrap values are higher, the
impact would be greater and would lead to a mis-reporting
of that particular process.

We now turn to the question of evaluating second or
subsequent processes. Everything so far discussed will still
apply, the only difference being that there will be an additional input in the form of completed units transferred from
the previous process. These units are always 100% complete,
and ready for the process that receives them; there is no
question of calculating a 'degree of completeness'. Whether
they are incorporated into the process and transferred to a
subsequent process, whether they are part of work in progress, whether they are a normal or abnormal loss or gain,
whether they are lost at the beginning, during, or at the end
of the process, they are always 100% complete.

The transfer is to be regarded as a fourth element which
we call 'previous process units'. In the following illustration
we have used a columnar presentation which eliminates
repetitive titling.

*Illustration*

The following details relate to Process 2 for a
particular month:

|  | Units | £ |
|---|---|---|
| Opening Work in Progress | 1 600 | 276 |
| Degree of completion: | | |
|   Materials 70% | | |
|   Labour   60% | | |
|   Overhead 60% | | |
| Transferred from Process 1 | 10 200 | 460 |
| Transferred to Process 3 | 9 200 | |
| Additional costs in period: | | |
|   Material | | 224 |
|   Labour | | 661·50 |
|   Overhead | | 882 |
| Production scrap | 800 | |
| Degree of completion: | | |
|   Materials 100% | | |
|   Labour    70% | | |
|   Overhead  70% | | |
| Closing Work in Progress | 1 800 | |
| Degree of completion: | | |
|   Material 60% | | |
|   Labour   40% | | |
|   Overhead 40% | | |

Normal process loss is 10% of production.
Production scrap is sold for £0·02 per unit

We are required to prepare an evaluation, and to complete the entries in the process account. Figure 51 demonstrates a method of preparation, together with the relevant
process account and abnormal gain and loss account. Four
notes are appended to that figure to explain some of the
calculations. The abnormal gain and loss account has not
been totalled because the transfer to profit and loss account
would not be carried out until the end of the financial year.
As an interim measure it is an effective guide to the way in
which expected and actual yields compare.

| Cost element | Units this Period | Opening W.I.P. % | E.U. | Gain/Loss % | E.U. | Closing W.I.P. % | E.U. | Total E.U. | Added Value £ | Cost per Unit £ | Value Closing W.I.P. £ | Value Gain or Loss £ |
|---|---|---|---|---|---|---|---|---|---|---|---|---|
| Transfers from previous process | 7600 | — | — | 100 | (200) | 100 | 1800 | 9200 | 460 | 0·05· | 90 | (10) |
| Material | ·7600 | 30 | 480 | 100 | (200) | 60 | 1080 | 8960 | 224 | 0·025 | 27 | (5) |
| Labour | 7000 | 40 | 640 | 70 | (140) | 40 | 720 | 8820 | 661½ | 0·075 | 54 | (10·50) |
| Overhead | 7600 | 40 | 640 | 70 | (140) | 40 | 720 | 8820 | 882 | 0·10 | 72 | (14) |
| | | | | | | | | | | £0·25 | £243 | £(39·50) |

*Notes:* 1. E.U. = equivalent units.
2. Units this period = Units transferred less opening W.I.P. units = 9200 − 1600 = 7600.
3. Percentage applied in opening W.I.P. column is work to be done this period to complete opening. W.I.P., e.g. materials 70% complete last period require 30%·to complete this period.
4. Gain/Loss column is for the net units, i.e. normal loss this period is 10% (10 200 + 1600 − 1800) = 1000. Actual loss is 800. Abnormal gain = 200 units.

PROCESS No. 2 ACCOUNT

| | Units | £ | | Units | £ |
|---|---|---|---|---|---|
| Opening W.I.P. | 1 600 | 276·00 | Transfers to Process 3 at £0·25% | 9 200 | 2 300 |
| Transfers from Process 1 | 10 200 | 460·00 | | | |
| Material | | 224·00 | Normal loss | 1 000 | — |
| Labour | | 661·50 | Closing W.I.P. | 1 800 | 243 |
| Overhead | | 882·00 | | | |
| Abnormal gain | 200 | 39·50 | | | |
| | 12 000 | £2 543·00 | | 12 000 | £2 543 |

ABNORMAL GAIN AND LOSS ACCOUNT

| | | |
|---|---|---|
| | Period gain from Process 2 | 39·50 |
| | Process 2 scrap sales 800 units at £0·02 p.a. | 16·00 |

FIGURE 51

## Accounting and recording entries

These are shown in Figure 52 where each block represents a ledger account and follows the general pattern established in previous chapters.

Lines 1, 2 and 3 represent the inputs to processes or by-products, with line 4 showing the transfer of completed units from one process to the next or to finished goods stock, as shown by line 5.

The dotted line at Note 'A' shows the alternative pos-

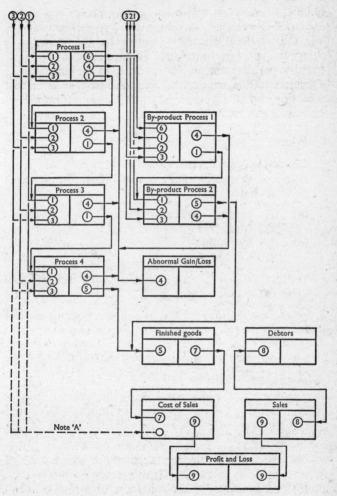

FIGURE 52

sibility, whereby an organisation may decide not to incorporate administration, selling and distribution expenses into the overhead absorption rate. The alternative is to charge it against profit through a control account.

This block diagram should be studied in conjunction with a separate text on accountancy and the later chapter on cost accounting bookkeeping to establish the more formal debit and credit entries.

### Exercises

1  Define each of the terms given below, when used in connection with materials, in a business operating on a process cost basis:

(*a*)  (i)  Normal losses and gains
       (ii)  Abnormal losses and gains
(*b*)  (i)  By-products
       (ii)  Joint products

How would you evaluate and deal with each of these items in the process accounts?                          (ICMA)

2  In process costing, the finished product of one process becomes the raw materials input for the next process. At what price can the transfer be made? Explain the variations of which you are aware and carefully explain the effects of each.

3  The manufacture of product A, by the Alphega Processing Company Ltd, is completed by means of three consecutive processes. You are required to prepare, for the month of April, and using the following information:

(*a*)  the work ·in progress account for Processes 1, 2 and 3.
(*b*)  the accounts for abnormal loss, abnormal gain and finished goods stock.

During April the input to Process 1 of basic raw material was 5000 units at a cost of £0·2 per unit. Total production overhead of £3200 was charged to the costs of each process for the month as a percentage of the direct wages incurred. There were no opening or closing work in progress stocks. In the finished goods stock, there were, however, the following balances:

| April 1 19.1 | £1200 |
|---|---|
| April 30 19.1 | 1500 |

Information for the month for the individual processes was as follows:

|  | Process 1 | Process 2 | Process 3 |
|---|---|---|---|
| Normal loss as % of Input | 5 | 10 | 5 |
| Output in units | 4700 | 4300 | 4050 |
|  | £ | £ | £ |
| Scrap value per unit | 0·10 | 0·50 | 0·60 |
| Additional direct materials | 700 | 800 | 1300 |
| Direct wages | 300 | 500 | 800 |
| Direct expenses | 275 | 191 | 256 |

Discuss briefly the principles to be observed and the various bases available for evaluating work in progress stock for balance sheet purposes. (ICMA)

4 XY Limited operates a chemical process which jointly produces four products A, B, C and D. Product B is sold without further processing, but additional work is necessary on the other three before they can be sold. Budgeted data of production, stocks, sales, selling prices and costs for the year were as follows:

|  | Production lb | Closing stocks | Sales lb |
|---|---|---|---|
| Product A | 150 000 | 10 000 | 140 000 |
| B | 110 000 | 15 000 | 95 000 |
| C | 60 000 | 5 000 | 55 000 |
| D | 180 000 | Nil | 180 000 |

There were no opening stocks of the four products. Closing stocks were ready for sale.

|  | Selling prices | Cost of additional work to make product saleable |
|---|---|---|
|  | £ per lb | £ per lb |
| **Product A** | 0·70 | 0·10 |
| **B** | 0·60 | — |
| **C** | 0·60 | 0·20 |
| **D** | 1·35 | 0·35 |

Production costs of the joint process were £180 000, and other costs were:

| Administration—fixed | £45 000 |
|---|---|
| Selling—fixed | £35 000 |
| Selling—variable £0·01 per lb sold | |

An overseas customer has expressed interest in buying from the existing production 50 000 lb each, in one year, of any or all of products A, C and D before they have been further processed by XY Ltd. He has offered to pay the following prices:

| Product | A | C | D |
|---|---|---|---|
| Price per lb | £0·65 | £0·52 | £0·90 |

On such sales, variable selling costs would be only £0·006 per lb. The fixed administration and selling costs would remain as stated above.

The costs of the joint process are to be apportioned to the individual product costs on the following three bases:

(a)  the weight of products produced;
(b)  the sales value of products produced;
(c)  the sales value of products produced less the cost of the additional work incurred to make products saleable.

You are required, on each of the above bases, to calculate for the year:

   (i)  the gross profit per product (i.e. before deducting administration and selling overhead);

 (ii)  the total gross profit;

(iii)  the total net profit;

 (iv)  which products you would recommend XY Ltd to sell to the overseas customer, before further processing at the prices quoted above, in order to increase its net profit;

  (v)  the annual net profit of XY Ltd if your advice at (iv) above was followed and quantities sold were as offered by the overseas customer.     (ICMA)

5  (*a*)  State the characteristics which distinguish process costing from job costing.

    (*b*)  Glux is produced by refining crude chemicals through a process which involves a weight loss of 15%. During Period 2, 8800 lb of chemicals which cost 80p per lb were introduced into the process, which yielded 7000 lb of Glux. Wages booked to the process amounted to £1200 and overheads apportioned to it amounted to £1140. The waste from the process was sold for 20p per lb. Prepare accounts to show the result of producing Glux during Period 2.     (ACCA)

6  The work in progress account for Process 3 for October is being prepared, and given below are the debit items of that account. You are required to:

  (*a*)  complete the work in progress account;

  (*b*)  prepare the abnormal loss account.

Your calculations should be shown in the form of an evaluation statement.

### Process 3  Work in Progress A/c

| October | Units | £ | £ |
|---|---|---|---|
| 1  Balance brought forward | | | |
| Previous process units | 1 000 | 350 | |
| Direct material | | 160 | |
| Direct wages | | 52 | |
| Production overhead | | 88 | 650 |
| | | | |
| 31  Input during month | | | |
| Previous process units | 10 200 | 5 000 | |
| Direct material | | 1 780 | |
| Direct wages | | 900 | |
| Production overhead | | 1 816 | 9 496 |

The following information is available: a system of average pricing is in operation; normal loss in process for the month is 1000 units; and the stage reached in Process 3 was as follows:

| | Scrapped during month | Work in progress October 31 |
|---|---|---|
| Number of units | 1200 | 1200 |
| | % | % |
| Direct material | 90 | 60 |
| Direct wages and production overhead | 60 | 50 |

The value of units scrapped was £0·25 per unit; the value received from those units considered to be part of normal loss was regarded as a reduction in the cost of the input from Process 2. All finished output has been transferred to Process 4.                    (ICMA)

# Other Cost Ascertainment Methods

The preceding four chapters have examined the major methods of job and unit cost ascertainment in general use. This chapter considers two other cost ascertainment systems:

1 Unit costing, used where an organisation has a specific and natural unit of output. For example, the textile industry may use the metre; a coal mine, the ton of coal; a brick works, a thousand bricks.
2 Operating costing, used where an organisation needs to find the cost of providing a service. This service might be the provision of steam, or canteen facilities, or, within a firm or industry, providing transport, gas or electricity.

### Unit costing

Sometimes this is referred to as *output costing*, and it is used where the object is to ascertain the cost of a given unit. Analysis of expenditure tends to be simpler because expenditure is on one type of product; but the product may be produced in various sizes or standards, and the analysis of expenditure in these cases will need to be more detailed.

Although at first glance it may appear to be applicable only to the extractive industries, or brickworks and textiles, the system may apply also to breweries, flour mills and so on, and can be seen as a form of process costing. We could find it used in organisations where separate articles are made in separate departments or cost centres, and also where distinct operations are separated departmentally.

## Material

In unit costing, a normal system of stores and stores control is usually found, though in many instances of unit production, the amount and specification of materials tends to be a constant factor of input; as a result there is less need for the more sophisticated systems found in job and batch production. We could even see the formal stores requisitioning system being dispensed with.

In its place we find standard specifications of material being issued from stock at predetermined intervals. Thus, instead of a requisitioning system, a very well-organised production data system may be needed.

## Labour

The collection and allocation of labour costs tends to be relatively straightforward. The nature of manufacture necessitates information about average unit cost. Therefore, some method of recording arrival and departure time, together with a basis for splitting that time between direct and indirect, will be necessary. Some form of recording idle time and other non-productive time by direct operatives will also be required.

## Overheads

Sophisticated systems of apportionment and absorption tend to be of less importance with unit costing systems. Expenses are associated with a particular part of production or with a department, and are thus directly allocatable. The common or non-allocatable expenses associated with the general organisation may be gathered into a control account.

The absorption rate for these will be based on the cost unit, since we know that such units are likely to be homogeneous.

In many cases of unit costing, we may find that only the works or factory expenses are directly allocatable. This would imply that the administration, selling and distribution expenses would be the subject of the absorption base mentioned above.

## Cost control in unit costing

In a unit costing system it is usual to prepare a regular working or operating statement to show the inputs, outputs and cost per unit. When prepared, say, weekly or monthly and with comparative figures, such a statement can provide control information. In the example of, say, a coal mine, the statement would show the inputs of wages, working expenses and other administration, against the extracted output tonnage of coal. When this tonnage is divided into the individual elements and total of costs, the result is the cost per ton unit. If this is compared with, say, the previous period or the same period last year, or cumulative to date with the same figures for the previous year, an invaluable guide is provided.

Thus, costs should not be collected and collated in an overall manner. It may well be advantageous to have detailed analyses of materials, a grade or occupation break-down of labour and a split between the fixed and variable elements of labour and expense, in order to discern trends and make the working or operating statement more valuable as information for management.

### Working example

The Upshire Brick Company Ltd. manufactures bricks of a local character. They are all of the same shape and size with some slight colour variation which is not considered important enough to warrant a separate cost ascertainment system.

The following information is extracted for the three months up to April. The figures in brackets against each item indicate the overall unit cost to the end of the previous quarter.

We are required to prepare, in a tabular form, a working statement together with comparative information.

|  |  | £ | £ |
|---|---|---|---|
| *Materials:* | Sand | 1 000 | (0·66) |
|  | Lime | 500 | (0·36) |
|  | Additive | 3 000 | (1·98) |
|  | Stores | 3 000 | (2·12) |
| *Labour:* | Claydigging | 3 246 | (2·15) |
|  | Sandsifting | 2 194 | (1·61) |
|  | Moulding | 4 706 | (3·07) |
|  | Cleaning and Stacking | 3 854 | (2·51) |
| *Expenses:* | Claydigging | 2 060 | (1·41) |
|  | Sand Sifting | 1 343 | (1·04) |
|  | Moulding | 1 680 | (1·17) |
|  | Cleaning and Stacking | 2 917 | (2·06) |
| *Other charges:* | Administration | 4 146 | (2·75) |
|  | Selling | 3 817 | (2·61) |
|  | Stock yard and Distribution | 3 037 | (1·98) |

| | |
|---|---|
| Opening stock of bricks—units | 235 000 |
| Closing stock of bricks—units | 380 000 |
| Bricks sold—units | 1 355 000 |

A working or operating statement from that information is given in Figure 53. It will be seen that there are a number of ways in which information can be produced for management control purposes. Perhaps one of the most important aspects is the column of comparative figures shown on the right-hand side.

## Operating costing

This is a system of cost ascertainment used to find the cost of providing a service. The method is different from that used in ascertaining manufacturing data and costs, but has

| WORKING STATEMENT | | | | 3 months to April |
| --- | --- | --- | --- | --- |

**PRODUCTION STATEMENT**

| | | |
| --- | --- | --- |
| Bricks sold | | 1 355 000 |
| *Plus* Closing stocks | | 380 000 |
| | | 1 735 000 |
| *Less* Opening stocks | | 235 000 |
| Production this period | | 1 500 000 |

| Details | Cost | | Unit cost | |
| --- | --- | --- | --- | --- |
| | Element £ | Total £ | This period £ | To end previous quarter £ |
| *Materials* | | | | |
| Sand | 1 000 | | 0·67 | 0·66 |
| Lime | 500 | | 0·33 | 0·36 |
| Additive | 3 000 | | 2·00 | 1·98 |
| Stores | 3 000 | | 2·00 | 2·12 |
| | | 7 500 | 5·00 | 5·12 |
| *Labour and expenses* | | | | |
| Clay digging | 3 246 | | 2·17 | 2·15 |
| | 2 060 | | 1·37 | 1·41 |
| | | 5 306 | 3·54 | 3·56 |
| Sand sifting | 2 194 | | 1·46 | 1·61 |
| | 1 343 | | 0·90 | 1·04 |
| | | 3 537 | 2·36 | 2·65 |
| Moulding | 4 706 | | 3·14 | 3·07 |
| | 1 680 | | 1·12 | 1·17 |
| | | 6 386 | 4·26 | 4·24 |
| Clean and stack | 3 854 | | 2·57 | 2·51 |
| | 2 917 | | 1·94 | 2·06 |
| | | 6 771 | 4·51 | 4·57 |
| *Other charges* | | | | |
| Administration | 4 146 | | 2·76 | 2·75 |
| Selling | 3 817 | | 2·54 | 2·61 |
| Stacking and distribution | 3 037 | | 2·03 | 1·98 |
| | | 11 000 | 7·33 | 7·34 |
| Total cost and unit cost | | £40 500 | £27·00 | £27·48 |

FIGURE 53

a marked similarity to the method of unit costing described above.

The unit of cost, whilst being the same within the industry, will differ from location to location but will refer to the type of service rendered.

Transport organisations or transport departments use the 'passenger mile' or 'ton mile' to denote the unit. By the former unit, we mean the cost of carrying a single passenger for one mile. By the latter unit we mean the cost of carrying a ton weight over a distance of one mile. Similarly, hospitals may be costed on the basis of the 'patient-bed day', and a boiler-house producing steam for use within an organisation may take as its unit the cost of producing a thousand pounds of steam.

In every case the cost unit is different but all have the same common feature: the cost per unit is derived by dividing the total number of units into the total costs of providing the service.

Let us examine the transport example more closely. One of the units in use may be the ton-mile, a unit devised to take into account both the distance travelled and the weight carried. If costs were calculated on distance covered without regard to weight carried, the system would be inequitable since it would give the same result or charge for carrying one ton as for carrying one pound over the same distance. A system based on weight only would produce similar inequalities.

### Illustration

If 10 tons are carried a distance of 5 miles we have 50 ton miles. But if the load was made up of three different weights to be carried over three different distances the calculation would be as follows:

$$
\begin{aligned}
3 \text{ tons carried for 5 miles} &= 15 \text{ ton miles} \\
5 \text{ tons carried for 4 miles} &= 20 \text{ ton miles} \\
2 \text{ tons carried for 2 miles} &= \phantom{0}4 \text{ ton miles}
\end{aligned}
$$

*Total ton miles*                    39

giving quite a different result. This calculation is usually referred to as an 'absolute ton mile'.

*Accounting records and transport operations*

Because the emphasis of operating costing is on expense as distinct from raw materials, labour and overhead, the collection and collation system must be devised within the general accounting system.

A different but nevertheless concise approach is also needed to what we may term 'output data'. We would find that expenditures would be collated under three main headings:

1 Operating charges including such expenses as drivers' wages, petrol and oil.
2 Maintenance charges, including expenditures incurred in vehicle maintenance, such as cleaning, overhauls, spares and tyres.
3 Fixed charges for all the expenditures incurred whether the vehicle is operating or not and which have little or no relationship with weight or passengers carried. These will include such items as road tax, insurance and depreciation.

Notice that under the first heading we group expenditures which are almost proportionally variable; the second heading contains those expenditures which may increase the more the vehicle is used, but which do not necessarily increase in direct proportion.

All these expenses are brought together in a monthly cost summary under the three headings, in such a way that when divided by ton miles or passenger miles, they yield the operating cost per ton or per passenger. Comparison will again be an important aspect of control, highlighting trends and differences and enabling management to take corrective action where necessary.

Examples of two necessary documents are shown in Figures 54 and 55. They are a journey Log Sheet, to record

| Trip No. | Route Detail | | Tonnage | | Mileage | Time |
|---|---|---|---|---|---|---|
| | From | To | Deliver | Collect | | |
| 1 | | | | | | |
| 2 | | | | | | |
| 3 | | | | | | |
| 4 | | | | | | |
| 5 | | | | | | |
| 6 | | | | | | |
| 7 | | | | | | |
| 8 | | | | | | |
| 9 | | | | | | |
| 10 | | | | | | |
| | | Totals | | | | |

LOG SHEET

Route Number _____   Date _____
Time Out _____   Time In _____   Vehicle _____
Mileage Out _____   Mileage In _____   Driver _____
Route Supplies _____   Petrol _____   Mate _____
Traffic Conditions Out _____   Oil _____
In _____

TRIP RECORD

FIGURE 54

the actual deliveries and mileages, and a monthly cost summary. It will be observed that a complete record is being built up for each vehicle and its use over time. From that experience, invaluable information for management control via cost reporting and analysis can be processed.

*Internal services operating costing*

Similar procedures and techniques can be developed for internal service operations such as the canteen. This will be especially important if the policy of the firm is to provide a substantial subsidised main meal and work-break.

```
                        MONTHLY COST SUMMARY
   FIXED CHARGES                            Month Ending _____
   Insurance                               Vehicle No. _____
   Road Tax                                Mileage    _____
   Depreciation                            Tonnage    _____
   Interest
   Others
              Total  £ _____        Charge per month   £ _____

   OPERATING CHARGES

   Driver _____ Hours @ _____ per hour _____
   Mate   _____ Hours @ _____ per hour _____
   Fuel   _____ gallons @ _____ per gallon _____
          _____ gallons @ _____ per gallon _____
          _____ gallons @ _____ per gallon _____
   Oil    _____ pints @ _____ per pint _____
                          TOTAL THIS MONTH      £ _____

   MAINTENANCE CHARGES

   Overhaul  _____
             _____
             _____
   Spares    _____
             _____
             _____
   Tyres     _____
             _____
             _____
   Other Charges _____
             _____

                     TOTAL THIS MONTH          £ _____
              TOTAL RUNNING COST FOR MONTH      £ _____
               TOTAL TON/MILES FOR MONTH          _____
               OPERATING COST PER TON MILE      £ _____
```

FIGURE 55

Expenditures may be grouped under the following headings:

1 'Provisions' rather than 'raw material', to include cigarettes and confectionery;
2 Labour services. (We will not have to worry about allocatable or direct cost, because everyone working in the canteen is part of the canteen service.)

3   Direct expense to cover such things as knives, forks, spoons, plates, cups, saucers and scouring powder;
4   Site or establishment charge, usually an apportionment from the pool of common non-allocatable expenditures incurred by the organisation as a whole. Almost certainly it will include such charges as rates, insurance and general managerial salaries and expenses. Electricity, gas and water are usually metered directly to the canteen. Depreciation would also be a directly allocatable charge based on the value of the equipment located there.

*The application in use*

One may ask, why attempt to cost an internal service operation separately? The answer is, cost effectiveness. We are always aware that there may be room for improvement, a better way of obtaining more value for the same expenditure.

The canteen manager, or manageress, will need to make the menu as attractive as possible by introducing variety and rotation; even though it may be subsidised, no worker will continue to pay even a small sum for dull, repetitive meals. By expanding the range the possibilities of price advantage through bulk buying may increase, and by introducing a meal coding system it will be possible to evaluate the popularity of certain meals or combinations. From this information a basis for effective buying could be established.

To enable management to achieve this and other similar ends it will be necessary to produce an operating cost statement which is expense-based, as is the transport cost statement.

**Exercises**

1   The following particulars are extracted from the records of Block Makers Ltd, and refer to the production for April 19.1

*Materials used:*

| | |
|---|---|
| Sharp sand | £0·32 per 1000 blocks |
| Clinker | 440 tons at £10 per ton |
| Infill | 310 tons at £4 per ton |
| General stores materials | £2080 |

*Labour*

| | |
|---|---|
| Mixing and screening | £2850 |
| Blockmaking | 4760 |

*Works expenses* are absorbed at the rate of 20% on direct labour.

*Administration expenses* are absorbed at the rate of £1 per 1000 blocks sold.

There was an opening stock of 200 000 blocks and a closing stock of 300 000 blocks. Sales of 1 900 000 blocks at £10 per 1000 were made during April 19.1.

You are required to prepare a monthly cost statement showing the total cost, the cost per 1000 blocks made and the profit per 1000 blocks sold.

2  Your company owns a lorry which is engaged on a regular run from your factory to a customer 35 miles away. This lorry has a capacity of 10 tons and does two round trips a day, fully loaded on the outward journey and empty on the return journey. Your company operates thirteen accounting periods in the year, each lasting four weeks. The following information is available for the four weeks ending March 24:

| | |
|---|---|
| Drivers' wages | £35 per week |
| Repairs (variable) for 4 weeks | £66 |
| Oil (variable) | £4 |
| Garaging per day | £1 |

Other information:

| | |
|---|---|
| Vehicle cost new, excluding tyres | £2 750 |
| Anticipated life of vehicle | 100 000 miles |
| Vehicle insurance | £130 per annum |

| | |
|---|---|
| Cost of set of tyres | £375 |
| Anticipated life of tyres | 25 000 miles |
| Petrol consumption | 14 miles per gallon |
| Petrol cost | 35p per gallon |
| Licence | £65 per annum |
| Sundry overhead expense (fixed) | £442 per annum |
| Estimated sale proceeds of lorry when traded in | £250 |

Using the information, you are required:

(*a*)   to compile a vehicle operating statement showing running costs, standing costs and total costs for the four weeks ending March 24.

(*b*)   Express these costs in terms of cost per mile and cost per ton mile.

(*c*)   Using these cost rates, calculate the price you would quote for a week-end job involving a round trip of 100 miles, a load of 8 tons on both the outward and the return journey, and drivers' wages of £12, and giving a contribution to other standing costs of £10.

(ICMA)

3   Draw up a *pro forma* cost statement for a canteen subsidised by the company, serving a firm of 1500 employees. What measures of efficiency would you use in such a case, and on what basis would canteen prices be fixed?

(ICMA)

# 11

# Cost Accounting Bookkeeping

Cost accountancy is not a separate branch, but an integral part of, the whole field of accountancy and financial management. Studies have shown that in arriving at costs for jobs, processes, units or services, we must ensure that all cost is accounted for. That is, the costs absorbed into a particular method of cost ascertainment, must be reconciled or integrated with the total expenditures made and incomes received in operating the whole business as recorded in the company's accounts.

Let us view the matter from the point of view of an accountant newly appointed by a manufacturing organisation. Apart from satisfying himself that the accounting system meets some minimum standard of stewardship, he will be concerned with establishing a means of scorekeeping. He intends to do so by carrying out analyses of expenditure on a departmental or product basis as the means to achieving some measure of control. Three possibilities are open to him. They are:

1  To work on a system sometimes called 'third entry', that is, to extract relevant information from the existing financial accounting system. This presupposes that the existing bookkeeping system is in a state that will enable information to be extracted and analysed with a fair degree of confidence. As a start it has much to recommend it, but it should be regarded only as a short-term measure.

2 To open a separate cost accounts ledger with its own control accounts. This would include all the expenditure and income accounts normally forming the basis of the trading and profit and loss accounts. Thus all the accounts normally forming the basis of the balance sheet will be kept separately in the financial ledger. The two ledgers will be related through the medium of an overall ledger control account. For this reason the system is usually referred to as 'interlocked accounting'.

3 To keep all the accounts in one ledger but to modify the manner in which some of the entries are made. Control accounts will still feature quite prominently but the system will operate as an integrated whole. This is usually referred to as an 'integrated accounting system'.

It will be seen as we progress through this chapter that using an integrated accounting system has decided advantages.

In this chapter we examine the interlocked and integrated accounts systems. That is not to say that the third entry method has no merit, but that for present purposes it can only be regarded as being based on an extraction from financial records; confidence in a cost reporting system built on this method must necessarily be low.

It is assumed that at this stage the reader has reached a reasonable level of competence with double-entry bookkeeping. If this is not the case, a standard text should be studied before proceeding any further with this chapter.

## Interlocked accounts

We have noted that this method requires two distinct ledgers to be maintained and interlocked by a ledger control account.

To show how this works we will adopt the simple transactions shown in Figure 56 in journal form.

Looking at transaction (*a*) we note that an entry

> DR   Purchases
> CR   Creditors

would be made in the normal financial books of account. We also note that these purchases were made in respect of raw material stock and work in progress. We could then also have made an entry in another ledger:

> DR   Raw material stock
> DR   Work in progress
> CR   Memorandum

but this would be an unsatisfactory duplication of entries in two sets of ledgers. Glancing again at our example we see that, in fact, purchases and raw material stock are a duplication; if we modify the whole transaction to:

> DR   Some account in the financial ledger
> CR   Creditors
> DR   Stock
> CR   Some account in the cost accounts ledger

then we have eliminated the major duplication and need only to decide on some title for the account which appears above as 'Some account in the . . . ledger'. We call that which appears in the financial ledger, a financial control account, and that which appears in the cost accounts ledger, the cost accounts ledger control account. The transaction will now appear as:

> DR   Financial ledger control
> CR   Creditors
> DR   Stock
> CR   Cost ledger control

| Text ref. | Account name | | |
|---|---|---|---|
| (a) | Purchases<br>　To Creditors<br>Being purchases for:<br>　Raw material stock　　£800<br>　Work in progress　　　£200 | 1000 | 1000 |
| (b) | Gross Wages<br>　To Cash<br>　　Social Security<br>　　Income Tax<br>Being wages and salaries for:<br>　Work in progress　　£1900<br>　Works overhead　　　200<br>　Administration overhead　400 | 2500 | 2100<br>200<br>200 |
| (c) | Rates<br>Heat and light<br>Telephones<br>Stationery<br>　To Expense creditors<br>Being expenses apportioned to:<br>　Works overhead　　　£1600<br>　Administration overhead　500 | 600<br>800<br>500<br>200 | 2100 |
| (d) | Debtors<br>　To Sales<br>Being sales for period | 7000 | 7000 |
| 1 | Creditors<br>　To Cash<br>Being payment for previous period<br>　purchases | 7000 | 7000 |
| 2 | Cash<br>　To Debtors<br>Being receipts against previous period sales | 8000 | 8000 |
| 3 | Fixed Assets<br>　To Creditor<br>Being purchase of new equipment | 4000 | 4000 |
| 4 | Depreciation<br>　To Provision for depreciation<br>Being period depreciation on production<br>　equipment | 300 | 300 |

FIGURE 56

Similarly for transaction (*b*), the entry in the financial books

> DR Gross wages
> CR Cash
> Social Security
> Income Tax

would be replaced by the entry

> DR Financial ledger control
> CR Cash
> Social Security
> Income Tax

In the cost accounts ledger the entry would be

> DR Work in progress
> Works overhead
> Administration overhead
> CR Cost ledger control

The effect of imposing this method on all the transactions shown in Figure 56 is demonstrated in journal form in Figure 57.

To complete the illustration, the journal entries are now shown more formally in typical ledger form. Figure 58 (*a*) shows the entries made in a facsimile financial ledger and Figure 58 (*b*) the entries in a facsimile accounts ledger. The last three entries on Figure 57 represent the following: 5 stands for the value of stores requisitions covering the issue of raw material to production; 6 stands for the amount of works overhead absorbed by work in progress; 7 stands for the amount of overhead apportioned to cost of sales as administration overhead.

Further examination reveals that not only are financial entries 1, 2 and 3 made independently of the cost systems, but that additional entries 5, 6 and 7 can now also be made, independently of the financial system.

| Text ref. | Account Name | Financial books of account | | Cost ledger accounts | |
|---|---|---|---|---|---|
| | | Dr. | Cr. | Dr. | Cr. |
| (a) | Financial Ledger Control | 1000 | | | |
| | Creditors | | 1000 | | |
| | Raw material stock | | | 800 | |
| | Work in Progress | | | 200 | |
| | Cost ledger control | | | | 1000 |
| (b) | Financial Ledger Control | 2500 | | | |
| | Cash | | 2100 | | |
| | Social Security | | 2100 | | |
| | Income Tax | | 200 | | |
| | Work in Progress | | | 1900 | |
| | Works overhead | | | 200 | |
| | Administration overhead | | | 400 | |
| | Cost ledger control | | | | 2500 |
| (c) | Financial ledger control | 2100 | | | |
| | Creditors | | 2100 | | |
| | Works overhead | | | 1600 | |
| | Administration overhead | | | 500 | |
| | Cost ledger control | | | | 2100 |
| (d) | Debtors | 7000 | | | |
| | Financial ledger control | | 7000 | | |
| | Cost ledger control | | | 7000 | |
| | Sales | | | | 7000 |
| (1) | Creditor | 7000 | | | |
| | Cash | | 7000 | | |
| (2) | Cash | 8000 | | | |
| | Debtor | | 8000 | | |
| (3) | Asset | 4000 | | | |
| | Creditor | | 4000 | | |
| (4) | Financial ledger control | 300 | | | |
| | Provision for depreciation | | 300 | | |
| | Works overhead | | | 300 | |
| | Cost ledger control | | | | 300 |
| (5) | Work in Progress | | | 480 | |
| | Raw material stock | | | | 480 |
| (6) | Work in Progress | | | 1900 | |
| | Works Overhead | | | | 1900 |
| (7) | Cost of Sales | | | 872 | |
| | Administration Overhead | | | | 872 |

FIGURE 57

IN THE FINANCIAL LEDGER

*Financial Ledger Control*

| | | | | | |
|---|---|---|---|---|---|
| (*a*) | Creditors | 1000 | (*d*) | Debtors | 7000 |
| (*b*) | Wages | 2500 | | | |
| (*c*) | Creditors | 2100 | | | |
| (4) | Depreciation | 300 | | | |

*Creditors Control*

| | | | | | |
|---|---|---|---|---|---|
| (1) | Cash | 7000 | (*a*) | Purchases | 1000 |
| | | | (*c*) | Expenses | 2100 |
| | | | (3) | Assets | 4000 |

*Cash*

| | | | | | |
|---|---|---|---|---|---|
| (2) | Debtors | 8000 | (*b*) | Payroll | 2100 |
| | | | (1) | Creditors | 7000 |

*Social Security Deductions*

| | | | | |
|---|---|---|---|---|
| | | (*b*) | Payroll | 200 |

*Income Tax Deductions*

| | | | | |
|---|---|---|---|---|
| | | (*b*) | Payroll | 200 |

*Debtors Control*

| | | | | | |
|---|---|---|---|---|---|
| (*d*) | Sales | 7000 | (2) | Cash | 8000 |

*Assets*

| | | | |
|---|---|---|---|
| (3) | New Equipment | 4000 | |

*Provision for Depreciation*

| | | | |
|---|---|---|---|
| | | (4) This period | 300 |

FIGURE 58 (a)

This interlocked ledger system requires a certain basic set of ledgers and accounts, together with a procedure for use. These may be summarised as follows:

1 Fixed asset accounts to allow for recording permanent possessions such as buildings, plant, equipment, motor vehicles and so forth. There will also be accounts to record depreciation against those assets.

2 Share capital accounts, including capital and revenue reserves, together with accounts to record fixed interest and debt capital.

## IN THE COST ACCOUNTS LEDGER

### Cost Ledger Control

| (d) Sales | 7000 | (a) Purchases | 1000 |
| | | (b) Payroll | 2500 |
| | | (c) Expenses | 2100 |
| | | (4) Depreciation | 300 |

### Raw Material Stock

| (a) Purchases | 800 | (5) Issue to W.I.P. | 480 |

### Work in Progress (W.I.P.)

| (a) Purchases | 200 | | |
| (b) Wages | 1900 | | |
| (4) Material ex stock | 480 | | |
| (6) Works overhead | 1900 | | |

### Works Overhead

| (b) Wages | 200 | (6) Recovery to W.I.P. | 1900 |
| (c) Expenses | 1600 | | |
| (4) Depreciation | 300 | | |

### Administration Overhead

| (b) Wages | 400 | (7) Recovery to Cost of Sales | 872 |
| (c) Expenses | 500 | | |

### Sales

| | | (d) Deliveries | 7000 |

### Cost of Sales

| (7) Administration overhead | 872 | | |

FIGURE 58 (b)

3  Debtor and creditor accounts, in total and by name of individual customer and supplier.
4  The cash and/or bank account.
5  The financial accounts ledger control account to record transactions that affect the cost accounting ledger.

The foregoing, together with certain balances maintained in the cost accounts ledger, will form the basis for producing the balance sheet.

In the cost accounting ledger:

1 Stores ledger control account, to record purchases received and materials issued to work in progress, leaving a balance of materials in stock.
2 Work in progress control account, to record issues of material from stores, allocations of direct labour and overhead and, transfers of completed work to finished goods. The balance represents uncompleted work.
3 Finished goods stock account, to record the cost value of goods received from work in progress and transferred to cost of goods sold account or costing profit and loss account. The balance represents the value at cost of goods unsold.
4 Wages control account.
5 Various overhead control accounts, to record the actual cost of overhead expenditures and the amounts absorbed into cost at various points. The balance represents overhead under- or over-absorbed.
6 The cost accounts ledger control account, to record transactions that affect the financial account ledger.

The foregoing will form the basis of the manufacturing, trading and profit and loss accounts. Account balances remaining open will be used, together with the balances in the financial accounting ledger, to form the balance sheet. The control accounts in both ledgers will be supported by detailed records, such as:

(*a*) debtors control, or sales ledger control, supported by individual accounts for each customer;

(b) creditors control, or bought ledger control, supported by individual accounts for each supplier;

(c) stores control supported by individual accounts for each item of material;

(d) work in progress control, supported by individual job cards or batch cards for each job, product, component, sub-assembly, assembly, or for each individual process;

(e) finished goods stock control, supported by individual accounts for each type of saleable product;

(f) overhead control, supported by individual accounts or standing orders for each category and classification of overheads.

We now consider a specimen set of transactions for the cost accounts ledger only. Each transaction is followed by the debit and credit, which are then entered in the cost accounts ledger as displayed in Figure 59. A trial balance is extracted and the costing profit and loss computed as shown in Figure 60.

### Illustration

The following balances are shown in the cost accounts ledger as at October 1:

|  | DR £ | CR £ |
|---|---|---|
| Work in progress control | 7 840 | |
| Finished goods stock control | 5 860 | |
| Works overhead control | 400 | |
| Administration overhead control | 200 | |
| Stores ledger control | 10 500 | |
| Cost accounts ledger control | | 24 800 |
| | £24 800 | £24 800 |

(These balances are the opening ledger balances
for the beginning of the period)

#### Work in Progress Control

| | | | | | |
|---|---|---|---|---|---|
| Oct. 1 | Opening balance | 7 840 | (g) | Finished goods | 120 000 |
| (b) | Direct labour | 61 200 | | Balance C/D | 7 040 |
| (d) | Works overhead | 18 700 | | | |
| (f) | Material issues | 39 300 | | | |
| | | £127 040 | | | £127 040 |
| Nov. 1 | Balance B/D | 7 040 | | | |

#### Finished Goods Stock Control

| | | | | | |
|---|---|---|---|---|---|
| Oct. 1 | Opening balance | 5 860 | (a) | Cost of sales | 118 500 |
| (g) | Work in progress | 120 000 | | Balance C/D | 7 360 |
| | | £125 860 | | | £125 860 |
| Nov. 1 | Balance B/D | 7 360 | | | |

#### Works Overhead Control

| | | | | | |
|---|---|---|---|---|---|
| Oct. 1 | Opening balance | 400 | (d) | Work in progress | 18 700 |
| (c) | Indirect labour | 2 800 | | Balance C/D | 2 000 |
| (j) | Stores issues—repairs | 1 500 | | | |
| (l) | Cost accounts control | 16 000 | | | |
| | | £20 700 | | | £20 700 |
| Nov. 1 | Balance B/D | 2 000 | | | |

#### Administration Overhead Control

| | | | | | |
|---|---|---|---|---|---|
| Oct. 1 | Opening balance | 200 | (e) | Cost of sales | 6 200 |
| (m) | Cost accounts control | 5 800 | | | |
| | Balance C/D | 200 | | | |
| | | £6 200 | | | £6 200 |
| | | | Nov. 1 | Balance B/D | 200 |

#### Stores Ledger Control

| | | | | | |
|---|---|---|---|---|---|
| Oct. 1 | Opening balance | 10 500 | (f) | Work in progress | 39 300 |
| (i) | Purchases | 36 000 | (j) | Works overhead | 1 500 |
| (k) | Carriage inwards | 600 | | Balance C/D | 6 300 |
| | | £47 100 | | | £47 100 |
| Nov. 1 | Balance B/D | 6 300 | | | |

#### Cost Ledger Account Control

| | | | | | |
|---|---|---|---|---|---|
| (h) | Sales | 132 000 | Oct. 1 | Opening balance | 24 800 |
| | Balance C/D | 15 200 | (a) | Wages | 64 000 |
| | | | (i) | Purchases | 36 000 |
| | | | (k) | Carriage inwards | 600 |
| | | | (l) | Works expenses | 16 000 |
| | | | (m) | Admin. expenses | 5 800 |
| | | £147 200 | | | £147 200 |

#### Gross Wages Control

| | | | | | |
|---|---|---|---|---|---|
| (a) | Cost accounts control | 64 000 | (b) | Work in progress | 61 200 |
| | | | (c) | Works overhead | 2 800 |
| | | £64 000 | | | £64 000 |

#### Cost of Sales

| | | | | | |
|---|---|---|---|---|---|
| (e) | Admin. overhead | 6 200 | | | |
| (n) | Finished Goods Sold | 118 500 | | | |

#### Sales

| | | | | | |
|---|---|---|---|---|---|
| | | | (h) | Cost Accounts control | 132 000 |

FIGURE 59

## TRIAL BALANCE—OCTOBER 31

| | | |
|---|---|---|
| Work in Progress Control | 7 040 | |
| Finished Goods Stock Control | 7 360 | |
| Works Overhead Control | 2 000 | |
| Administration Overhead Control | | 200 |
| Stores Ledger Control | 6 300 | |
| Cost Accounts Ledger Control | | 15 200 |
| Cost of Sales | 124 700 | |
| Sales | | 132 000 |
| | £147 400 | £147 400 |

## COSTING PROFIT AND LOSS

| | | | |
|---|---|---|---|
| Cost of Sales | 124 700 | Sales | 132 000 |
| Profit C/D | 7 300 | | |
| | £132 000 | | £132 000 |
| | | Nov. 1 Profit B/D | 7 300 |

FIGURE 60

The transactions for October were as follows:

| | | £ |
|---|---|---|
| (a) | Gross wages | 64 000 |
| | (DR wages control, CR cost accounts ledger control) | |
| (b) | Direct wages | 61 200 |
| | (DR W.I.P. control, CR wages control) | |
| (c) | Indirect wages—works | 2 800 |
| | (DR works overhead control, CR wages control) | |
| (d) | Works overhead allocated to production | 18 700 |
| | (DR W.I.P. control, CR works overhead control) | |
| (e) | Administration overhead allocated | 6 200 |
| | (DR cost of sales, CR administration overhead control) | |

£

(*f*)   Stores issued to production                          39 300
(DR  W.I.P. control, CR   stores ledger control)

(*g*)   Goods finished during the period               120 000
(DR   finished goods stock control, CR   W.I.P. control)

(*h*)   Finished goods delivered to customer         132 000
(DR   cost accounts ledger control, CR   sales)

(*i*)   Materials purchased                              36 000
(DR   stores ledger control, CR   cost accounts ledger control)

(*j*)   Stores issued to factory repair orders            1 500
(DR   works overhead control, CR   stores ledger control)

(*k*)   Carriage inwards on materials purchased         600
(DR   stores ledger control, CR   cost accounts ledger control)

(*l*)   Works expenses                                16 000
(DR  works overhead control, CR  cost accounts ledger control

(*m*)   Administration expenses                       5 800
(DR  administration overhead control, CR  cost accounts ledger control)

(*n*)   Finished goods sold at cost                   118 500
(DR   cost of sales, CR   finished goods stock control)

We should observe one or two other features:

1   That a sales account has been opened to receive the value of sales invoices.
2   That a cost of sales account has been opened to receive the cost value of sales and the amount of overhead absorbed from administration. The sales expenses absorption could be treated in the same manner.
3   That carriage inwards is regarded as part of the cost of acquiring materials.
4   The trial balance serves two purposes: firstly, as a check on the validity of the additions, deductions and double-entry concept, and secondly, as evidence that the cost accounts ledger is in balance, when comparing the

balance on the cost accounts ledger control with the financial accounts ledger control. The balance in the financial accounts ledger control should be *debit* £15 200 in the case of this illustration.

## The need for reconciliation

With the system of interlocked accounts, two completely independent ledgers have been created from which two independent statements of profit can be produced. It is possible that different profits may result. Why should that happen?

1  The closing stock value used in producing the financial statement may be arrived at by taking a physical count. In the cost accounts it may be the value arrived at by the use of techniques outlined in Chapter 3.
2  Financial statements may assume all wages are to be accounted for in the period. Cost accounting statements may be based on wage analysis with indirect wages debited to overhead control.
3  Financial statements may list expense expenditures as a charge against profits. Cost accounting statements may be produced on the basis of techniques of overhead absorption outlined in Chapter 5.

For these reasons alone it would be necessary to reconcile the two profit statements. Clearly, if transactions are carried through in the manner illustrated in Figures 57 and 58 the need for reconciliation diminishes or disappears. Where that full process is not carried out, or where it is company policy to have independent profit statements despite the interlocking of accounts, reconciliation becomes necessary.

To observe how a reconciliation may be achieved we shall examine a simple example:

*Illustration*

During the year a company's profits have been calculated from the cost accounting system at £23 063. The final accounts prepared from the financial books of account disclose a figure of £16 624. Given the following information, we are required to prepare a comparative reconciliation statement:

*Profit and Loss account—year to March 31*

| | | | |
|---|---:|---|---:|
| Opening stocks | 82 154 | Sales | £346 500 |
| Purchases | 247 179 | | |
| | 329 333 | | |
| *Less:* | | | |
| Closing stocks | 75 121 | | |
| | £254 212 | | |
| Direct wages | 23 133 | | |
| Factory overhead | 20 826 | | |
| Gross profit c/d | 48 329 | | |
| | £346 500 | | £346 500 |
| | | | |
| Administration | | Gross profit b/d | 48 329 |
| expenses | 9 845 | Income from | |
| Selling expenses | 22 176 | investments | 316 |
| Net profit | 16 624 | | |
| | £48 645 | | £48 645 |

The cost accounting records show:

1  a stock ledger closing balance of £78 197;
2  direct wages analysis, in total, of £24 867;
3  a factory overhead absorption account with transfers to production of £19 714;
4  an administration expenses recovery of 3% on selling price;
5  that selling expenses are recovered at 5% on selling price.

(ICMA question adapted)

RECONCILIATION STATEMENT

| Detail | Financial books | | Cost Accounting books | | Difference |
|---|---|---|---|---|---|
| Opening stocks | 82 154 | | 82 154 | | — |
| Purchases | 247 179 | | 247 179 | | — |
| | 329 333 | | 329 333 | | — |
| *Less* Closing stocks | 73 121 | | 78 197 | | 3 076 |
| | | | | | |
| Materials used | | 254 212 | | 251 136 | +3 076 |
| Direct wages | | 23 133 | | 24 867 | −1 734 |
| Factory overhead | | 20 826 | | 19 714 | +1 112 |
| Cost of production | | 298 171 | | 295 717 | +2 454 |
| | | | | | |
| Administration expenses | 9 845 | | 10 395 | | −550 |
| Selling expenses | 22 176 | | 17 325 | | +4 851 |
| | | 32 021 | | 27 720 | +4 301 |
| | | | | | |
| Cost of sales | | 330 192 | | 323 437 | +6 755 |
| Sales | | 346 500 | | 346 500 | — |
| | | | | | |
| Operating profit | | 16 308 | | 23 063 | +6 755 |
| Sundry income | | 316 | | — | −316 |
| | | | | | |
| Total net profit | | £16 624 | | £23 063 | +£6 439 |

*Note:* (1) 3% × £346 500 = £10 395 Administration Expenses.
(2) 5% × £346 500 = £17 325 Selling Expenses.
(3) Financial books of account profit £16 624
   Additional profit on reconciliation to cost
   accounting books of account          6 439
                                       _____
                                       £23 063
                                       _____

## FIGURE 61

The reconciliation is shown as a three-column comparative
table in Figure 61 to illustrate where the differences occur
and their 'plus' or 'minus' status. It is important that great
care is taken to identify the figures from which differences
are to be expressed for it is very easy to switch at any point
and arrive at an incorrect answer.

**The integrated ledger system**

Although the control system of accounting just examined has decided advantages, the question of the duplication of work remains. Where the manufacturing centre is far removed from the financial accounting centre, there is good reason for having this system. However, when a firm has all its organisation in one place there is greater advantage in the total integration of all accounting entries.

In order to integrate, we need to dispense with the operation of the two major control accounts, the financial ledger control account and cost ledger control account, and amalgamate all the accounts within one ledger. In so doing we reorganise the manner and method of keeping accounts, and aim to produce a set of financial accounts which is suitable for stewardship purposes, but which is also more informative, more descriptive and thus more in line with the need for scorekeeping.

Let us examine the first transaction again. The normal bookkeeping entry reads:

DR   Purchases
CR   Creditors

Using the interlocked method this becomes:

DR   Financial ledger control
CR   Creditors in the financial accounts ledgers
DR   Raw material stock
DR   Work in progress
CR   Cost ledger control in the cost accounts ledger

To integrate, we drop the main accounts and the entry becomes:

DR   Raw material stock
DR   Work in progress
CR   Creditors

which is similar to the first entry for normal bookkeeping, but which has the bonus of additional information about purchases.

This method retains the control account feature of the interlocked system as far as stocks, work in progress and overheads are concerned, as well as the necessary back-up details already discussed under interlocked ledgers.

Let us examine the operation of this system by considering the following information:

The Westmoreland Engineering Company Ltd. has the following balances in its ledgers at October 31:

|  | £ | £ |
|---|---|---|
| Ordinary share capital |  | 320 000 |
| Stores control | 72 000 |  |
| Work in progress control | 68 000 |  |
| Finished goods control | 52 000 |  |
| Fixed assets | 220 000 |  |
| Provision for depreciation |  | 20 000 |
| Profit and loss |  | 128 000 |
| Cash at bank | 40 000 |  |
| Debtors control | 48 000 |  |
| Creditors control |  | 32 000 |
|  | £500 000 | £500 000 |

Transactions during the month of November were:

| 1 | Wages—cash drawn for wages | 48 380 |  |
|---|---|---|---|
|  | employers' Social Security contributions | 5 390 |  |
|  | employees' Social Security contributions | 2 370 |  |
|  | Income Tax (PAYE) | 5 160 |  |
|  |  |  | £61 300 |
|  | Direct labour | | 58 300 |
|  | Indirect labour—works | | 3 000 |
| 2 | Credit purchases—materials and components | | 66 920 |
| 3 | Administration expenses—wages and salaries | | 5 200 |
|  | credit purchases | | 2 000 |
|  | cash purchases | | 800 |

| 4 | Works expenses | —wages and salaries | 10 500 |
| | | credit purchases | 14 000 |
| | | cash purchases | 500 |
| 5 | Selling and distribution expenses—wages and salaries | | 9 600 |
| | | —credit purchases | 400 |
| 6 | Stores issued—to production | | 72 540 |
| | | —for repair and other work | 1 500 |
| 7 | Cheques received from customers | | 192 860 |
| 8 | Cheques paid to suppliers | | 68 100 |
| 9 | Depreciation on fixed assets—November | | 900 |
| 10 | Cost value of finished goods transferred | | 142 840 |
| 11 | Sales on credit | | 200 000 |
| 12 | Factory cost of goods sold | | 146 400 |
| 13 | Works overhead recovered at 50% on direct labour | | |

We are required to write up the ledger accounts for the
month of November. Administration, selling and distribution costs are transferred to cost of sales account at 5% of
sales value.

We are to take out a trial balance and compute the profit
to date. (AIA Final—adapted)

Before going on to produce the ledger accounts let us consider each transaction. The figure in bold type refers to the
item number of the transaction in the foregoing information.

**1**

| DR | Gross wages control | £61 300 |
| CR | Social Security | 7 760 |
| CR | Income Tax | 5 160 |
| CR | Cash | 48 380 |
| DR | Work in progress control | 58 300 |
| DR | Works overhead control | 3 000 |
| CR | Gross wages control | 61 300 |

This apparent duplication procedure should always be
carried out. There will be many instances in actual practice
where the total of gross wages is not fully allocated.

2

|     |                                |        |
|-----|--------------------------------|--------|
| DR  | Stores ledger control          | 66 920 |
| CR  | Creditors control              | 66 920 |

This entry will be supported by individual entries to specific material and component cards held in stock ledgers. There will also be individual entries to the account of each supplier which, in total, will equal the creditor's total.

3

|     |                                    |        |
|-----|------------------------------------|--------|
| DR  | Administration overhead control    | 8 000  |
| CR  | Cash (for salaries and purchases)  | 6 000  |
| CR  | Creditors control (for purchases)  | 2 000  |

4

|     |                                    |        |
|-----|------------------------------------|--------|
| DR  | Works overhead control             | 25 000 |
| CR  | Cash (for salaries and purchases)  | 11 000 |
| CR  | Creditors control (for purchases)  | 14 000 |

5

|     |                                           |        |
|-----|-------------------------------------------|--------|
| DR  | Selling and distribution overhead control | 10 000 |
| CR  | Cash (for salaries)                       | 9 600  |
| CR  | Creditors control (for purchases)         | 400    |

In Transactions **3**, **4** and **5**, the analysis for Social Security contributions and Income Tax deduction has been omitted for the sake of clarity. It should be noted that the same procedure as demonstrated in Transaction **1** would apply.

The debit to the various overhead controls would be supported by individual cards, or standing orders for each category and classification of overhead. In this illustration we have assumed, for the sake of clarity, that all overhead costs are allocatable. In practice some overheads are common, and thus subject to an apportionment process. In these circumstances, a general overhead control is opened in the ledger. Subsequent apportionments would be cleared from it to the service department or cost centre overhead control.

6

|     |                          |        |
|-----|--------------------------|--------|
| DR  | Work in progress control | 72 540 |
| DR  | Works overhead control   | 1 500  |
| CR  | Stores control           | 74 040 |

**7**

| DR | Cash | 192 860 | |
| CR | Debtors control | | 192 860 |

**8**

| DR | Creditors control | 68 100 | |
| CR | Cash | | 68 100 |

**9**

| DR | Works overhead control | 900 | |
| CR | Provision for depreciation on fixed assets | | 900 |

The assumption made here is that 'fixed assets' refers to plant and equipment used in the manufacturing process. Analysis of the plant register would reveal which fixed asset is in use for what purpose, and would thus be the basis for a more appropriate charge.

**10**

| DR | Finished goods control | 142 840 | |
| CR | Work in progress control | | 142 840 |

**11**

| DR | Debtors control | 200 000 | |
| CR | Sales | | 200 000 |

This entry will be supported by individual entries to each customer's personal account which, in total, will equal the total shown on the debtors' control.

**12**

| DR | Cost of sales | 146 400 | |
| CR | Finished goods control | | 146 400 |

**13**

| DR | Work in progress | 29 150 | |
| CR | Works overhead control | | 29 150 |

The figure used is calculated at 50% of the direct labour figure of £58 300, which is charged to work in progress for the month.

The next two sets of entries are necessary to comply with

### Ordinary Share Capital

| | | | | | |
|---|---|---|---|---|---|
| Nov. 30 | Balance C/F | £320 000 | Nov. 1 | Balance B/F | £320 000 |
| | | | Dec. 1 | Balance B/F | 320 000 |

### Stores Control

| | | | | | |
|---|---|---|---|---|---|
| Nov. 1 | Balance B/F | 72 000 | (6) | Issues | 74 040 |
| (2) | Purchases | 66 920 | Nov. 30 | Balance C/F | 64 880 |
| | | £138 920 | | | £138 920 |
| Dec. 1 | Balance B/F | 64 880 | | | |

### Work in Progress Control

| | | | | | |
|---|---|---|---|---|---|
| Nov. 1 | Balance B/F | 68 000 | (10) | Finished Goods | 142 840 |
| (1) | Labour | 58 300 | Nov. 30 | Balance C/F | 85 150 |
| (6) | Materials | 72 540 | | | |
| (13) | Overheads | 29 150 | | | |
| | | £227 990 | | | £227 990 |
| Dec. 1 | Balance B/F | 85 150 | | | |

### Finished Goods Control

| | | | | | |
|---|---|---|---|---|---|
| Nov. 1 | Balance B/F | 52 000 | (12) | Goods Sold at Cost | 146 400 |
| (10) | Work in Progress | 142 840 | Nov. 30 | Balance C/F | 48 440 |
| | | £194 840 | | | £194 840 |
| Dec. 1 | Balance B/F | 48 440 | | | |

### Fixed Assets

| | | | | | |
|---|---|---|---|---|---|
| Nov. 1 | Balance B/F | 220 000 | Nov. 30 | Balance C/F | 220 000 |
| Dec. 1 | Balance B/F | 220 000 | | | |

### Provision for Depreciation on Fixed Assets

| | | | | | |
|---|---|---|---|---|---|
| Nov. 30 | Balance C/F | 20 900 | Nov. 1 | Balance B/F | 20 000 |
| | | | (9) | November charge | 900 |
| | | £20 900 | | | £20 900 |
| | | | Dec. 1 | Balance B/F | 20 900 |

### Profit and Loss

| | | | | | |
|---|---|---|---|---|---|
| | | | Nov. 1 | Balance B/F | 128 000 |

### Cash

| | | | | | |
|---|---|---|---|---|---|
| Nov. 1 | Balance B/F | 40 000 | (1) | Wages | 48 380 |
| (7) | Debtors | 192 860 | (3) | Administration: Salaries and expenses | 6 000 |
| | | | (4) | Works salaries and expenses | 11 000 |
| | | | (5) | Selling and Distribution Salaries | 9 600 |
| | | | (8) | Creditors | 68 100 |
| | | | Nov. 30 | Balance C/F | 89 780 |
| | | £232 860 | | | £232 860 |
| Dec. 1 | Balance B/F | 89 780 | | | |

### Debtors Control

| | | | | | |
|---|---|---|---|---|---|
| Nov. 1 | Balance B/F | 48 000 | (7) | Cash | 192 860 |
| (11) | Sales | 200 000 | Nov. 30 | Balance C/F | 55 140 |
| | | £248 000 | | | £248 000 |
| Dec. 1 | Balance B/F | 55 140 | | | |

FIGURE 62

### Creditors Control

| | | | | | | |
|---|---|---|---|---|---|---|
| (8) | Cash | 68 100 | Nov. 1 | Balance B/F | | 32 000 |
| Nov. 31 | Balance C/F | 47 220 | (2) | Goods | | 66 920 |
| | | | (3) | Administration expenses | | 2 000 |
| | | | (4) | Works expenses | | 14 000 |
| | | | (5) | Selling and Distribution expenses | | 400 |
| | | £115 320 | | | | £115 320 |
| | | | Dec. 1 | Balance B/F | | 47 220 |

### Gross Wages Control

| | | | | | |
|---|---|---|---|---|---|
| (1) | Payroll | £61 300 | (1) | Allocation | £61 300 |

### Social Security Contributions

| | | | | | |
|---|---|---|---|---|---|
| Nov. 30 | Balance C/F | £7 760 | (1) | Payroll | £7 760 |
| | | | Dec. 1 | Balance B/F | 7 760 |

### Income Tax (PAYE)

| | | | | | |
|---|---|---|---|---|---|
| Nov. 30 | Balance C/F | 5 160 | (1) | Payroll | 5 160 |
| | | | Dec. 1 | Balance B/F | 5 160 |

### Works Overhead Control

| | | | | | |
|---|---|---|---|---|---|
| (1) | Indirect Labour | 3 000 | (13) | Recovery at 50% × £58 300 | 29 150 |
| (4) | Salaries and expenses | 25 000 | Nov. 30 | Balance C/F | 1 250 |
| (6) | Materials | 1 500 | | | |
| (9) | Depreciation | 900 | | | |
| | | £30 400 | | | £30 400 |
| Dec. 1 | Balance B/F | 1 250 | | | |

### Administration Overhead Control

| | | | | | |
|---|---|---|---|---|---|
| (3) | Salaries and expenses | 8 000 | (14) | Recovery at 5% × £200 000 | 10 000 |
| Nov. 30 | Balance C/F | 2 000 | | | |
| | | £10 000 | | | £10 000 |
| | | | Dec. 1 | Balance B/F | 2 000 |

### Selling and Distribution Overhead Control

| | | | | | |
|---|---|---|---|---|---|
| (5) | Salaries and expenses | £10 000 | (15) | Recovery at 5% × £200 000 | £10 000 |

### Sales

| | | | | |
|---|---|---|---|---|
| | | (11) | Debtors | 200 000 |

### Costs of Sales

| | | |
|---|---|---|
| (12) | Finished Goods at Cost | 146 400 |
| (14) | Administration Overhead | 10 000 |
| (15) | Selling and Distribution Overhead | 10 000 |
| | | £166 400 |

FIGURE 62 (Continued)

the instruction given at the end of the transactions list, that is, that administration, selling and distribution overheads are transferred to cost of sales, at 5% of sales value.

**14**

| DR | Cost of sales | 10 000 |
| CR | Administration overhead control | 10 000 |

Being 5% on sales of £200 000

**15**

| DR | Cost of sales | 10 000 |
| CR | Selling and distribution overhead control | 10 000 |

Being 5% on sales of £200 000

The transactions are entered into the accounts in the integrated ledger as demonstrated in Figure 62. The procedure for balancing off and carrying down the balance has been observed with the exception of three accounts: profit and loss, sales, and cost of sales. Under normal circumstances the balances on the latter two accounts would have been transferred to the profit and loss account. It has not been done in this instance, so as to highlight the point that the integrated ledger can show calculation of profit on operations. This is a firm improvement over the normal financial book-keeping method which requires a fairly lengthy procedure to arrive at the same answer. In the integrated system there is a continuous process of transfer of value from one account to another, eventually reaching a total cost figure in the cost of sales account. A trial balance and profit and loss account are shown in Figure 63.

## The advantages of integrated accounting

1 Periodic reconciliations are unnecessary.
2 The probability of error is greatly reduced because cost accounting reporting is usually shorter-term than financial accounting reporting. Thus, errors tend to be found

## TRIAL BALANCE—NOVEMBER 30

| | | |
|---|---:|---:|
| Ordinary Share Capital | | 320 000 |
| Stores Control | 64 880 | |
| Work in Progress Control | 85 150 | |
| Finished Goods Control | 48 440 | |
| Fixed Assets | 220 000 | |
| Provision for Depreciation on Fixed Assets | | 20 900 |
| Profit and Loss | | 128 000 |
| Costs | 89 780 | |
| Debtors | 55 140 | |
| Creditors | | 47 220 |
| Social Security Contributions | | 7 760 |
| Income Tax | | 5 160 |
| Works Overhead Control | 1 250 | |
| Administration Overhead Control | | 2 000 |
| Sales | | 200 000 |
| Cost of Sales | 166 400 | |
| | £731 040 | £731 040 |

## PROFIT AND LOSS
*Period to November 30*

| | | | |
|---|---:|---|---:|
| Cost of Sales | 166 400 | Sales | 200 000 |
| Profit | 33 600 | | |
| | £200 000 | | £200 000 |

FIGURE 63

quickly and corrective action to eliminate repetition is immediate.

3　The information made available by an integrated system is produced quickly. Thus, management can be notified very speedily of the outcome of decisions, external influences and internal conditions.

4　The elimination of unnecessary transfers and analysis makes for greater use of existing resources and for cost reductions.

### Conclusion

It may be observed that integrated accounting implies a change in the relationship between financial and cost accounting recording and information processing. Here is a method of preparing fast and accurate data, from common information produced in scorekeeping rather than stewardship form. In recent years there has been an increased willingness to accept this concept, probably brought about by the greater use of mechanical and electronic data-processing equipment. One of the important features of the use of such equipment is the need to integrate information in order to achieve the most economic, or 'least cost' operation.

There are, furthermore, some rather exciting developments taking place which will change the way in which accounting information should or must be produced: inflation or price-change accounting and the impact of the entry into Europe are two examples. Without doubt, these and other matters will raise problems which will call for fast, accurate answers.

### Exercises

1　You are required to prepare for S Manufacturing Limited for the year ended October 31:

(a) The following control accounts in the cost ledger:

> Raw materials stores
> Work in progress
> Finished goods

(b) A reconciliation statement to reconcile the profits shown in the financial and cost accounts.

The summarised Manufacturing, Trading, Profit and Loss, and Appropriation accounts for the year in the financial accounts are given below:

| | £ | £ |
|---|---:|---:|
| Raw materials: | | |
| Opening stock | 24 130 | |
| Purchases | 51 480 | |
| | 75 610 | |
| Closing stock | 27 310 | |
| | | 48 300 |
| Direct wages | | 18 400 |
| Production overhead | | 40 620 |
| Production cost incurred | | 107 320 |
| Work in progress—opening stock | 32 820 | |
| closing stock | 30 240 | |
| | | 2 580 |
| Cost of goods manufactured—carried down | | £109 900 |
| Finished goods: | | |
| Opening stock | 65 860 | |
| Cost of goods manufactured | 109 900 | |
| | 175 760 | |
| Closing stock | 73 370 | |
| Cost of goods sold | | 102 390 |
| Gross profit carried down | | 97 610 |
| Sales | | £200 000 |

| | |
|---|---:|
| Administration overhead | 25 400 |
| Selling and distribution overhead | 18 700 |
| Financial expenses | 10 000 |
| | 54 100 |
| Net profit carried down | 43 510 |
| | |
| Gross profit brought down | £97 610 |
| | |
| Retained profit balance brought down | 25 670 |
| Net profit this year | 43 510 |
| | |
| | £69 180 |
| *less:* dividends | 15 340 |
| taxation | 18 680 |
| | 34 020 |
| | |
| Balance—retained profit carried down | £35 160 |

The following information from the cost accounts is given:

| | £ |
|---|---:|
| Control account balances brought down at beginning of the year: | |
| Raw materials stores | 24 620 |
| Work in progress | 32 170 |
| Finished goods | 64 920 |
| Transactions for the year: | |
| Raw material issued | 48 730 |
| Cost of products produced | 115 640 |
| Cost of products sold | 107 730 |
| Abnormal loss in raw material stores | 510 |

Production overhead has been absorbed at a rate of 250% of direct wages. A notional rent of £5000 has been charged into the cost accounts.

Describe briefly a system of accounting which would obviate the need to reconcile the profits shown in the financial and cost accounts. (ICMA adapted)

2 C Limited operates an integrated accounting system. You are required to:

(a) open and write up the accounts for May 19.1
(b) prepare a profit and loss account for May 19.1.

The trial balance at May 1 19.1 was as follows:

|  | £000s | £000s |
|---|---|---|
| Raw material stock | 138 | |
| Work in progress | 34 | |
| Finished goods stock | 62 | |
| Debtors | 200 | |
| Creditors | | 140 |
| Expense creditors | | 58 |
| Wages accrued | | 11 |
| PAYE tax | | 45 |
| Bank | 40 | |
| Freehold buildings | 360 | |
| Plant and machinery at cost | 240 | |
| Provision for depreciation, plant and machinery | | 60 |
| Issued share capital | | 600 |
| General reserve | | 120 |
| Profit and loss account | | 40 |
| | £1074 | £1074 |

The following information is given of the transactions that took place in May 19.1:

|  | £000s |
|---|---|
| Sales | 320 |
| Purchase of raw material | 92 |
| Raw materials returned to supplier | 4 |
| Production overhead incurred | 88 |
| Selling and distribution costs incurred | 42 |
| Administration costs incurred | 37 |
| Direct wages incurred | 42 |
| Raw materials issued to production | 80 |
| Raw materials issued to production maintenance | 10 |
| Raw materials returned to stores from production | 2 |
| Abnormal loss in production | 5 |
| Cost of finished goods sold | 210 |
| Payments received in respect of sales | 330 |
| Payments made for raw materials purchased | 101 |
| Discounts allowed | 11 |

|                                        | £000s |
| -------------------------------------- | ----- |
| Discounts received                     | 3     |
| Payments made to expense creditors     | 140   |
| Direct wages paid                      | 34    |
| PAYE tax deducted from wages           | 16    |

You are informed that:

(a)  depreciation of plant and machinery is provided for at 10% of cost per annum;

(b)  production overhead is absorbed on the basis of 250% of direct wages incurred;

(c)  selling and distribution costs and administration costs incurred in May 19.1, are charged against the profits of May 19.1;

(d)  work in progress was valued on May 31 19.1 at £39 000.       (ICMA)

3   'The cost ledger is made up of a series of control accounts.' What do you understand by this statement?

4   The cost accounts of AB Limited for the financial year show a profit of £17 002, and the following differences between cost and financial accounts are known to exist:

|                                               | £    |
| --------------------------------------------- | ---- |
| Directors' fees in financial accounts only    | 1250 |
| Interest on capital in cost accounts only     | 2000 |
| Company taxation                              | 6220 |

Work in progress valuation is known to be £1740 higher in cost accounts than in financial accounts; depreciation provision is £850 higher in cost accounts than in financial accounts; and total expenses of £27 000 are shown in financial accounts but overhead cost is absorbed at 150% on direct labour of £19 250 in the cost accounts.

Prepare a reconciliation statement showing the profit disclosed by the financial accounts.   (ACCA adapted)

# Part III

# Control Techniques

# 12

# Budgets and Budgetary Control

We commence the study of this technique with two definitions from the ICMA Terminology:

1 A *budget* is 'a financial and/or quantitative statement, prepared and approved prior to a defined period of time, of the policy to be pursued during that period for the purpose of attaining a given objective. It may include income, expenditure and the employment of capital.'

(ICMA)

2 *Budgetary control* is 'the establishment of budgets relating the responsibilities of executives to the requirements of a policy, and the continuous comparison of actual with budgeted results, either to secure by individual action the objectives of that policy or to provide a firm basis for its revision'. (ICMA)

Thus, the budget will define the target, and budgetary control will show whether or not that target has been achieved.

## The budget

Budgeting has the following advantages:

1 It requires management to carry out in advance, and on a continuous basis, a study of the resources available and the problems associated with their use.

2 It provides a basis on which policies can be continuously examined, revised and restated as guidelines for the total organisation.
3 It co-ordinates and correlates efforts. The procedure necessary for systematic budgeting reveals weaknesses at a very early stage.

There are limitations to be weighed against the advantages:

1 Planning or forecasting is not an exact science. A great deal of wide-ranging judgement is required to establish the basis of the forecast.
2 The enthusiasm of everyone in the organisation is needed for the plan to have any chance of success.
3 The benefits of budgeting do not appear overnight or indeed over a year. It always takes time to evaluate and correct a new system.

## Before budgeting

In order to start the process from a firm basis, three things are necessary:

1 The organisation chart. This defines the functional responsibility and the level of authority of each person. We may say that where such persons are managers, their activity justifies a budget.
2 A classification of accounts. This is a vocabulary within which everyday terms take on a specific meaning. For example, one of the matters that has to be settled at an early stage is the responsibility for the apportionment of common costs. Thus the accounts classification manual will show, for example, the point of charge for rates. If, in the initial instance, rates are classified as an administrative expense, then they become part of the administrative budget.

3 A budget committee. This will consist of the managers of the major functions. The principal functions of that committee are to:

    (*a*)   Receive and review budgets
    (*b*)   Suggest revisions and amendments
    (*c*)   Approve original, revised or amended budgets
    (*d*)   Recommend action to improve effectiveness
    (*e*)   Co-ordinate the individual functional budgets into the master budget.

These three prerequisites give the budgeting process strength and direction. The organisation chart tells us who will budget. The accounts classification will show that person what is to be budgeted. The budget committee will approve or reject that budget in the light of the overall objectives of the organisation.

### The total or master budget

The outcome of the budgeting process will be the collation of a series of functional budgets into a total or master budget. Its form will be that of a set of final accounts and a balance sheet, giving top management an evaluation or forecast of the position the organisation will be in, or will reach, at some point in the future.

The accountant has a major role in the budgeting process. He will be required, as manager, to produce a functional budget for the operation of the accounting services. He will also evaluate the individual functional budgets and co-ordinate them with the master budget format.

A complete set of functional budgets will generally consist of:

1 *The sales budget.* This should give forecasts in sales units by area, product, customer grouping, or whatever

combinations are required by the policy directive. It should also give some indication of the credit ratings of customers, as the basis for preparing a debtors budget. The sales budget will need to be supported by the functional budgets for:

(*a*)   Salesmen and commission
(*b*)   Sales office and selling expenses
(*c*)   Advertising and market research

2   *The production budget.* This will need to be prepared from several other functional budgets such as:

(*a*)   Machine and labour utilisation
(*b*)   Stock policy
(*c*)   Purchasing and material consumption, including an indication of suppliers' credit policy
(*d*)   Labour—direct and indirect
(*e*)   Works expenses

3   *The administrative budget.* This will cover the main functional areas such as accounting, secretarial services, canteen, personnel and so forth.

4   *The distribution budget.* This will include distribution and warehouse forecasts for salaries, wages and expenses.

5   *The capital expenditure programme*, to cover proposed new and replacement equipment.

6   *The cash budget*, to show the flow of receipts and expenditures.

7   The budgeted profit and loss account.

8   The budgeted balance sheet.

Figure 64 demonstrates the interrelationship of these budgets. The size of the block assigned to each budget is an indication of the time scale: the smaller the block, the earlier it is needed. Thus the block allocated to the budgeted

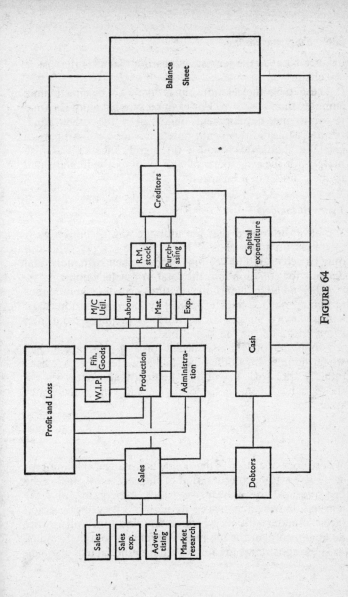

FIGURE 64

balance sheet is the largest, indicating that it is the last in the chain.

The actual interrelationship is likely to be much more complex than is shown. For example, we have not shown a research and development budget. On the other hand, retail organisations will not have a machine utilisation budget. We should also notice the significance of the cash budget, for the availability of cash resources is fundamental to the running of a business.

## Types of budgets

We have discovered that the ultimate aim of budgeting is to obtain an assessment of likely future activity. This can only be achieved if all sections produce their own individual budgets for collation into the total or master budget.

A *functional* budget is one relating to any of the functions or managerial activities as defined by the organisation chart.

A *summary* budget is one which is prepared from, and summarises, all the functional budgets.

The *master* budget is a special form of summary budget which summarises all the other budgets after they have been initially approved. It will only be finally approved when it shows achievement of the objective laid out in the policy statement.

## Limiting factors

Where does one start in the policy and budget-making process? It is with a consideration of the constraints facing the organisation, the industry in which it operates, and the markets in which it places its goods. Every organisation faces some constraints which at any one time will restrict its ability to plan for the most desirable or optimal results.

These constraints are known as 'limiting factors', 'principal budget factors' or 'key factors', and they include, for example, the availability of raw material, the availability of cash, the availability of the right grade of labour, or the demand for the product the firm produces.

In some industries, notably those producing domestic and household goods, the predominant factor is sales; in the heavier industries, production is often predominant, since their survival depends on capacity and technical knowledge rather than sales. There is no general rule to be followed, except to say that the predominant factors must be established at the earliest moment and used as the basis for policy and budget processes.

One should not however assume that, once found and established, the limiting factor will remain constant. It can change almost from day to day and thus needs to be carefully incorporated into the reporting process.

## Budget compilation

We now go through some of the main budgets to obtain a broad picture of budget compilation.

### The sales budget

This will consider the immediate past performance in conjunction with sales analysis and market research. Feasibility tests will need to be applied to forecasts to establish their validity. For example, a sales budget that forecasts the sales of two million lawnmowers per year when there are only one million lawns is clearly a nonsense.

This budget is the responsibility of the sales manager, but he will delegate this responsibility down through his district and area managers or branch managers to the salesman. This is a 'grass roots' operation that takes every advantage of the experience of the person covering the area. Budgets would probably be produced by the salesmen in the form illustrated in Figure 65.

The use of this or a similar document will allow functional budgets for each section, area and district to be built

| Product | Jan. | Feb. | Mar. | Apr. | May | June | July | Aug. | Sept. | Oct. | Nov. | Dec. | Total |
|---|---|---|---|---|---|---|---|---|---|---|---|---|---|
| Scales I<br>Scales II<br>Scales III | | | | | | | | | | | | | |
| Shears II<br>Cutters | | | | | | | | | | | | | |
| | | | | | | | | | | | | | |

SALES FORECAST　Year to December 19—

Territory＿＿＿＿＿＿＿＿＿＿＿　District＿＿＿＿＿＿＿

Sales Representative＿＿＿＿＿＿＿　Area＿＿＿＿＿

FIGURE 65

up until an estimate of the total sales figure is reached. The same form could also be used to build up a territorial analysis in the form suggested in Figure 66.

At every stage adjustments will have been made to incorporate the functional budget into the sales budget, and at the final stage full consideration must be given to such matters as:

(a) general business environment and conditions in the industry;
(b) the anticipated share of the market;
(c) economic and political conditions, especially in connection with export markets and the availability of particular components;
(d) the financial effect of customer payment or debtor policy;
(e) the production possibilities and capacities.

| Territory | Customer type | January | | February | | / / | December | | Total | |
|---|---|---|---|---|---|---|---|---|---|---|
| | | Qty. | £ | Qty. | £ | | Qty. | £ | Qty. | Total |
| NORTH | 1 | | | | | | | | | |
| | 2 | | | | | | | | | |
| | 3 | | | | | | | | | |
| | Total | | £ | | £ | | | £ | | £ |
| SOUTH | 1 | | | | | | | | | |
| | 2 | | | | | | | | | |
| | 3 | | | | | | | | | |
| | Total | | £ | | £ | | | £ | | £ |
| EAST | 1 | | | | | | | | | |
| | 2 | | | | | | | | | |
| | 3 | | | | | | | | | |
| | Total | | £ | | £ | | | £ | | £ |
| WEST | 1 | | | | | | | | | |
| | 2 | | | | | | | | | |
| | 3 | | | | | | | | | |
| | Total | | £ | | £ | | | £ | | £ |
| TOTAL | | | £ | | £ | | | £ | | £ |

TERRITORIAL SALES FORECAST — 19____

FIGURE 66

## Production budgets

Before the sales budget is accepted, the ability of the production department to achieve a range of capabilities must be forecast. The objective will be to keep men and machines operating at the highest possible level of activity throughout the year consistent with the requirements of sales forecasts and stock policy. For this purpose several interrelated functional budgets will be necessary. They may include the following:

(*a*) plant or machine utilisation
(*b*) manpower
(*c*) materials and purchasing requirements
(*d*) opening and closing stocks of raw material, work in progress, and finished goods at each period.

MACHINE UTILISATION BUDGET

Department_____  Period_____

Machine Group_____  Planned
Hours per week_____  Maintenance_____
Weeks per period_____

| Machine Number | Machine Hours | | | Product Hours Required | | | Over or Under Util. |
|---|---|---|---|---|---|---|---|
| | Basic | Planned M't'ce | Net Available | Product Units | Unit Hours | Total Product Hours | |
| | | | | | | | |
| | | | | | | | |
| | | | | | | | |
| Totals | | | | | | | |

FIGURE 67

MANPOWER BUDGET    Period_____

Production Output Hours    Department_____

Product A            @         Unit hours =       Hrs. total
       B
       C
       D
Total Hours Requirement

| GRADE | MALE | | | | FEMALE | | | | TOTAL | |
|---|---|---|---|---|---|---|---|---|---|---|
| | Under 18 | | Over 18 | | Under 18 | | Over 18 | | | |
| | No. | Hrs. | No. | Hrs. | No. | Hrs. | No. | Hrs. | No. | Hrs. |
| Direct | | | | | | | | | | |
| Skilled | | | | | | | | | | |
| Semi-skilled | | | | | | | | | | |
| Unskilled | | | | | | | | | | |
| | | | | | | | | | | |
| Indirect | | | | | | | | | | |
| Shop labour | | | | | | | | | | |
| Maintenance | | | | | | | | | | |
| Cleaners | | | | | | | | | | |
| Totals | | | | | | | | | | |

FIGURE 68

Figure 67 indicates the way in which plant utilisation forecasts may be collated. Figure 68 suggests a way in which manpower could be estimated. The validity of both these estimates will be subject to scrutiny and feasibility testing in conjunction with the final outcomes of the sales budget.

Clearly, the sales and production budgets must match, in order to ensure that neither men nor machinery are over- or under-used.

The relationship between these two budgets and the opinions evaluated in converting them to net normal availability are the basis for the direct labour budget in financial terms.

## Materials, purchasing and stocks budgets

A matcrials budget will indicate the quantity and value o the direct materials required for a given range of products. It enables the purchasing department to set up buying schedules, and it indicates the impact on cash resources of the requirements of suppliers or creditors. It will be the basis for re-evaluating factors such as Minimum and Maximum Stock Levels, Re-order Levels and Re-order Quantities and for deciding whether a particular stock policy is feasible. However the whole matter very much depends on the production and sales forecasts, for until they are agreed it will not be possible to determine material requirements.

## The cash budget

This is probably the most fundamental budget of all, bringing together all the other factors in cash terms, and indicating:

1   the projected availability of cash at particular periods;
2   when funds are likely to be low;
3   the point at which additional funds will be required.

A cash budget will involve detailed forecasts of anticipated cash receipts and cash disbursements for the period covered by the budget, and probably for a short time beyond it. The information on which the cash budget is based comes from the following sources:

1 the sales budget, with a debtors budget, indicating cash receipts;
2 materials budget, with a creditors budget indicating cash expenditure;
3 payroll, or total labour budget;
4 fixed asset or capital replacement and investment budget;
5 total expenses budget, and a secondary creditors budget;
6 policy budget, which will reveal such items as tax, dividends, interest, and, possibly, anticipated new sources of funds such as new share issues, debenture issues, mortgages, and so forth.

Cash budgets need to be prepared with care and a great deal of experience and are usually reasonably reliable and accurate for short periods. For the longer term it is a wise move to install a system known as 'roll over' cash budgeting: this requires a monthly review, with revisions incorporated into the forward estimate.

## The budget period and continuous budgeting

It is reasonable to assume that many organisations will want to prepare their budgets for the same period as that covered by their accounts, i.e. one year. In doing so, they may divide that annual budget into the shorter control periods used in most other cases. For example, the year may be divided into:

(a) the twelve calendar months;
(b) four quarters divided into one five-week, and two four-week periods;
(c) thirteen four-week periods.

The method used will depend on the organisation's usual practice, the type of business they are involved in, and over what time period they feel a major control should operate. A firm in the heavy capital goods or contracting industry, with orders extending over, say, three years, will have very different ideas from an organisation involved in an industry that experiences short-term seasonal fluctuations. We might find the former happily preparing five-year budgets and the latter six-monthly budgets.

The term 'budget period' is usually taken to mean the total length of a period, whilst the term 'control period' usually implies the shorter period. We have observed that planning and control are directed towards some future target towards which the organisation is feeling its way.

The budgeting system we have set up involves the whole organisation in an end-of-budget-period reappraisal in order to set the budget for the next period. It is somewhat puzzling when we also see that such a process is done in an apparently isolated 'per period' form. To overcome this rather insular approach, 'roll over' or 'continuous' budgeting has been adopted by many organisations. Figure 69 shows, in diagrammatic form, how this would work.

At the end of January in the first year, three actions are taken:

1  Compare January budget with January actual results.
2  As a result, leave or revise, in part or in whole, the budget for the remaining eleven months.
3  Add the budget for January of the second year.

Thus, at the beginning of February of the first year, a new twelve-month budget is in existence covering the next twelve months. This 'continuous' or 'roll over' process ensures that objectives, estimates and targets are being subjected to constant reappraisal.

The procedure may also be used for formulating more

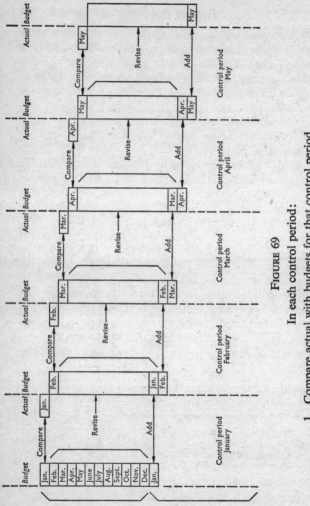

FIGURE 69

In each control period:

1 Compare actual with budgets for that control period
2 Take effective action and revise budget
3 Revise where necessary the budgets for the budget period
4 'Roll over' the budget by one control period.

effectively the longer-term budgets of, say, five, ten or even twenty years. These budget periods may be necessary in the heavy capital goods or contracting industries.

We now consider two practical applications of some of the matters discussed above.

### Example 1

XYZ Ltd manufactures three products P1, P2 and P3. These are made in three production departments D1, D2 and D3, from four materials M1, M2, M3 and M4. The following information is supplied:

Standard product cost detail:

| Material | | Used in department | Cost per unit £ | *Products* P1 | P2 | P3 |
|---|---|---|---|---|---|---|
| Material | M1 | D1 | 0·50 | — | 1 | 2 |
| | M2 | D2 | 0·20 | 1 | — | 2 |
| | M3 | D2 | 0·25 | 2 | 1 | — |
| | M4 | D3 | 0·15 | 2 | 2 | 1 |
| Rejection on final inspection at end of process | | | | 5% | 10% | 10% |
| Budget details: | | | | | | |
| Sales for the year (£000s) | | | | 260 | 580 | 450 |
| Unit sale price (£) | | | | 5 | 10 | 6 |
| Finished goods stocks (000s units): | | | | | | |
| January 1 | | | | 5 | 10 | 15 |
| December 31 | | | | 10 | 15 | 30 |

| | *Materials* M1 | M2 | M3 | M4 |
|---|---|---|---|---|
| Raw materials stocks (000s units) | | | | |
| January 1 | 30 | 40 | 10 | 60 |
| December 31 | 40 | 30 | 20 | 50 |

You are required to prepare:

(*a*) Standard material cost per product;

(*b*) The production budget, production cost budgets for direct materials, by department, and finally, the purchasing budget for the year.                    (ICMA)

Figure 70 shows a suggested approach and layout.

### Example 2

The month-by-month forecasts of a company for the five months May to September are as follows:

| | | | £000s | | |
|---|---|---|---|---|---|
| | *May* | *June* | *July* | *Aug* | *Sept* |
| Materials consumed | 60 | 70 | 80 | 102 | 90 |
| Wages | 32 | 32 | 32 | 40 | 32 |
| Depreciation | 7 | 7 | 7 | 7 | 7 |
| Factory expenses | 5 | 5 | 5 | 5 | 5 |
| Rent | 3 | 3 | 3 | 3 | 3 |
| Salaries and office expenses | 32 | 32 | 32 | 32 | 32 |
| Advertising and publicity | 12 | 14 | 10 | 16 | 20 |
| Sales Commission | 8 | 9 | 10 | 13 | 11 |
| | 159 | 172 | 179 | 218 | 200 |
| Sales | 160 | 180 | 200 | 260 | 220 |
| Profit | 1 | 8 | 21 | 42 | 20 |
| Closing stock—raw material | 70 | 80 | 90 | 70 | 60 |

The following additional information is given:

1  On average, payment is made to suppliers one month after delivery.
2  The lag in payment of wages is one eighth of a month.
3  Factory expenses are paid during the month in which they were incurred.
4  Rent is paid quarterly on the last day of March, June, September and December.
5  Salaries and office expenses are paid in the month in which they arise.
6  Advertising and publicity expenditure is paid monthly, but two months' credit is taken.

### STANDARD MATERIAL COST

| Material | Dept. | Unit rate | P1 Unit | P1 £ | P2 Unit | P2 £ | P3 Unit | P3 £ | Total £ |
|---|---|---|---|---|---|---|---|---|---|
| M1 | D1 | £0·50 | — | — | 1 | 0·50 | 2 | 1·00 | 1·50 |
| M2 | D2 | 0·20 | 1 | 0·20 | — | — | 2 | 0·40 | 0·60 |
| M3 | D2 | 0·25 | 2 | 0·50 | 1 | 0·25 | — | — | 0·75 |
| M4 | D3 | 0·15 | 2 | 0·30 | 2 | 0·30 | 1 | 0·15 | 0·75 |
| | | | | £1·00 | | £1·05 | | £1·55 | £3·60 |

### PRODUCTION BUDGET—UNITS

| | P1 | P2 | P3 |
|---|---|---|---|
| Sales value (£000's) | 260 | 580 | 450 |
| Unit sales value (£) | 5 | 10 | 6 |
| Sales units (000's) | 52 | 58 | 75 |
| *Plus* Closing stocks FG (000's) | 10 | 15 | 30 |
| *Less* Opening stocks FG (000's) | 5 | 10 | 15 |
| | 57 | 63 | 90 |
| *Add* Back rejections at 5%; 10%; 10% | 3 | 7 | 10 |
| Production units (000's) | 60 | 70 | 100 |

### PRODUCTION COST AND PURCHASE BUDGET

| | M1 | M2 | M3 | M4 | Total |
|---|---|---|---|---|---|
| *Material unit price* | £0·50 | £0·20 | £0·25 | £0·15 | |
| Opening stock (RM units—000's) | 30 | 40 | 10 | 60 | |
| Closing stock (RM units—000's) | 40 | 30 | 20 | 50 | |
| Change in stocks | +10 | −10 | −10 | −10 | |
| Production units (000's) | | | | | |
| P1— 60 | — | 60 | 120 | 120 | |
| P2— 70 | 70 | — | 70 | 140 | |
| P3—100 | 200 | 200 | — | 100 | |
| Total purchase units (000's) | 280 | 250 | 180 | 350 | |
| Total purchase value (000's) | £140 | £50 | £45 | £52·5 | £287·5 |
| *Department Production* | D1 | D2 | | D3 | |
| *Costs (£000's)* | £140 | £95 | | £52·5 | £287·5 |

FIGURE 70

WORKING SCHEDULES

| Note No. | | May | June | July | Aug. | Sept. |
|---|---|---|---|---|---|---|
| 1 | To establish purchases and creditors | | | | | |
| | Opening Stock | — | 70 | 80 | 90 | 70 |
| | Closing Stock | 70 | 80 | 90 | 70 | 60 |
| | Change in Stock | ÷70 | +10 | +10 | −20 | −10 |
| | +Materials consumed | +60 | +70 | +80 | ⊦102 | +90 |
| | ─Purchases | 130 | 80 | 90 | 82 | 80 |
| | Creditors paid 1 month after delivery | — | 130 | 80 | 90 | 82 |
| 2. | Wages | 32 | 32 | 32 | 40 | 32 |
| | Paid with 1,8 month lag. 7/8 now | 28 | 28 | 28 | 35 | 28 |
| | 1/8 1 month | | 4 | 4 | 4 | 5 |
| | Cash paid | | 32 | 32 | 39 | 33 |
| | *Depreciation—not a cash item* | | | | | |
| 3 | Factory expenses paid as shown | 5 | 5 | 5 | 5 | 5 |
| 4 | Rent. Paid quarterly | | 9 | — | — | 9 |
| 5 | Salaries and office expenses—paid as stated | 32 | 32 | 32 | 32 | 32 |
| 6 | Advertising and publicity | 12 | 14 | 10 | 16 | 20 |
| | Paid 2 months in arrears | | | 12 | 14 | 10 |
| 7 | Sales commission | 8 | 9 | 10 | 13 | 11 |
| | Paid 1 month in arrear | | 8 | 9 | 10 | 13 |
| 8 | Sales | 160 | 180 | 200 | 260 | 220 |
| | Received 2 months in arrears | | | 160 | 180 | 200 |
| 9 | Opening Cash balance | | | 52 | | |
| 10 | Payment for machinery | | | | | 30 |
| | Dividend and taxation | | | | 6 | |
| | Investment grants | | | | | 20 |

The amounts within the horizontal boxes for July, August and September constitute the cash budget for the three months as follows:

| Income | July | Aug. | Sept. |
|---|---|---|---|
| Opening cash balance b/f | 52 | 42 | 26 |
| Cash from Debtors. | 160 | 180 | 200 |
| Investment grants | | | 20 |
| | £212 | £222 | £246 |
| *Expenditure* | | | |
| Paid to creditors | 80 | 90 | 82 |
| Wages | 32 | 39 | 33 |
| Factory expenses | 5 | 5 | 5 |
| Rent | | | 9 |
| Salaries and office expenses | 32 | 32 | 32 |
| Advertising and publicity | 12 | 14 | 10 |
| Sales Commission | 9 | 10 | 13 |
| Machinery | | | 30 |
| Dividend and taxation | | 6 | |
| | 170 | 196 | 214 |
| Closing balance b/f | 42 | 26 | 32 |
| | £212 | £222 | £246 |

FIGURE 71

7 Sales commission is paid one month in arrears.
8 On average, debtors take two months' credit.
9 Cash balance at July 1 is £52 000.
10 In September £30 000 will be paid for machinery. A dividend and taxation payment of £6000 will be paid in August. Investment grants of £20 000 will be received in September.

You are required to prepare a cash budget for each of the three months to September 30. (ICMA)

Figure 71 shows how to approach this example. These examples indicate the wide-ranging detail that needs to be considered and amassed in order to install, start and maintain a budgeting system. With this type of question it is important that a neat set of working schedules are planned.

## Budgetary control

Three points emerge in the definition of budgetary control:

(*a*) the establishment of budgets;
(*b*) the continuous comparison of 'actual' with budget;
(*c*) individual action.

We could further précis these features to the single words *plan*, *compare* and *act*.

An overall management operation has three main objectives:

1 to control costs.
2 to control performance.
3 to control finance and obtain financial stability.

What of the comparison? This is the point at which the accounting service comes into play. By 'comparison' we mean the action of listing the actual expenditures and performances and comparing them with the budget; the deviations revealed by this comparison will be the basis for effective action.

### Fixed and flexible budgets

What we have evolved in our budget process so far is a fixed budget or, in other words, a budget designed to remain unchanged regardless of the level of activity. Although a fixed budget may be a very good instrument for forward planning in general terms, it is not really suitable in cases where the level of activity varies.

Let us consider a very simple example:

*Illustration*

| | |
|---|---:|
| Budgeted sales—5000 at £5 each | £25 000 |
| Budgeted cost of sales at £3 each | 15 000 |
| Gross profit | 10 000 |
| *Less:* Administration and selling expenses—all fixed | 5 000 |
| Net profit | £5 000 |
| The actual results were: | |
| Sales—4800 | £24 720 |
| Costs | 14 304 |
| Gross profit | 10 416 |
| Administration and selling expenses | 5 016 |
| Net profit | £5 400 |

No matter how close these two sets of figures *appear* to be, they are not comparable. The budget is posed in terms of one performance or activity level, while the actual results are on a totally different level. Thus one of the sets of figures must be adjusted so that comparison may be carried out.

The budget, being a forecast, is the most suitable candidate for adjustment because the *actual* result is an unalterable fact. By reorganising the budget in terms of the actual performance we would obtain the following:

*Comparison*

| | Activity level—4800 units | | |
| | Budget | Actual | Difference |
| | £ | £ | £ |
| Sales (Budget at £5 per unit) | 24 000 | 24 700 | +720 |
| Cost of sales (Budget at £3 per unit) | 14 400 | 14 304 | − 96 |
| Gross profit | 9 600 | 10 416 | +816 |
| Administration and selling expenses | 5 000 | 5 016 | −16 |
| Net profit | £4 600 | £5 400 | +£800 |

—from which the following analysis could be made:

1 Sales price increase from £5 to £5·15
   4800 units @ £0·15 more revenue:                    +£720
2 Production costs or cost of sales are just under £3 per
   unit @ £2·98
   4800 units at £0·02 less cost:                      +£96
3 Slight increase in forecast fixed costs:            −£16
4 Net profit increase as a result:                    +£800

The 'action points' may now be discerned:

1 Sales manager to investigate decrease in units: was it due to increased price? Do we adjust or revise budget for remainder of the year? Were forecasts optimistic?
2 Production manager to investigate costs. Look at forecast build-up of costs. Are we using different material, or different labour from forecast? Are performances up? Are wastage factors down? Were forecasts pessimistic? Do we need to adjust or revise budget for remainder of year?

3　Points for administration and sales managers to investigate: was forecast rounded down? Were any costs underestimated? Do we need to adjust or revise budget for the remainder of the year?

4　Budget committee: what will be the long-term effect on profit of the answers to the three points above?

We can now see the comparing process being carried out correctly and leading to a properly executed chain of events, decisions and actions. Two points should be noted:

1　The chain of events, decisions and actions, if taken on a comparison of the unadjusted budget, may have been different and completely misleading.

2　At no point is there an indication that sales management or production management or anyone is to blame.

This adjustment of budgets is known as flexible budgeting.

### A flexible budget

This is designed to change in accordance with the level of activity actually attained: the schedule of incomes and expenditures which comprise the budget is built up to take account of the varying effect of changing levels of activity or performance.

At what level do costs vary, and by how much? Figure 72 indicates in a simple fashion one of the ways in which a particular cost centre budget will need to be formulated. We see from this that it is possible to arrive at unit costs for different activity levels. This, or the absolute figures, may be used for flexing the budget so as to make it comparable to the actual results. The effect of the change of activity level on the changing levels of expenditure is shown in the graph in Figure 73.

| EXPENSE BUDGET | | | Dept. ___S___ Period ___1 Month___ | | | | | | |
|---|---|---|---|---|---|---|---|---|---|
| Activity level | | | 0·7 | 0·8 | 0·9 | 1 | 1·1 | 1·2 | 1·3 |
| Forecast units | | | 3500 | 4000 | 4500 | 5000 | 5500 | 6000 | 6500 |
| Expense | Code | V SV | £ | £ | £ | £ | £ | £ | £ |
| Shop Labour | 512 | SV | 270 | 280 | 290 | 300 | 310 | 320 | 330 |
| Shop Cleaning | 513 | SV | 270 | 280 | 290 | 300 | 310 | 320 | 330 |
| Progress | 514 | SV | 455 | 470 | 485 | 500 | 515 | 530 | 545 |
| Clerical | 515 | SV | 710 | 740 | 770 | 800 | 830 | 860 | 890 |
| Overtime Premium | 516 | V | 140 | 160 | 180 | 200 | 220 | 240 | 260 |
| Power | 543 | SV | 610 | 640 | 670 | 700 | 730 | 760 | 790 |
| Maintenance | 568 | V | 210 | 240 | 270 | 300 | 330 | 360 | 390 |
| Inspection | 569 | SV | 610 | 640 | 670 | 700 | 730 | 760 | 790 |
| Consumables | 572 | V | 280 | 320 | 360 | 400 | 440 | 480 | 520 |
| Stationery | 594 | V | 70 | 80 | 90 | 100 | 110 | 120 | 130 |
| Total Variable and Semi-variable | | | 3625 | 3850 | 4075 | 4300 | 4525 | 4750 | 4957 |
| Supervision | 536 | F | 400 | 400 | 400 | 400 | 400 | 400 | 400 |
| Managers | 538 | F | 700 | 700 | 700 | 700 | 700 | 700 | 700 |
| Production Control | 522 | F | 300 | 300 | 300 | 300 | 300 | 350 | 350 |
| Depreciation | 584 | F | 200 | 200 | 200 | 200 | 200 | 300 | 300 |
| Total Fixed | | | 1600 | 1600 | 1600 | 1600 | 1600 | 1750 | 1750 |
| Total Expense | | | 5225 | 5450 | 5675 | 5900 | 6125 | 6500 | 6725 |
| Rate per Unit | | | 1·493 | 1·362 | 1·261 | 1·180 | 1·114 | 1·083 | 1·035 |

FIGURE 72

It is not unreasonable to expect the manager concerned to be aware of the relationship that exists when forecasting expenses and to formulate a budget accordingly. This is one of the many objects of the exercise—that managers should recognise the relationship and be prepared to subject a particular cost to a more or less stringent control, knowing the probable effect on unit cost.

One could advance the idea that the fixed costs are not controllable by lower levels of management; that they are a *policy* cost, determined by the decision to start operations of a particular kind in a particular location, since this decision determines the rate of labour, the cost of transportation, the amount of rates and so forth. Therefore, to ask managers of small sections or cost centres to accept responsibility for and make the best use of such expenditures, rather contradicts the general rule that managers should

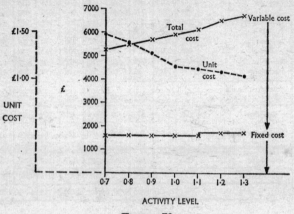

FIGURE 73

only be required to budget or forecast the expenditures for which they are responsible.

*Activity ratio*

Having discussed flexibility in some detail and concluded with the recognition of the problem, there remains the question of how to measure an activity. In the case of production, we will probably need a measure of productivity, or a ratio expressing the value of production against some acceptable base.

The bases that will be acceptable are those which can be measured or evaluated with reasonable certainty. They are:

1  Budgeted clock hours
2  Actual clock hours
3  Actual units of production
4  The unit standard hours per unit of production

From these four measures we can evaluate the two components of activity. They are *capacity* and *efficiency*, and their relationship is expressed as follows:

$$\text{Activity} = \text{Capacity} \times \text{Efficiency}$$

*Capacity* is the relationship between budgeted and actual clock hours:

$$\text{Capacity} = \frac{\text{Actual clock hours}}{\text{Budgeted clock hours}}$$

*Efficiency* is the relationship between the unit standard hour rate of actual production and actual clock hours:

$$\text{Efficiency} = \frac{\text{Actual production} \times \text{unit standard hours}}{\text{Actual clock hours}}$$

$$\text{Capacity} = \frac{\text{Actual clock hours}}{\text{Budgeted clock hours}} = \frac{4600}{100 \times 50} = 0 \cdot 92$$

$$\text{Efficiency} = \frac{\text{Actual Production} \times \text{Unit standard rate}}{\text{Actual clock hours}}$$

$$= \frac{5958}{4600} = 1 \cdot 295$$

$$\text{Activity} = \text{Capacity} \times \text{Efficiency} = 0 \cdot 92 \times 1 \cdot 295 = 1 \cdot 2$$

From this we see that although there were not so many capacity hours available as were forecast, the production rate or efficiency, measured in standard hours, was at a higher level than anticipated. Thus, activity is $0 \cdot 2$ or $20\%$ higher.

*Illustration*

| | |
|---|---:|
| Budgeted number of employees | 100 |
| Budgeted working hours per week | 50 |
| Actual clock hours | 4600 |

Actual production:

| | |
|---|---|
| Product 1 | 5000 |
| 2 | 500 |
| 3 | 1000 |

Unit standard hours:

| | |
|---|---|
| Product 1 | 12 mins |
| 2 | 75 mins |
| 3 | 4 hours 20 mins |

*Solution*

Actual production × unit standard hours

| Product | Production | Unit standard rate | Total hours |
|---|---|---|---|
| 1 | 5000 | 12 mins | 1000 |
| 2 | 500 | 75 mins | 625 |
| 3 | 1000 | 4 hours 20 mins | 4333 |
| | | | 5958 |

It may be that by forecasting a range of different relationships between capacity and efficiency in conjunction with known characteristics of the items of cost, we can produce a better forecast; but this is not a matter we shall pursue in this text.

**Exercises**

1　A draft budget for a company with four production centres included the following data for the year:

| Cost Centre | Directly allocated overhead £ | Apportioned Overhead % | Direct Labour hours |
|---|---|---|---|
| A | 32 800 | 20 | 60 000 |
| B | 45 200 | 40 | 75 000 |
| C | 28 400 | 10 | 30 000 |
| D | 14 400 | 30 | 100 000 |

The total overhead to be apportioned amounted to £352 000. As a result of technical developments it was decided to reorganise the production centres. A revised budget was therefore developed, incorporating the following changes from the draft budget:

(*a*) A new cost centre, E, was established.

(*b*) £13 000 of overhead previously allocated directly to cost centre A is to be transferred to cost centre E.

(*c*) An additional £30 000 of overhead is to be allocated directly to E.

(*d*) An additional £60 000 of overhead will be incurred and should be apportioned as follows:

| Cost centre | A | B | C | D | E |
|---|---|---|---|---|---|
| Percentage | — | 10 | 10 | 20 | 60 |

(*e*) Overhead will be absorbed on a machine hour rate for all cost centres except A. Revised budget hours are:

| Cost centre | A | B | C | D | E |
|---|---|---|---|---|---|
| Machine hours | — | 40 000 | 17 400 | 60 000 | 22 500 |
| Direct labour Hours | 50 000 | — | — | — | — |

You are required to calculate:

(i) Cost centre direct labour hour rates of overhead absorption on the draft budget;

(ii) Cost centre direct labour hour rates and/or machine hour rates of overhead absorption (as relevant) based on the revised budget;

(iii) The overhead chargeable to unit of product Z both under the draft budget and the revised budget.

The time taken in each cost centre for production of one unit of Z was budgeted as follows:

| Cost centre | Draft budget Direct labour hours | Revised budget Direct labour hours | Machine hours |
|---|---|---|---|
| A | 5 | 5 | — |
| B | 10 | — | 3 |
| C | 5 | — | 2 |
| D | 7 | — | 3 |
| E | — | — | 5 |

(ICMA)

2  D Limited is preparing a budget for the twelve months ending December 31. Based on the data given you are required to prepare budgets for production, personnel (direct wages only), direct material cost and purchases. Budgeted data available includes the following:

(a)  Stocks: to meet the expected needs of a sales campaign to be launched next year, stocks are to be increased this year.

| Direct materials | January 1 units | December 31 units |
|---|---|---|
| DM1 | 150 000 | 240 000 |
| DM2 | 60 000 | 96 000 |
| DM3 | 70 000 | 112 000 |
| DM4 | 90 000 | 144 000 |

| Finished goods | | |
|---|---|---|
| Product A | 3 000 | 8 000 |
| Product B | 7 000 | 17 000 |
| Product C | 9 000 | 19 000 |

(b)  Sales for the year at standard selling prices:

| Product A | £800 000 |
|---|---|
| Product B | £1 280 000 |
| Product C | £2 400 000 |

(c) Other data:

Direct labour hours 1 270 000
Fixed production overhead £1 143 000

Fixed production overhead is absorbed on a direct labour hour basis.

Administration overhead is absorbed at a rate of 50% of production cost.

Selling and distribution overhead is absorbed at a rate of 25% of production cost. Profit is calculated at a rate of 12½% of selling price.

(d) Standard cost data per unit of product include the following:

|  | Standard price per unit £ | Product A units | Product B units | Product C units |
|---|---|---|---|---|
| Direct materials: |  |  |  |  |
| DM 1 | 0·2 | — | 9 | 12 |
| 2 | 0·3 | 2 | 7 | — |
| 3 | 0·5 | 6 | 5 | 3 |
| 4 | 0·1 | 4 | — | 9 |
|  | Standard rate per hour £ | hours | hours | hours |
| Direct wages: |  |  |  |  |
| Department 1 | 0·8 | 5 | 3 | 6 |
| 2 | 0·6 | 5 | 3 | 6 |

(ICMA)

3  You are required to prepare for S Limited for the year commencing January 1, 19.1 the production budget and the purchases budget.

The company makes three products P1, P2 and P3 using three raw materials M1, M2 and M3 by three grades of labour, W1, W2 and W3; the following information is given:

Details for compilation of standard costs and selling prices:

|  | Standard price per lb | P1 | P2 per unit of product | P3 |
|---|---|---|---|---|
| Direct materials: | £ | lb | lb | lb |
| M1 | 0·25 | 56 | — | — |
| M2 | 0·40 | — | 145 | — |
| M3 | 0·60 | — | — | 95 |

|  | Standard rate per hour | hours | hours | hours |
|---|---|---|---|---|
| Direct wages: |  |  |  |  |
| W1 | 0·75 | 20 | — | — |
| W2 | 0·80 | — | 40 | — |
| W3 | 0·50 | — | — | 60 |

Production overhead is absorbed on a basis of direct labour hours:

Administration, selling and distribution expenses are absorbed on the basis of 25% of production cost.

Profit is calculated at $16\frac{2}{3}\%$ of selling price.

Budget details include:

|  | P1 £ | P2 £ | P3 £ |
|---|---|---|---|
| Sales for year at standard | 369 000 | 432 000 | 693 000 |
| Finished goods stocks valued at standard prime costs: |  |  |  |
| at January 1, 19.1 | 40 600 | 72 000 | 60 900 |
| at December 31, 19.1 | 34 800 | 90 000 | 69 600 |

|  | W1 | W2 | W3 |
|---|---|---|---|
| Direct labour hours: | 112 000 | 96 000 | 210 000 |

Production overhead: £313 500

|  | M1 £ | M2 £ | M3 £ |
|---|---|---|---|
| Raw materials: |  |  |  |
| Stocks valued at standard prices: |  |  |  |
| at January 1, 19.1 | 13 000 | 26 800 | 50 400 |
| at December 31, 19.1 | 13 750 | 28 400 | 48 000 |

(ICMA)

4 For a production department of a manufacturing company you are required to:

(a) prepare a fixed budget of overhead;

(b) prepare a flexible budget of overhead at 70%, 85% and 110% of budgeted volume;

(c) calculate a departmental hourly rate of overhead absorption. The budgeted level of activity of the department is 5000 hours per period and a study of the various items of expenditure reveals the following:

|  | £ | £ per hour |
|---|---:|---:|
| Indirect wages | — | 0·40 |
| Repairs: up to 200 hours | 100 | |
| for each additional 500 hours up to a total of 4000 hours | 35 | |
| additional from 4001 to 5000 hours | 60 | |
| additional above 5000 hours | 70 | |
| Rent and rates | 350 | |
| Supervision: up to 2500 hours | 400 | |
| additional for each 600 hours above 2500 and up to 4900 | 100 | |
| additional above 4900 hours | 150 | |
| Power: up to 3600 hours | | 0·25 |
| for hours above 3600 | | 0·20 |
| Consumable supplies | | 0·24 |
| Depreciation: up to 5000 hours | 650 | |
| from above 5000 hours to 6500 hours | 820 | |
| Cleaning: up to 4000 hours | 60 | |
| above 4000 hours | 80 | |
| Heat and light: from 2100 hours to 3500 hours | 120 | |
| from above 3500 hours to 5000 hours | 150 | |
| above 5000 hours | 175 | |

(ICMA)

5 The managing director of ACA Enterprises Ltd has
accepted your advice to operate a system of budgetary
control, and you have been given the task of collecting
the necessary data and co-ordinating the work involved
in preparing the budget which, it has been decided,
should be expressed in terms of activity levels of 90% to
110% in steps of 10%.

Analyses of past records adjusted to render the figures
comparable, followed by discussions with management,
have yielded the following information which it has been
agreed should form the basis for the manufacturing overhead budget for next year:

(a) 60 000 direct labour hours constitute 100% activity;
(b) The hourly direct labour rate is to be taken at
60p:
(c) Fixed costs for the year are estimated as follows:

| | |
|---|---|
| Depreciation | £2000 |
| Management and supervision | 8500 |
| Insurance | 500 |
| Maintenance | 1000 |

(d) Variable costs are estimated as follows:

| | |
|---|---|
| Indirect labour | £0·10 per hour |
| Consumable stores | 10% of direct labour cost |
| Canteen and welfare services | 5% of cost of direct and<br>indirect labour |

(e) Semi-variable costs for the past seven years have
been as follows:

| | |
|---|---|
| Year 1 | £7970 |
| 2 | 7640 |
| 3 | 8200 |
| 4 | 8710 |
| 5 | 9620 |
| 6 | 9300 |
| 7 | 9840 |

(*f*) Direct labour hours for the past seven years have been as follows:

|  |  |
|---|---|
| Year 1 | 47 000 hours |
| 2 | 44 000 |
| 3 | 49 000 |
| 4 | 53 000 |
| 5 | 62 000 |
| 6 | 59 000 |
| 7 | 64 000 |

You are required to prepare the manufacturing overhead budget for the next year, and calculate the manufacturing overhead allowance for next year, assuming 63 000 direct labour hours were worked.    (ACCA adapted)

# 13

# Standard Costing and Variance Analysis

In the previous chapter we saw that budgets and budgetary control are means of forecasting and obtaining reliable and prompt control information about the operations of an organisation.

If the budgets are based on some predetermined standards for materials, labour and overhead, and used in conjunction with the flexible budgeting process, one of the strongest bases for control and cost reduction will be created.

In any event, standards are an almost indispensable feature in the establishment of budgets, for both techniques make it possible for reports to be prepared which compare actual costs with predicted costs. By referring to Figure 74 we see the relationship between the twin techniques of budgetary control and standard costing. For by expressing the original forecast in terms of standard price and quantity, flexing it in accordance with the actual activity, and then comparing with actual costs, differences are expressed in more precise form. The differences, more formally referred to as 'variances', will be in a form which will allow further analysis of material, labour and overhead to be carried out.

The differences between 'budgets' and 'standards' are as follows:

1 Budgets are a broad statement of expectation. Standards are a detailed statement of expectation.

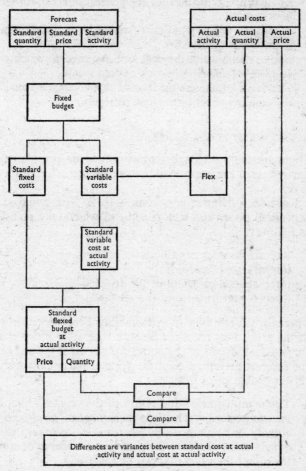

**FIGURE 74**

2 Budgets are guidelines for the general direction of business activity.

Standards tell us what costs should be if a certain performance is achieved.

3 Budgets emphasise the cost level required to operate at a given volume to achieve a desired result.

Standards emphasise the level of cost being achieved and the detailed effect of the desired result.

### Activity and level of attainment

These are the most important aspects to be considered in any system of predetermination based on projected performance.

Consider driving a car from A to B. The outcome is dependant on certain factors some of which may be listed as follows:

1 forecast weather conditions
2 forecast road conditions
3 forecast state of health of the driver
4 forecast performance of the vehicle.

There is a large area of vulnerability here which, in the actual event, may make the forecast look silly. But perhaps the most important of the points mentioned is the last one: the forecast performance of the vehicle. We could consider three possible views here:

1 The manufacturer's indication of the way in which the vehicle performs. This is a *theoretical* or *ideal* level of activity or attainment, which requires maximum effort at maximum efficiency. It constitutes a target to be aimed for rather than one that can be achieved.
2 Our experience of past performance, which suggests the level of activity that could be achieved; this presupposes

some knowledge of whether past performance was measurably good or bad. If this is not taken into account, our forecast of future performance could be complacent. We could call this the *achievable* level of activity or performance.

3 The performance which could be attained by making sure that the vehicle was in good condition. This requires all the factors to be efficiently co-ordinated so that the activity level can be forecast with reasonable accuracy. We could regard this as an *attainable* level.

The same process will need to be followed by every organisation setting up a system of standard costing. They will need to ask the question, 'What will be the level of activity or performance on which we will base our standards? Will it be ideal, achievable or attainable?'

### Cost standards

One of the definitions of cost that we have used is that it is the product of price and quantity. Therefore in any control system both aspects must be taken into account. There are some base units for establishing both price and quantity which we may regard as acceptable, and which we are not required to think about in our forecasting or predetermination process. Such matters as time, length and weight come to mind. Everyone is aware that there are sixty minutes to the hour, twelve inches to the foot, one thousand grammes to the kilogramme. All of these may be regarded as recognised or known or *acceptable cost standards*.

There are other acceptable bases of price and quantity which are peculiar to organisations. For example, the buyer will be aware of how much will have to be paid per ton of a specific material. A production engineer will be aware of how much of a specific material will be required to make a particular part or component. A work study engineer will be aware of the length of time that should be taken to perform a specific task. All of these may be regarded as specific or *calculated cost standards*.

A cost standard is, then, a prerequisite to the calculation of the budgeted or predetermined figure known as either a standard quantity or a standard price.

## Standard cost

'A predetermined cost calculated in relation to a prescribed set of working conditions, correlating technical specifications and scientific measurements of materials and labour to the price and wage rates expected to apply during the period to which the standard cost is intended to relate, with an addition of the appropriate share of budgeted overhead. Its main purposes are to provide bases for control through variance accounting, for the valuation of stocks and work in progress, and, in exceptional cases, for fixing selling prices.' (ICMA)

This indicates that a standard cost is:

(a) estimated in advance;
(b) based on some specification of quantity;
(c) based on some specification of price;
(d) based on some specification of conditions of activity or performance.

This definition almost exactly covers our discussion of cost standard, implying that standard cost and cost standard are one and the same thing.

It is perhaps unfortunate that the definition of standard cost fails to indicate that it may be standard cost *per unit* and thus the product of unit standard price and unit standard quantity. The use of the term 'standard cost' in its existing definition has been the cause of much confusion amongst students of cost accounting.

In what follows, the term 'cost standard' is used and standard price and standard quantity are seen as the vital factors.

## Cost standard period and limiting factors

As with budgeting, it is essential that a time period for the standard is established. That period must be of a sensible length and must allow for the need to change, modify and improve standards from time to time. One year is very often regarded as satisfactory, particularly if allied to the financial year of the organisation.

We must have due regard to conditions in the period in question. The production cycle, the market for the products, the volatility of price change, seasonal fluctuations and labour availability may be just a few of the limiting factors or constraints within which an organisation operates. It would not, for example, be a good idea to establish the standard price for a particular material for one year if it were known that supply and price were subject to violent or seasonal fluctuation. Thus, there is no general or accepted rule. To achieve maximum control, the period must be determined individually in each organisation.

Individual control periods are then established within the length of time regarded as the cost standard period. This shorter period will be the basis from which the comparative management information and control comparisons are made.

## The preparation of cost standards

The next consideration is the volume of business and the attainable level of activity or performance. We have observed that standard costing and budgeting control have certain basic principles in common. A decision as to the volume of business likely to be achieved is reflected through the sales budget to the production budget. The type and quantity of material required and the grade and skill of labour to be employed will be the basis of the production budget relative to the attainable activity level expected.

This implies that cost standards of material usage and price, labour rates and performance, and overhead absorption rates must be established. From these predetermined cost standards it will then be possible to establish two distinct bases of information:

1 A departmental cost standard statement in a form similar to Figure 75;
2 An output or operation cost standard statement in a form similar to Figure 76.

The illustration in Figure 75 indicates the way in which cost standards may be incorporated into departmental budgets, together with a possible basis on which some cost standards may be calculated.

The illustration in Figure 76 indicates the way in which the calculated cost standards may then be incorporated into a statement showing the cost standard for an individual part or component or sub-assembly. We note that department four, the subject of Figure 75, appears on the output cost standard at operations 1 and 5.

It should be clear that, given that the cost standards are compiled with care and reasonable knowledge, the budget, cost standards and actual operations may be bound to-

DEPARTMENTAL COST STANDARD STATEMENT

| Attainable capacity | 0·94 | Dept. No. | 4 |
| Attainable efficiency | 0·96 | Dept. Manager | J. L. Brown |
| Attainable activity | 0·90 | Period | Mar.–May |

| Cost element | Cost standards | | | Total | |
| | Units | Usage | Unit Rate | Cost | Element |
| --- | --- | --- | --- | --- | --- |
| | | | £ | £ | £ |
| *Direct Materials* | | | | | |
| Material 127 | Metres | 4 000 | 1·00 | 4 000 | |
| 134 | lbs | 7 000 | 0·20 | 1 400 | |
| 506 | galls. | 1 000 | 0·70 | 700 | |
| | | | | | 6 100 |
| *Direct Labour* | | | | | |
| Skilled—Male | hours | 6 000 | 1·00 | 6 000 | |
| Semi-skilled—Male | „ | 12 000 | 0·85 | 10 200 | |
| Skilled—Female | „ | 2 500 | 0·80 | 2 000 | |
| Semi-skilled—Female | „ | 10 000 | 0·60 | 6 000 | |
| | | | | | 24 200 |
| *Departmental Overhead* | | | | | |
| Supervision | | | | 1 000 | |
| Inspection | | | | 3 000 | |
| Maintenance | | | | 1 000 | |
| Labourers | | | | 1 500 | |
| Clerical | | | | 4 000 | |
| Tools | | | | 1 000 | |
| Consumables | | | | 1 000 | |
| Depreciation | | | | 2 000 | |
| | | | | | 14 500 |

Prepared by _____ Date_____

Approved by _____ Date_____

FIGURE 75

gether into a comprehensive analysis, reporting and control system.

## Setting direct material cost standards

There are three factors to be taken into account in determining the direct material cost standard. They are:

OUTPUT COST STANDARD

Part No. A726
Output Standard 100

| Deposit | Operation No. | Operation details | Cost standards Units | Usage | Unit rate | Materials £ | Labour £ | Overhead £ |
|---|---|---|---|---|---|---|---|---|
| 4 | 1 | Draw material No. 127 from stores<br>Cut to length<br>Overheads | Metres<br>Hours<br>Direct lab. | 40<br>75/60<br>£1·10 | 1·00<br>0·88<br>60% | 40·00 | 1·10 | 0·66 |
| 3 | 2 | Drill 2 holes 12 mm at 6 mm from each end<br>Overheads | Hours<br>Direct lab. | 40/60<br>0·40 | 0·60<br>80% | | 0·40 | 0·32 |
| 1 | 3 | Forms to shape<br>Overheads | Hours<br>Direct hours | 180/60<br>3 | 0·75<br>1·00 | | 2·25 | 3·00 |
| 7 | 4 | Burnish<br>Overheads | Hours<br>Direct lab. | 120/60<br>1·44 | 0·72<br>100% | | 1·44 | 1·44 |
| 4 | 5 | Paint to specification<br>Colour Materials 506<br>Labour<br>Overheads | Gallons<br>Hours<br>Direct lab. | 0·25<br>45/60<br>0·66 | 0·70<br>0·88<br>60% | 0·175 | 0·66 | 0·396 |
| | | | | | Totals | £40·175 | £5·85 | £5·86 |

Prepared by ——— Date ———

Approved by ——— Date ———

| Summary | Total | Each |
|---|---|---|
| Material | £40·175 | 0·402 |
| Labour | 5·850 | 0·058 |
| Overheads | 5·816 | 0·058 |
| | £51·841 | £0·518 |

FIGURE 76

1 the specification of the material to be used;
2 the quantity of that specified material;
3 the price to be paid for that quantity.

The specification of materials is usually laid down in the first instance by the designer but can be amended by compromise and co-operation with production engineering and method study. Once agreement has been reached on the precise materials that are to be used, someone will then calculate how much of that material will be required to produce a given quantity of parts or components.

This will require an analysis of the most economical shape and size of material available, together with the results that could be expected from it. If we were to apply the 'ideal', 'achievable' or 'attainable' criteria already discussed, then we would have to include some normal loss in calculating the quantity cost standard.

The last factor to be evaluated is price. When deciding the cost standard of material price, the basic problem is whether to use the price that is current at the time the standard is being set, or to forecast the average price for the period during which the standard will be in use.

To use a current price, especially during times of rapidly rising prices would mean that any comparison of actual price with standard price would show progressively increasing differences or variances. The cost standard would lose credibility as the basis for control.

It is better to attempt to forecast an average price. This is often difficult, because the prices used are controlled mainly by external factors and organisations have little ability to influence a particular material supply through large and/or consistent orders. Many ingenious and unique devices are employed in an attempt to overcome this problem, not the least of which is statistical analysis.

Having established standard prices, we then recognise that under conditions of rising prices:

1 There will probably be favourable differences in the first part of the control period and adverse differences in the latter part of the period.
2 When interpreting those differences it may be difficult to decide how many are due to price change and how many are due to error in estimating.

*Setting direct labour cost standards*

There are three factors to be taken into consideration when setting direct labour cost standards:

1 the method, equipment and grade of labour by which the task will be performed;
2 the estimated time that it will take an operative to perform the task;
3 the hourly rate at which that operative will be rewarded.

The first factor requires the highly specialised knowledge of a production engineer, and possibly a work study engineer. That person will need to take into consideration the work to be performed on the specified materials with the available equipment and labour.

The second factor follows on from the method of manufacture and requires an estimate of the time required for performing the task in hand. The basis for standard performance is a unit known as the *standard hour* and defined in the ICMA terminology as:

'A hypothetical unit pre-established to represent the amount of work which should be performed in one hour at standard performance.'

We see that in attempting to establish the cost standard for labour hours, certain conditions will have to be accepted and certain problems overcome, which we could summarise as follows:

1  What is the sequence of operations to be performed?
2  What equipment and tools will be used?
3  What grade of labour will normally be available to perform the task?
4  What conditions or constraints will be effective during the performance of the above three matters?
5  What allowances for fatigue, rest, personal time and so forth, will need to be made?

It now remains for us to formulate and apply a cost standard for pay rates. The basic problem is whether to use current rates of pay or some forecast average covering the whole year. We have already observed how vulnerable we may be in adopting current rates when we discussed material prices. Provided it is possible to forecast or budget for the factors making up the payroll, it may be possible to establish a calculated hourly rate of pay.

### Illustration

The following information is available for operations to be carried out in the main assembly department of a light engineering factory:

| | | Standard hours per unit | | | |
|---|---|---|---|---|---|
| | Budget Sales Units | Skilled Male | Semi-Skilled Male | Skilled Female | Semi-Skilled Female |
| Product 1 | 40 000 | 0·25 | 1·25 | 0·75 | — |
| 2 | 70 000 | 0·50 | 2·00 | 1·00 | 1·25 |
| 3 | 100 000 | 1·00 | 1·00 | 3·00 | 1·50 |

Stock policy:
Product 1—Increase finished stocks by 2250 units
2—      ,,      ,,      ,,   ,,  6000   ,,
3—Decrease   ,,      ,,   ,,  5000   ,,

Normal rejection—5% of all production
Attainable activity level—0·90

Current rates of pay:

| Skilled male | £1·00 per hour |
| Semi-skilled male | £0·85 ,, ,, |
| Skilled female | £0·80 ,, ,, |
| Semi-skilled female | £0·65 ,, ,, |

Minimum paid hours:
48 hours per week for 47 weeks
40 ,, ,, ,, ,, 5 weeks

Basic hours: 40 hours per week with overtime
paid at 'time and a half'

In this problem we observe that there are 47 working weeks of 48 hours and five other weeks of 40 hours. This latter forecast is to take account of paid annual and statutory holidays. Clearly, all costs must be included in order to evaluate a realistic hourly rate. Even with these straightforward and simple facts, the calculations are quite tedious, as Figure 77 demonstrates. It will be observed that the cost standard can be expressed as a 'rate per grade of operative' or a total rate for the department. Where production is likely to be balanced between the three products it is usual to use a departmental rate; where production is likely to be unbalanced between the three products, it would be more advisable to use the rate per grade of operative. The rate of pay used in the example is the current rate but, with local knowledge, this would be adjusted to take account of any known or forecast wage rate movements.

## Setting overhead absorption cost standards

The objective is to establish a standard overhead absorption rate for each department or cost centre, rather than the less acceptable blanket rate. The basic procedures for calculating these rates were discussed and examined in Chapter 5.

There are three factors to be considered before we can establish the cost standard. They are:

CALCULATION OF DEPARTMENTAL COST STANDARDS

Activity Level __0·90__                                Department __Main Assembly__

| | Product | | | Total |
|---|---|---|---|---|
| | 1 | 2 | 3 | |
| Sales units | 40 000 | 70 000 | 100 000 | |
| Stock change | +2 750 | +6 000 | −5 000 | |
| Good production | 42 750 | 76 000 | 95 000 | |
| *Add* Back Rejection 5% | 2 250 | 4 000 | 5 000 | |
| *Total Production* | 45 000 | 80 000 | 100 000 | |
| *Hours Required* | | | | |
| Skilled—Male | 0.25  11 250 | 0·50  40 000 | 1·00 100 000 | 151 250 |
| Semi-skilled—Male | 1·25  56 250 | 2·00 160 000 | 1·00 100 000 | 316 250 |
| Skilled—Female | 0·75  22 500 | 1·00  80 000 | 3·00 300 000 | 402 500 |
| Semi-skilled—Female | —      — | 1·25 100 000 | 1·50 450 000 | 550 000 |
| *Production hours* | 90 000 | 380 000 | 950 000 | 1 420 000 |

*Pay Hours and Staff Required*

| | Skilled Male | Semi-Skilled Male | Skilled Female | Semi-Skilled Female | Total |
|---|---|---|---|---|---|
| Unit Product hours = 0·90 Activity | 151 250 | 316 250 | 402 500 | 550 000 | 1 420 000 |
| *Add* back 1/9th | 16 805 | 35 139 | 44 722 | 61 111 | |
| Clock hours | 168 055 | 351 389 | 447 222 | 611 111 | |
| *No. of operatives:* 47 weeks @ 48 hours 5 weeks @ 40 hours = 2456 annual hours | 69 | 143 | 182 | 249 | |
| Clock hours | 168 055 | 351 389 | 447 222 | 611 111 | |
| *Add* back Overtime premium hours 47 weeks × 4 hrs = 7·6% 2456 hours | 12 772 | 26 706 | 33 989 | 46 444 | |
| *Total paid hours* | 180 827 | 378 095 | 481 211 | 657 555 | |
| Hourly rate | £1·00 | £0·85 | £0·80 | £0·65 | |
| *PAYROLL* | £180 827 | £321 381 | £384 969 | £427 411 | £1 314 588 |
| Cost Standard Rate per hour (Payroll/unit product hours) | £1·196 | £1·016 | £0·956 | ·£0·777 | £0·926 |

FIGURE 77

1 That there are overhead budgets for each department or cost centre;
2 That there is an appropriate unit of measurement for each department or cost centre. This will be in the form of direct labour cost, direct labour hours, machine hours and so on;
3 That we can distinguish the behaviour of overhead under varying conditions. In other words, the variable and fixed content can be separated.

The first factor has been discussed at length. It will be recalled that an overhead budget provides for the forecast expenditure at a specified or anticipated level of output, whilst a flexible budget provides for expenditures that may vary with that activity. The objective in both cases was to aim for the separation, and thus control, of fixed and variable costs. The budgeting system must establish the levels of expenditure for fixed and variable overhead cost for each department or cost centre, in order to provide the basis for a separate recovery rate. Some organisations do not go to this length and attempt to use a single combination recovery rate. Generally, this is confusing, and from a management information and control point of view is not to be recommended.

The second factor follows from the matters discussed above. It will be recalled that we prefer to use direct labour hours for a labour-intensive department or cost centre. On the other hand, in a machine-intensive department or cost centre, the machine hour would be more appropriate. When considered in conjunction with the need to establish separate budgets for fixed and variable overhead costs on a flexible basis, the importance of the unit of measurement becomes clear.

The third factor requires us to bear in mind the variability of cost. Figure 78 indicates a basic pattern of overhead

OVERHEAD RATE OF ABSORPTION—COST STANDARD

| Expense | Basis of Apportionment | Total | Production depts. | | | Service depts. | |
|---|---|---|---|---|---|---|---|
| | | | 1 | 2 | 3 | A | B |
| *Variable overheads* | | | | | | | |
| Directly allocatable | Direct | 46 000 | 10 000 | 12 000 | 16 000 | 5 000 | 3 000 |
| Common variable | Apportioned | 19 000 | 5 000 | 3 000 | 7 000 | 2 000 | 2 000 |
| Service costs—Dept. A | Apportioned | — | 2 000 | 4 000 | 1 000 | (7 000) | |
| Dept. B | Apportioned | — | 1 000 | 1 000 | 3 000 | | (5 000) |
| | | £65 000 | £18 000 | £20 000 | £27 000 | — | — |
| Unit of Recovery | | | Direct Labour £12 000 | Direct Labour Hours 16 000 | Machine Hours 13 500 | | |
| Recovery Rate | | | 150% | £1·25 p.h. | £2·00 p.h. | | |
| *Fixed Overheads* | | | | | | | |
| Directly allocatable | Direct | 9 000 | 4 000 | 2 000 | 1 000 | 1 000 | 1 000 |
| Common fixed | Apportioned | 15 000 | 5 000 | 4 000 | 3 000 | 2 000 | 1 000 |
| Service costs—Dept. A | Apportioned | — | 1 000 | 1 000 | 1 000 | (3 000) | |
| Dept. B | Apportioned | — | 500 | 1 000 | 500 | | (2 000) |
| | | £24 000 | £10 500 | £8 000 | £5 500 | — | — |
| | | | 87·5% | £0·50 | £0·41 | | |
| | | | 97·2% | £0·55 | £0·45 | | |
| | | | 79·5% | £0·45 | £0·37 | | |

*Recovery Rate:*
1. Based on above unit of measurement
2. If activity decreases 10%
3. If activity increases 10%

FIGURE 78

behaviour; that is, as the activity increases, the recovery rate for fixed overheads diminishes.

The characteristics of overhead behaviour are important in establishing a cost standard of overhead absorption. It is accomplished by selecting some activity as the basis for charging overheads to jobs, products, processes or units. We are aware that variable expenses can be measured and controlled at any volume with the aid of the flexible budget, but fixed expenses can only be absorbed by operating at the activity level used to establish the rate of recovery.

## Variance analysis

Having established cost standards for each of the three elements of cost we proceed to the comparative aspect of the control process. Comparison is carried out through the technique known as 'variance analysis' which may be defined as:

> 'The method of ascertaining the difference of actual costs from planned costs, and for analysing the various causes of such differences for effective management action.'

Before going on to discuss the method let us remind ourselves once again of the salient features of cost. They are:

1 cost is price times quantity.
2 cost has three elements: material, labour and overhead.
3 cost has three characteristics: variability, normality and controllability.

From these three features we are able to point out certain differences or variances that will occur in a system of variance analysis. These three features and the basic variance titles are displayed in Figure 79. The terms to describe each

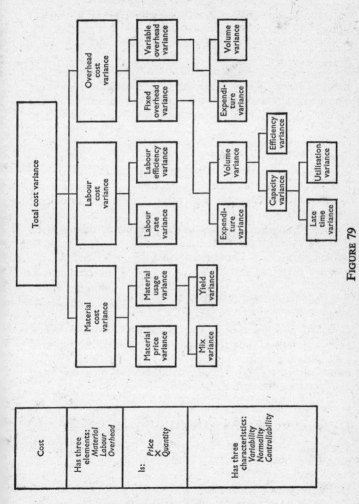

FIGURE 79

variance in this Figure are those which occur in normal usage.

## Some basic definitions

Before proceeding to the method of variance calculation we need to understand with clarity the meanings of the various titles and descriptions used in the rest of this chapter.

Standard cost—SC   The most important title of all: it means the *actual* output produced valued at the *standard* price per unit. Standard price per unit is interpreted as the unit quantity cost standard valued at the unit price cost standard.

Budgeted cost—BC   The *budgeted* quantity to be produced at the *standard* price per unit.

Actual cost—AC   The *actual* quantity produced at the *actual* price per unit.

Standard quantity—SQ   The *budgeted* quantity which should have been produced or used for the actual output.

Budgeted quantity—BQ   The *budgeted* quantity which should have been produced or used for the *budgeted* output.

Actual quantity—AQ   The *actual* quantity which was used to produce the *actual* output.

## The basic methods of variance analysis

There are two ways in which a variance can be isolated or calculated. They are:

1   by the use of a formula;
2   by the use of normal double-entry bookkeeping methods.

*The formula method*

For the analysis of *price variance* we use the basic formula AQ(SP−AP), that is:

$$\text{Actual quantity} \times \begin{pmatrix} \text{the difference between} \\ \text{standard price per unit and the} \\ \text{actual price per unit} \end{pmatrix}$$

—where the actual quantity must be expressed in the same unit as the price. Thus, if the price per unit is rate per hour, then the actual quantity must be expressed in hours. If the price per unit is expressed in composite form, such as standard number of hours per unit multiplied by the rate per hour, then the actual quantity must be expressed in the same terms.

For the analysis of *quantity variances* we use the basic formula SP(SQ−AQ), that is:

$$\text{Standard price per unit} \times \begin{pmatrix} \text{The difference between the} \\ \text{standard quantity of units} \\ \text{that should be used and the} \\ \text{actual quantity of units that} \\ \text{were used} \end{pmatrix}$$

We shall examine the use of these formulas by referring to the example and solution illustrated in Figure 80. Here is a situation where three factors are given:

(*a*) The cost standard per unit.
(*b*) The actual output units.
(*c*) The actual cost of producing the output units.

1 We calculate a simple price difference per pound of input and note that the difference is adverse. This is because we are paying more per pound than was anticipated by the cost standard.

Cost standard per unit — 100 lb at £0·10 per lb.
Actual output          — 500 units.
∴ Standard cost = 500 units × 100 lb per unit at £0·10 per lb
                                                          = £5,000
Actual cost of 500 units = 40,000 lb at £0·12 per lb    = 4,800

                                    Total variance    £200(F)

| | Cost | Price | Quantity |
|---|---|---|---|
| **1.** | Price Difference<br>per unit<br>SP — AP<br>= £0·10 — £0·12 | £0·02(A) | |
| **2.** | Quantity Difference<br>per unit<br>SQ — AQ<br>100 lbs — 40,000/500 | | 20 lbs(F) |
| **3.** | Unit price differences<br>for total lbs<br>used — 40,000 lbs.<br>ie AQ(SP — AP) | 40,000 × £0·02(A)<br>= £800(A) | |
| **4.** | Unit quantity difference<br>at Standard price<br>per unit<br>ie SP(SQ — AQ) | | £0·10 (50,000 — 40,000)<br>= £1,000(F) |
| **5.** | Total variance<br>SPAQ — APAQ = AQ(SP — AP) — SP(SQ — AQ)<br>£200 F     = £800 A     — £1000 F | | |

FIGURE 80

2  We calculate a simple difference in pounds per unit of
   output and note that it is favourable. This is because we
   are using fewer pounds per unit than were anticipated
   by the cost standard.
3  We expand the price difference by multiplying by the
   actual amount of output units.
4  Similar action is taken with the quantity difference.
5  From points 3 and 4 we see that:

(a) Price differences (SP — AP) are extended by the actual units of output expressed in the same terms, i.e. AQ(SP — AP); the price difference of cost, if we multiply the expression through, is AQSP — AQAP.

(b) Quantity differences (SQ — AQ) are extended by the standard price and all expressed in the same terms, i.e. SP(SQ — AQ); the quantity difference of cost, if we multiply the expression through, is SPSQ — SPAQ.

From the two points above we note that three expressions are used:

1 AQSP or SPAQ: that is, the standard cost, already defined as the actual quantity produced at the standard price per unit.

2 AQAP: that is, the actual cost, already defined as the actual quantity produced at the actual price per unit.

3 SPSQ: that is, the budgeted cost, already defined as the budgeted or standard quantity to be produced at the standard price per unit.

We have now succeeded in tying together in one package the actual cost, the flexible budget, and the standard cost technique.

*The double-entry bookkeeping method*

The second method of calculating standard cost variances is the formula method carried through to a logical conclusion in the books of account. If we cannot carry out a double-entry transaction to incorporate our findings as an integral part of the accounting system, the analysis must lose credibility.

The same example has been used as for the formula method and the outcome is illustrated in Figure 81.

Opening stock of R.M.: 20 000 lbs @ £0·10 per lb.
Cost standard per unit: 100 lbs @ £0·10 per lb.
Actual output: 500 units.
Actual cost of purchases: 40 000 lbs @ £0·12 per lb.

*CREDITORS (at Actual Cost)*

|  |  |  |  |  |
|---|---|---|---|---|
|  |  | Goods at cost 40 000 lb @ £0·12 per lb |  | £4800 |

*R. M. STOCK (at Standard Cost = AQ × SP)*

| | | | | | |
|---|---|---|---|---|---|
| Opening stock @ £0·10 | 30 000 | £3 000 | Price variance 40 000 lb × (£0·10 − £0·12) | | £800 |
| Purchases @ £0·12 | 40 000 | 4 800 | Issue to W.I.P. standard cost 500 × 10 × £0·10 | 50 000 | 5 000 |
| Material usage @ £0·10 | 10 000 | 1 000 | Balance C/F | 30 000 | 3 000 |
| | 80 000 | £8 800 | | 80 000 | £8 800 |

*MATERIAL PRICE VARIANCE*

| | | | |
|---|---|---|---|
| Stock | £800 | | |

*WORK IN PROGRESS (at Standard Cost = AQ × SP)*

| | | | |
|---|---|---|---|
| Material issues | 50 000 | £5 000 | |

*MATERIAL USAGE VARIANCE*

| | | |
|---|---|---|
| | Unused Materials returned to stock: 50 000 lb issued 40 000 lb used 10 000 lb at £0·10 | £1 000 |

FIGURE 81

We note that an opening stock of raw materials has been created to start us off. The following points should be noted:

1　Following receipt of the invoice from the supplier we would calculate any price change and immediately amend stock value by placing the difference or variance in the material price variance account. This has the effect of pricing stock at standard cost, i.e. the actual quantity of materials in stock at the standard price.

　　The important point to note here is that stock accounts

should always be maintained at standard cost. Some schools of thought would not agree with this procedure, and would leave the price variance calculation until such time as the materials are issued to work in progress. To do so would have the effect of holding stock at a multitude of prices, and hence destroy the essential validity of the standard costing system.

2 The same comments must apply to the other two forms of stocks, work in progress and finished goods.

It may seem a little odd that in calculating the material usage variance we did not DR stock and CR work in progress. One can argue that if the materials were not used, then work in progress should receive the benefit. But to do so would again destroy the essential validity of standard costing. For we have accepted in formulating our cost standards that a certain output *should* cost a certain sum. That fact is recorded in the work in progress account as shown in Figure 81. The efficient usage of materials is reflected quite separately in the material usage account.

3 Thus, the two accounts recording variances, stocks and outputs being expressed in standard cost terms, are essential parts of a reporting analysis and control system.

## The basic variances

The six basic variances are:

| | |
|---|---|
| Material price variance | Material usage variance |
| Labour rate variance | Labour efficiency variance |
| Overhead expenditure variance | Overhead volume variance |

We will use some simple examples and calculate solutions by using both the formula and the bookkeeping method. The bookkeeping method will be shown in the form of journal entries.

*Material variances*

During the month of March, 1000 units of output were
produced using 6200 metres of steel. This was purchased for
Part No. 67 at a price of £595. The cost standard for part
No. 67 is 7 metres per unit at £0·10 per metre. We are
required to calculate the total, price and usage variances.

Formula method

*Material cost variance:*

| | | |
|---|---|---|
| SPAQ | 1000 units. 7 metres per unit £0·10 pm | £700 |
| APAQ | 6200 metres | £595 |

Total variance    £105(F)

(Note that the term 'SPAQ' takes on the same meaning as
used in the calculations for Figure 80.)

*Material price variance:*

$AQ(SP - AP)$

$$6200 \text{ metres} \left( £0·10 \text{ per metre} - \frac{£595}{6200} \right)$$

$$= £620 - £595 = \qquad\qquad £25(F)$$

*Material usage variance:*

$SP(SQ - AQ)$

£0·10 per metre (1000 units × 7 metres per unit
− 6200 metres)

£0·10 (7000 − 6200)

$$£0·10 \times 800 \text{ metres} = \qquad\qquad £80(F)$$

£105(F)

Bookkeeping method

| | | | |
|---|---|---|---|
| DR | Stock | £595 | |
| CR | Creditors | | £595 |
| | on receipt of goods (6200 metres) | | |
| DR | Stock | £25 | |
| CR | Material price variance | | £25 |
| | to adjust purchases to standard cost | | |
| DR | W.I.P. | £700 | |
| CR | Stock | | £700 |
| | on the issue of 7000 metres at £0·10 per metre | | |
| DR | Stock | £80 | |
| CR | Material usage variance | | £80 |
| | on the return to stock of unused materials; 800 metres at £0·10 per metre | | |

## Labour variances

In an assembly department, ten men are employed for 40 hours per week at a payroll cost of £492. In a certain period 1000 units of output are produced whose unit cost standard is 30 minutes per unit at £0·95 per hour. Calculate the total, labour rate and efficiency variances.

### Formula method

**Labour cost variance:**

| | | |
|---|---|---|
| SPAQ | 1000 units × 0·5 hrs × £0·95 per hour | £475 |
| APAQ | Payroll | £492 |
| | Total cost variance | £17(A) |

**Labour rate variance:**

AQ (SP − AP)

$$400 \text{ hrs} \left( £0·95 \text{ p.h.} - \frac{£492}{400} \right)$$

$$= £380 - £492 = \qquad\qquad £112(A)$$

**Labour efficiency variance:**

SP (SQ − AQ)

$$£0·95 \text{ per hour} \left( \begin{array}{c} 1000 \text{ units at } 0·5 \\ \text{hrs per unit} \end{array} - \begin{array}{c} 400 \\ \text{hrs} \end{array} \right)$$

$$£0·95 (500 - 400) = \qquad\qquad £95(F)$$

$$£17(A)$$

### Bookkeeping method

| | | | |
|---|---|---|---|
| DR | Wages control | £492 | |
| CR | Cash | | |
| | with payroll (400 hours) | | £492 |
| DR | Labour rate variance | £112 | |
| CR | Wages control | | £112 |
| | to adjust payroll cost | | |
| | to standard cost | | |
| DR | W.I.P. | £475 | |
| CR | Wages control | | £475 |
| | 500 hrs at £0·95 | | |
| DR | Wages control | £95 | |
| CR | Labour efficiency variance | | £95 |
| | to balance wages control | | |
| | with favourable efficiency | | |
| | variance | | |

*Overhead variances*

The cost standard rate of recovery in an assembly department is £1·50 per hour. In a certain week in which the output of 1000 units produced was worth 500 hours, the actual overhead expenditure was £870 and the actual clock hours were 400. We are required to calculate the total cost, overhead expenditure and overhead volume variances.

This example is very simple and takes no account of the fixed and variable elements. We are thus regarding overhead as a single element. We shall need to re-examine this matter later in the chapter.

Formula method

*Overhead cost variance:*

| | | |
|---|---|---|
| SPAQ | 500 hours at £1·50 per hour | £750 |
| APAQ | 400 hours | 870 |
| | | £120(A) |

*Overhead expenditure variance:*

AQ (SP − AP)

$$400 \text{ Clock hours} \left( \frac{£1·50}{\text{per hour}} - \frac{£870}{400} \right)$$

| | |
|---|---|
| 600 − 870 = | £270(A) |

*Overhead volume variance:*

SP  (SQ − AQ)

| | |
|---|---|
| £1·50 per hour (500 hrs  − 400 hrs) = | £150(F) |
| | £120(A) |

Bookkeeping method

| | | | |
|---|---|---|---|
| DR | Overhead control | £870 | |
| CR | Cash or creditors | | £870 |
| DR | Overhead expenditure variance | £270 | |
| CR | Overhead control | | £270 |
| | to adjust overhead control | | |
| | to standard cost | | |
| | (870 − 270) = (400 × £1·50) | | |

DR  W.I.P.                                £750
CR  Overhead control                               £750
    500 hours at £1·50 per hour
    (the overhead absorption)
DR  Overhead control              £150
CR  Overhead volume variance                  £150
    with the over-absorption
    of overhead due to volume
    change

The volume change with respect to overhead analysis should be very carefully noted. In this particular example we have a situation where the cost standard was calculated at £1·50 per hour on some known activity level, related to the fact that 1000 units could be produced in 500 hours. In the event they were produced in 400 hours. But due to the way in which standard costing is used, production was charged with the 500 hours at £1·50 per hour although the output was produced in less time. This fact is represented by the favourable variance shown against volume variance.

The three examples may now be brought together to form a simple operating statement as illustrated in Figure 82. This form of presentation, could include some comments as to possible causes and relationships and thus be a valuable part of the total control mechanism. The types of causes and relationships to be found in a variance analysis system are usually interactive—one thing may be leading to another. For example:

(a) Adverse material price variance with a favourable material usage variance may indicate that to pay more for a better quality material would lead to economies in material usage.

(b) Adverse labour rate variance with a favourable labour efficiency variance may indicate that where higher-rated operatives are used, the work is performed in less time.

### ASSEMBLY DEPARTMENT

Activity Level _____        Week No. _____

Output Units _____ 1000 _____        Date        _____

---

*Cost Standard per unit*

| | |
|---|---|
| Materials—7 metres at £0·10 per metre | £0·70 |
| Labour—30 minutes at £0·95 per hour | 0·475 |
| Overhead—30 minutes at £1·50 per hour | 0·75 |

Cost standard per unit        £1·925 .

---

*Actual Costs:*

| | | |
|---|---|---|
| Material | £595 | |
| Labour | 492 | |
| Overhead | 870 | |
| | | £1957 |
| Standard cost of actual output £1·925 for 1000 units | | 1925 |
| TOTAL VARIANCE | | £32(A) |

| *Variance Analysis* | F | A | |
|---|---|---|---|
| Material —Price | £25 | | |
| —Usage | 80 | | |
| Labour —Rate | | £112 | |
| —Efficiency | 95 | | |
| Overhead—Expenditure | | 270 | |
| —Volume | 150 | | |
| | £350 | £382 | |
| TOTAL VARIANCE | | | £32(A) |

FIGURE 82

We should always attempt to establish such relationships in an endeavour to make our presentations that much more valid. They should however only be made on known relationships, and not on intuitive guesses or on unsupported opinions.

### The more advanced variances

Having looked at the six basic variances we must now pass on to a consideration of other variances in a standard costing system. They are:

1 Material usage variance analysed between mix variance and yield variance. This form of analysis will be necessary for processes which involve mixing a specified recipe of materials. Cake-making or paint-making are two examples.
2 Labour efficiency variance analysed between real efficiency and idle time. This is an attempt to discover the real work hours which produced the known output, as opposed to the hours paid for.
3 Overhead volume variance, analysed between capacity variance and efficiency variance. Here we are equating volume with activity and thus attempting to discover the make-up of activity.
4 Overhead capacity variance, analysed between idle time and usage. This is an attempt to discover the real work capacity available for production as opposed to the total capacity available.
5 As a separate point for consideration with points 3 and 5 above, we shall need to look at overhead variances in terms of fixed and variable overhead.

*Mix and yield variances*

This analysis is associated with material usage where two or more materials are used to manufacture the end-product. The examples of cake-making and paint-making have already been given, but, clearly, any production method involving processing or recipes will require consideration of this. Let us consider a simple example.

## Illustration

A certain product is made by mixing together the following ingredients:

Abel: 60 lb at £2·00 per lb
Baker: 30 lb at £1·00 per lb
Chass: 10 lb at £3·00 per lb

In one week when 500 lb of product were obtained the following material usage occurred:

Abel: 350 lb at an actual cost of £640
Baker: 200 lb at an actual cost of £212
Chass: 50 lb at an actual cost of £200

We are required to identify and calculate the appropriate variances.

It will be observed that 600 lb were used to produce 500 lb of output. We will thus need to consider what *should* have been used as opposed to what *was* used, and this forms the basis of yield analysis. Note also the proportions indicated by the cost standard: the recipe calls for 60 lb of Abel to 30 lb of Baker to 10 lb of Chass for every 100 lb of input. A glance at the actual usage shows that these proportions were not maintained. This forms the basis of the mix analysis, which is usually displayed in table form as shown in Figure 83.

Let us examine the make-up to observe the origin of the figures.

MATERIAL VARIANCE ANALYSIS

Product ————
Week Ending ————

| Material | Prop'n | (1) Actual Quantity Actual Mix Actual Price $AQ_A AP$ | | (2) Actual Quantity Actual Mix Standard Price $AQ_A SP$ | | | (3) Actual Quantity Standard Mix Standard Price $AQ_S SP$ | | | (4) Standard Quantity Standard Mix Standard Price $SQ_S SP$ | | |
|---|---|---|---|---|---|---|---|---|---|---|---|---|
| Abel | 60 | 350 lb. | £640 | 350 lb. | £2 | £700 | 360 lb. | £2 | £720 | 300 lb. | £2 | £600 |
| Baker | 30 | 200 lb. | 212 | 200 lb. | £1 | 200 | 180 lb. | £1 | 180 | 150 lb. | £1 | 150 |
| Chass | 10 | 50 lb. | 200 | 50 lb. | £3 | 150 | 60 lb. | £3 | 180 | 50 lb. | £3 | 150 |
| | | 600 lb. | £1052 | | | £1050 | 600 lb. | | £1080 | 500 lb. | | £900 |

*Material price variance* £2 (A)

*Material mix variance* £30 (F)

*Material yield variance* £180 (A)

*Material usage variance* £150 (A)

*Total cost variance* £900 − £1052 = £152 A

= £2 (A) + £30 (F) + £180 (A) = £152 A

FIGURE 83

*Material price variance*

This is calculated from the basic formula already discussed, AQ(SP — AP). For material Abel:

$$\begin{aligned}
\text{Actual quantity} & \quad 350 \text{ lb} \\
\text{Standard price} & \quad £2 \text{ per lb} \\
\text{Actual price} & \quad £640 \text{ for } 350 \text{ lb}
\end{aligned}$$

$$\text{Therefore } 350\left(£2 - \frac{£640}{350}\right)$$
$$= £700 - £640 = £60(A)$$

These are the figures on the first line in columns 1 and 2 of the table. The headings of these two columns are $AQ_A AP$ and $AQ_A SP$, which is an expansion of the formula AQ(SP — AP).

Thus, the first two columns give the overall price variance. As the actual price column is greater than the standard price column the variance is adverse.

*Material usage variance*

This is calculated from the basic formula already discussed, SP(SQ — AQ). For material Abel the following information is given:

$$\begin{aligned}
\text{Standard price} & \quad £2 \text{ per lb} \\
\text{Standard quantity} & \\
\quad 60\% \text{ of } 500 \text{ lbs} & \quad 300 \text{ lb} \\
\text{Actual quantity} & \quad 350 \text{ lb}
\end{aligned}$$

$$\text{Therefore } £2(300 - 350)$$
$$= £600 - £700 = £100 \text{ (A)}$$

These are the figures on the first line in columns 2 and 4. The headings of these two columns are $AQ_A SP$ and $SQ_S SP$, which is an expansion of the formula SP(SQ — SQ). Thus the difference between columns 2 and 4 gives the overall material usage variance. As the 'actual quantity' column has a higher value than the 'standard quantity' column, the variance is adverse.

We see that usage has two components, mix and yield. How are we to discover their individual value? The answer is to go back to the material usage formula $SP(SQ - AQ)$.

In this example, quantity has a two-fold aspect:

(*a*) Given that the actual input of material is correct, what proportion of each recipe material should have been used? We can see that this will mean an amendment to the formula, such that SQ will mean the standard proportion of actual input material used; we abbreviate this to $AQ_S$. In addition, AQ will now mean the actual proportion of actual input material used; we abbreviate this to $AQ_A$.

Combining these two aspects we obtain $SP(AQ_S - AQ_A)$. So, for material Abel,

| | | |
|---|---|---|
| SP | Standard price | £2 per lb |
| $AQ_S$ | Standard proportion of actual input 60% of 600 lb | 360 lb |
| $AQ_A$ | Actual proportion of actual input | 350 lb |
| | Therefore £2(360 − 350) | |
| | = £720 − £700 = £20 (F) | |

These are the figures on the first line of the table under columns 2 and 3. The headings of these two columns are $AQ_A SP$ and $AQ_S SP$, which are an expansion of the formula derived above as $SP(AQ_S - AQ_A)$. Thus the the difference between columns 2 and 3 gives the material mix variance. In this case, as the $AQ_S SP$

column is greater than the $AQ_ASP$ column, the variance is favourable.

(b)  Given that the actual input material is correct, then how does its yield compare with the forecast input and yield? To answer this we again require an amendment to the general material usage formula such that SQ will mean the standard proportion of standard input; we abbreviate this to $SQ_S$. Also, AQ will now mean the standard proportion of the actual input material. (We have just used this in the mix calculation, abbreviating this to $AQ_S$.) Combining these two aspects we obtain $SP(SQ_S - AQ_S)$. So, for material Abel:

| | | |
|---|---|---|
| SP | Standard price | £2 per lb |
| $SQ_S$ | Standard proportion of standard input | |
| | 60% of 500 lb | 300 lb |
| $AQ_S$ | Standard proportion of actual input | |
| | 60% of 600 lb | 360 lb |

$$\text{therefore } £2(300 - 360)$$
$$= £600 - £720 = £120(A)$$

These are the figures on the first line of the table under columns 3 and 4. The headings of these two columns are $AQ_SSP$ and $SQ_SSP$, which are an expansion of the formula $SP(SQ_S - AQ_S)$ above. Thus, the difference between columns 3 and 4 gives us the material yield variance. In this case, as the $AQ_SSP$ column is greater than the $SQ_SSP$ column, the variance is adverse.

### Normal and abnormal gains and losses

The remaining problem is concerned with the matter of normal and abnormal losses. We have already noted that the mix and yield calculation is typical of a process cost situation.

### Illustration

A product MASH is produced by mixing together

> 4 tons of M at £3 per ton
> 3 tons of A at £1 per ton
> 2 tons of S at £2 per ton
> 1 ton of H at £6 per ton

In one week when 4617 tons of MASH were produced the actual material usage and cost were as follows:

> M 1800 tons for £5720
> A 1700 tons for £1580
> S   900 tons for £2000
> H   600 tons for £3700

There is a normal loss of 10% of input materials. We are required to identify and calculate the appropriate variances.

A solution is demonstrated in Figure 84. The approach is the same as in the previous example. The major difference occurs in the calculation of the standard total quantity of input as the basis for column 4. It will be noted that the actual yield is 4617 tons. If we assume that this is equivalent to a 90% yield after deductions of a normal loss of 10%, then the input material needed to produce it is $(4617/9) \times 10$, which is 5130.

The other interesting point concerns the yield variance. We observe from the table that an abnormal gain of 117 tons can be calculated. It is also possible to calculate the price per standard ton of *yield*, as shown, at £2·77 per ton. The product of the two calculations is the yield variance.

MATERIAL VARIANCE ANALYSIS

Product ——
Week ending ——

| Material | Prop'n | (1) Actual Quantity Actual Mix Actual Price AQ₁AP | | (2) Actual Quantity Actual Mix Standard Price AQ₁SP | | | (3) Actual Quantity Standard Mix Standard Price AQₛSP | | | Standard Quantity Standard Mix Standard Price SQₛSP | | |
|---|---|---|---|---|---|---|---|---|---|---|---|---|
| M | 4 | 1 800 | £5 720 | 1 800 | £3 | £5 400 | 2 000 | £3 | £6 000 | 2 052 | £3 | £6 156 |
| A | 3 | 1 700 | 1 580 | 1 700 | £1 | 1 700 | 1 500 | £1 | 1 500 | 1 539 | £1 | 1 539 |
| S | 2 | 900 | 2 000 | 900 | £2 | 1 800 | 1 000 | £2 | 2 000 | 1 026 | £2 | 2 052 |
| H | 1 | 600 | 3 700 | 600 | £6 | 3 600 | 500 | £6 | 3 000 | 513 | £6 | 3 078 |
| | | 5 000 | £13 000 | | | £12 500 | 5 000 | | £12 500 | 5 130 | | £12 825 |

Material price variance £500 (A)

Material mix variance £0

Material usage variance £325 (F)

Material yield variance £325 (F)

Total material cost variance £12 825 − £13 000 = £175 (A)

N.B. 4617 tons = 90% yield ∴ 5130 tons = Input.

| | |
|---|---|
| *Less* Normal Loss at 10% | 500 |
| Normal yield | 4500 |
| Actual yield | 4617 |
| Abnormal gain | 117 tons |

Cost per Standard ton:

| | | |
|---|---|---|
| 4 tons of M at £3 p.t. = | £12 | |
| 3 tons of A at £1 p.t. = | 3 | |
| 2 tons of S at £2 p.t. = | 4 | |
| 1 ton of H at £6 p.t. = | 6 | |
| 10 tons | £25 | |
| 1 ton (10%) Normal loss | — | |
| 9 tons of mix cost | £25 | = £2·77 tons for 117 tons of Abnormal Gain = £325 (F) |

FIGURE 84

## Labour efficiency and idle time

It is necessary to take account of idle time in order to calculate a true efficiency variance. It is normal, when calculating a cost standard, to calculate the activity hours on an 'attainable' base. Thus, allowances will have been made in the standard hours for such factors as changing tools and drawing materials, cleaning machines and so on. The standard hour will include an acceptable portion of time which, while not truly productive, must none the less be allowed for in achieving some attainable norm. Other lost time detracts from efficiency. Such factors as waiting for a job, abnormal machine breakdowns, parts not available, and so forth, may indicate inefficiency and should be shown quite separately as idle time hours. If they are allowed to clutter up or conceal the true efficiency, a certain distraction occurs which may well lead management on to a false trail of investigation. The calculation for idle time is simple and is demonstrated using the following information:

### Illustration

In an assembly department, ten men are employed for 40 hours per week at a payroll cost of £492. In a certain period 1000 units of output are produced whose unit cost standard is 30 minutes per unit at £0·95 per hour. The 400 clock hours making up the payroll included 50 idle time hours. Calculate the usual variances.

*Labour cost variance:*

| | | |
|---|---|---|
| SPAQ | 1000 units 0·5 hrs £0·95 | £475 |
| APAQ | Payroll | 492 |
| | Total cost variance | £17(A) |

*Labour rate variance:*

AQ(SP − AP)

$$400 \text{ hrs} \left( £0·95 - \frac{£492}{400} \right)$$

$$= £380 - £492 = \qquad £112(A)$$

*Idle time variance:*
SP × Idle time hours
£0·95 × 50 =                                    £47·50(A)

*Labour efficiency variance:*
SP(SQ—AQ)

$$£0·95 \left( \begin{array}{c} 1000 \text{ units at} \\ 0·5 \text{ hrs per unit} \end{array} - \begin{array}{c} 400 \text{ hrs} \\ less \\ \text{Idle hrs} \end{array} \right)$$

£0·95 (500 — 350) =                        £142·50(F)
                                            ─────────
                                             £17·00(A)
                                            ═════════

We note that the idle time variance is subtracted before calculating the efficiency variance. The actual hours during which 500 standard hours' *worth* of work was produced is then decreased by idle time to give the basis for calculating true efficiency.

## Overhead variances

An important comment was made in the last sentence. It was, 'the actual hours during which 500 standard hours' *worth* of work was produced'. This will prove to be a useful concept in the more sophisticated variance analysis we are about to examine.

Invariably the actual fixed overhead and the actual activity hours will differ from the budget and give rise to:

(a) an expenditure variance, where the actual fixed overhead differs from the budgeted fixed overhead in absolute terms.

(b) a volume variance where the actual activity hours have given rise to a change in overhead absorption. This could occur for one of two basic reasons: firstly, there could be a change in capacity. If this changed capacity includes idle time, it must be extracted and analysed separately before the true efficiency can be measured.

Secondly, there could be a change in efficiency, or in other words, in 'the actual hours during which the standard hours' *worth* of work was performed'.

*Illustration*

| | |
|---|---|
| Cost standard per unit | 1 hour |
| Budgeted output | 2000 units |
| Budgeted fixed overhead | £5000 |
| Fixed overhead absorption rate | $\dfrac{£5000}{2000 \times 1} = £2.50$ per hour |
| Actual output | 1800 units |
| Actual clock hours | 1900 hours |
| Idle time hours included in actual hours | 200 hours |
| Actual fixed overhead | £4950 |

The effect of these factors on overhead absorption is demonstrated by calculating the following variances:

*Fixed overhead cost variance:*

| | |
|---|---|
| SPAQ   1800 units × 1 hour × £2·50 per hour | £4500 |
| APAQ   Actual fixed overheads | £4950 |
| | £450(A) |

*Fixed overhead expenditure variance:*
Budgeted fixed overhead
*Less* actual fixed overhead
£5000 − £4950                                                    £50(F)

*Fixed overhead volume variance*
To measure the activity change from budget, we
   use the formula SP(SQ − AQ), where
   SQ = budgeted or standard activity hours
   AQ = actual activity hours *or* standard hours'
        worth of actual work

$£2.50 \left( \dfrac{\text{budgeted activity}}{\text{2000 hours}} - \dfrac{\text{actual activity}}{\text{1800 hours}} \right)$        = £500(A)

£450(A)

The fixed overhead volume variance can then be further

analysed in three ways, by using the original formula, but modifying the meanings of each term. The important points to remember are:

(a) that we are attempting to analyse the under- or over-absorption of fixed overheads whose rate was established on a budgeted level of expenditure and activity.

(b) that we are dealing with the actual hours taken to perform *standard hours' worth of work.*

1 *Fixed overhead capacity variance:* SP(SQ — AQ)
   where SQ = budgeted hours of capacity
        AQ = actual hours of capacity
             (i.e. clock hours)
        £2·50 (2000 — 1900)                    = £250(A)

2 *Fixed overhead idle hours variance:* SP(SQ — AQ)
   where SQ = adjusted standard clock hours
        AQ = actual production clock hours
        £2·50 (1900 — 1700)                    = £500(A)

3 *Fixed overhead efficiency variance:* SP(SQ — AQ)
   where SQ = the adjusted standard production hours
             after idle time
        AQ = Standard hours' worth of work produced
        £2·50 (1700 — 1800)                    = £250(F)
                                                 ———
                                               £500(A)
                                                 ═══

Two things will be noted. Firstly, the addition of the above three analyses gives the same figure as for volume variance. This should be no surprise, since they represent the further analysis of volume. Secondly, note the progression from budgeted hours to standard hours' worth of work through the above three steps; volume variance is

$$SP (SQ - AQ)$$
$$SP (2000 - 1800)$$

whilst idle time, capacity and efficiency are respectively

$$SP (2000 - 1900)$$
$$SP (1900 - 1700)$$
$$SP (1700 - 1800)$$

This relationship can be an extremely useful *aide mémoire* in fixed overhead variance analysis.

Variable overhead absorption rates are also based on the two calculations for budgeted variable overhead and budgeted activity. In this case, however, we would expect them to move in step, because of their variability. Nevertheless, in practice, we would find that divergence does occur and has two causes:

(a) An expenditure variance. Because the proportional relationship anticipated has not occurred, the actual total cost is different from budget.

(b) An efficiency variance which has again upset the proportional relationship, the result being that more or less standard hours' worth of work have been produced in the actual hours.

*Illustration*

| | |
|---|---|
| Cost standard per unit | 1 hour |
| Budgeted output | 2000 units |
| Budgeted variable overhead | £3000 |
| Variable overhead absorption rate | $\dfrac{£3000}{2000 \times 1} = £1\cdot50$ per hour |
| Actual output | 1800 units |
| Actual hours worked | 1700 hours |
| Actual variable overhead | £2680 |

The effect of these facts on overhead absorption is demonstrated by calculating the following variances:

*Variable overhead cost variance:*

| | | |
|---|---|---|
| SPAQ | 1800 units × 1 hour × £1·50 per hour | £2700 |
| APAQ | Actual variable overhead | 2680 |
| | | £20(F) |

*Variable overhead expenditure variance:* AQ(SP − AP)
where AQ = the number of hours that would be
used as the basis for overhead
absorption (i.e. work hours)

$$1700 \left( £1·50 - \frac{£2680}{1700} \right)$$

$$£2550 - £2680 \qquad\qquad = £130(A)$$

*Variable overhead efficiency variance:* SP(SQ − AQ)
where SQ = the standard work hours availabl̶
on which overhead *could* be ab̶ ̶ ̶d.
AQ = the standard hours' worth of wo̶
produced on which the overhead
*was* absorbed
£1·50 (1700 − 1800)
£1·50 × 100 = £150(F)

£20(F)

From the addition of these analytical variances we are able
to agree the total cost variance.

## Sales variances

An examination of the technique of variance analysis could
not be considered complete unless it could demonstrate the
ultimate effect on profit. There can be no profit unless there
are sales, and clearly, sales are just as likely to be affected
by variations as are the elements of cost.

Sales variances may be either revenue- or profit-based.
The latter are usually considered to be the more informative
Basically there are two broad areas of variance:

1 Variances due to a difference between actual and budgeted sales price.
2 Variances due to a difference between forecast and
actual volume of sales. Furthermore in a situation
where more than one product is sold, there will be a
mix and yield variance.

Let us consider a single-product sales situation to start with:

### Illustration

| | |
|---|---|
| Budgeted sales units | 2000 |
| Budgeted unit selling price | £5·50 |
| Cost standard per unit | £3·75 |
| Actual sales units | 2400 |
| Actual selling price per unit | £5·50 |

On the assumption that the cost standard per unit is constant, and that variances for actual cost have been extracted elsewhere, the sales variances are calculated from a profit point of view, the idea being to calculate the difference between actual and budgeted sales as it affects total profit.

Total sales variance affecting *profit*
  SPSQ: 2000 (£5·00 − £3·75)     = £2500
  Actual profit: 2400 (£5·50 − £3·75)   = £4200
                                 —————
                                 £1700(F)

Sales *profit* variance in price
  AQ (standard profit − actual profit):
  2400 (£1·25 − £1·75)       = £1200(F)

Sales *profit* variance in volume
  Standard profit (SQ − AQ):
  £1·25 (2000 − 2400)
  £1·25 × 400              =  £500(F)
                                 —————
                                 £1700(F)

Having established the relationship between sales and profit in this example we go on to the more practical aspect of the multi-product sales situation within which variations due to mix and yield become apparent.

*Illustration*

The monthly sales budget for Traders Ltd shows the following forecasts:

| Product | Quantity | Selling price | Unit cost standard |
|---------|----------|---------------|--------------------|
| Mini    | 6000     | £5            | £4                 |
| Minor   | 3000     | £10           | £7                 |
| Maxi    | 1000     | £20           | £15                |

During a particular month the following sales were recorded: Mini, 7200 at £37 440; Minor, 2800 at £27 440 and Maxi, 800 at £16 800. We are required to calculate the usual variances.

Figure 85 shows the calculation. It will be observed that the method of analysis used is the same as that for material mix and yield. The total units actually sold and the budgeted proportion of each product to total budgeted sales is the basis for the individual product sales shown in column 3.

## Operating statements

The calculations have been completed. The necessary entries have been posted to the specific accounts in the integrated ledger. A trial balance has been extracted and the books of account found to be in balance. But the most important part of the exercise is to analyse and report to management and to let people know exactly what is happening. Balancing the books lends credibility and confidence to the system but action can only be originated through processed information.

The accountant therefore has to consider the specific way in which this reporting is to be done, bearing in mind the person who is to receive the information. Apart from using an operating statement, there are no hard and fast rules except to use commonsense.

Operating statements must be designed to be as informa-

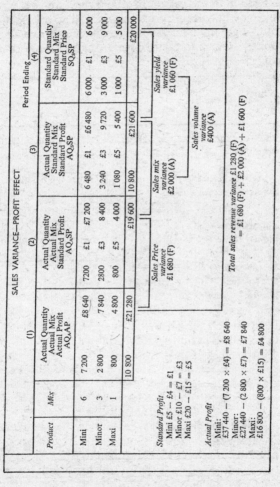

SALES VARIANCE—PROFIT EFFECT

Period Ending _____

|  |  | (1) Actual Quantity Actual Mix Actual Profit AQ,AP | | (2) Actual Quantity Actual Mix Standard Profit AQ,SP | | (3) Actual Quantity Standard Mix Standard Profit AQ₅SP | | (4) Standard Quantity Standard Mix Standard Price SQ,SP | |
|---|---|---|---|---|---|---|---|---|---|
| Product | Mix |  |  |  |  |  |  |  |  |
| Mini | 6 | 7 200 | £8 640 | 7200 £1 | £7 200 | 6 480 £1 | £6 480 | 6 000 £1 | 6 000 |
| Minor | 3 | 2 800 | 7 840 | 2800 £3 | 8 400 | 3 240 £3 | 9 720 | 3 000 £3 | 9 000 |
| Maxi | 1 | 800 | 4 800 | 800 £5 | 4 000 | 1 080 £5 | 5 400 | 1 000 £5 | 5 000 |
|  |  | 10 800 | £21 280 | | £19 600 | 10 800 | £21 600 | | £20 000 |

Sales Price variance £1 680 (F)

Sales mix variance £2 000 (A)

Sales yield variance £1 060 (F)

Sales volume variance £400 (A)

Total sales revenue variance £1 280 (F)
= £1 680 (F) + £2 000 (A) + £1 600 (F)

*Standard Profit*
Mini £5 − £4 == £1
Minor £10 − £7 == £3
Maxi £20 − £15 == £5

*Actual Profit*
Mini:
£37 440 − (7 200 × £4) == £8 640
Minor:
£27 440 − (2 800 × £7) == £7 840
Maxi:
£16 800 − (800 × £15) == £4 800

**Figure 85**

tive as possible to the person to whom they are addressed. It should not be necessary to point out that information sent out to a general manager will be different in size, detail and content from information sent to, say, a cost centre foreman.

PROFIT AND LOSS ACCOUNT

To: Board of Directors                                  Period:_____
    Divisional Managers                                  Date: _____

Capacity Factor _____        Efficiency Factor _____   Activity_____

Budgeted Sales                   _____ units at £ _____
                                 _____ units at    _____
                                 _____ units at
        Total Budgeted Sales                                £

Cost Standard per unit of sales
                                 _____ units at £ _____
                                 _____ units at    _____
                                 _____ units at
        Total Cost of Sales                          £

Budgeted Profit                                                    £
Sales Variances                  Price
                                 Volume _____

Standard Profit for Actual Sales                                  £

Cost Variances                   Favourable        Adverse

Material    price
            mix
            yield
Labour      rate
            efficiency
            rate time
Variable
overhead    expenditure
            capacity
Fixed
overhead    expenditure
            capacity
            efficiency

        Net cost variance                                         £

        Actual profit                                             £

Prepared by _____                              Date _____

FIGURE 86

If one general rule is to be made then it would probably be that the more senior the person, the less detail is required —the rationale being that in an *effectively* organised firm, the day-to-day supervision is delegated downwards, and the more senior staff are only presented with broad outlines.

In order to illustrate this, two sample operating statements are shown. Figure 86 is a profit and loss operating statement for presenting information to the Board of Directors and probably divisional managers. Comparing it to the profit and loss account which will be prepared and which will form the basis of the operating statement, one may wonder if it has not been made too simple. However there is sufficient detail contained in this report to enable the

| PRODUCTION STATEMENT | | | | Dept. _____ | |
|---|---|---|---|---|---|
| Deliveries to F. G. Stock _____ units | | | | Period _____ | |
| Change in W.I.P. Stock _____ units | | | | Date _____ | |
| Production Units _____ | | | | | |
| Capacity factor _____ | | Efficiency factor _____ | | Activity _____ | |

| | Hours | | | Unit output | Unit hours |
|---|---|---|---|---|---|
| | Paid | Worked | Standard | | |
| Budget | | | | | |
| Actual | | | | | |

| Controllable cost | Cost | | Variance | |
|---|---|---|---|---|
| | Flexed budget | Actual | Price | Quantity |
| Direct material | | | | |
| Direct labour | | | | |
| Supervision | | | | |
| Clerical | | | | |
| Tools | | | | |
| Consumables | | | | |
| Totals | | | | |

Compilers comments (basis of figures only)

Prepared by _____   Date _____

FIGURE 87

Board of Directors to discuss the general direction and motivation of the organisation.

On the other hand, Figure 87 illustrates the type of production operating statement that would be sent to a cost centre supervisor or departmental foreman. If any criticism is to be levelled at this report it would probably be that it is too simple, that more detail will be required at this level for effective action to be taken where required.

The methods of ascertaining cost and the techniques of control are fascinating. But all may be made useless by producing a poorly-designed operating statement addressed to the wrong person and containing the wrong information.

## Exercises

1   CT Products Ltd manufactures a wide range of household products including ceramic tiles. Each tile is 4 ins by 3 ins, and for a batch of 5000 square feet, after allowing for normal breakage, the standard mix of raw material is as follows:

| Raw material | Quantity lb | price per lb £ |
|---|---|---|
| X | 1000 | 0·30 |
| Y | 400 | 1·00 |
| Z | 600 | 0·50 |

For the four weeks ending April 27, the actual output was 864 000 tiles from 15 mixes. The following raw materials were used:

| Raw material | Quantity lb | price per lb £ |
|---|---|---|
| X | 16 000 | 0·28 |
| Y | 5 000 | 1·05 |
| Z | 9 000 | 0·52 |

Raw materials were taken into stock at actual prices and issued at standard prices. There were no opening or closing stocks of raw material in stores or work in progress.

You are required to:

(a) calculate the direct materials cost variance;
(b) analyse the direct materials cost variance to show price, mixture, usage and yield for each material and in total. (ICMA)

2 From the data given below for October you are required to
(a) Calculate the direct wage variance;
(b) Analyse the variance in terms of wage rates, labour mix, labour efficiency and idle time;
(c) Show the following accounts in the cost ledger: direct wages, and work in progress for direct labour only.

S Limited manufactures one standard product in Department 6. The standard labour force of the department consists of:

| Grade | Number of employees | Rate per hour |
|-------|---------------------|---------------|
| A | 100 | £1·20 |
| B | 80 | £1·00 |

During October, S Limited experienced a shortage of certain grades of labour. In Department 6 the actual labour force was:

| Grade | Number of employees | Rate per hour |
|-------|---------------------|---------------|
| A | 84 | £1·20 |
| | 6 | £1·25 |
| B | 86 | £1·00 |
| | 4 | £0·95 |

The standard performance for the department is 50 units per hour. An 8-hour day is in operation and there were 4 working weeks of 5 days each in October. Actual production during the month was 8200 units. A breakdown of a key machine resulted in 3 hours of lost production.

(ICMA)

3 The following information relates to the activities in Period 4 of a production department in a manufacturing company:

|  | Overhead | |
|---|---|---|
|  | *Budgeted* | *Actual* |
| *Fixed* | £ | £ |
| Rent and rates | 2 600 | 2 600 |
| Insurance | 400 | 420 |
| Supervision | 2 800 | 2 845 |
| Depreciation of machinery | 1 850 | 1 850 |
|  | 7 650 | 7 715 |
| *Variable* | | |
| Indirect labour | 3 510 | 2 980 |
| Consumable supplies | 1 170 | 1 070 |
| Maintenance | 990 | 765 |
| Fuel | 2 430 | 1 910 |
| Power and light | 1 350 | 1 290 |
|  | 9 450 | 8 015 |
| Total | £17 100 | £15 730 |

The budgeted hours were 9000 per period, but during Period 4 actual hours worked were 7600 and the value in standard hours of actual output was 8100.

You are required to calculate for Period 4
(a) standard fixed overhead rate per hour;
(b) standard variable overhead rate per hour;
(c) total overhead variance;

(*d*)   overhead volume variance divided into:
volume efficiency variance
capacity usage variance
overhead price variance (assuming that this is
related to fixed costs only)
overhead efficiency variance
overhead utilisation variance (assuming that this is
related to variable costs only).

Prepare also a tabulation to show each item of overhead
with its overhead variance. Also indicate the items that
would be controllable by the manager of the production
department if it were treated as a budget centre. (ICMA)

4   Using the prime cost data given below for the month of
March, you are required to calculate the following
variances:

(*a*)   Material cost; material price; material usage.
(*b*)   Wage cost; wage rate; labour efficiency; labour
idle time.

Standard prime cost data for one unit of product Z are
as follows:

|  | *Ref.* | *lb* | *price per lb* |
|---|---|---|---|
| Materials | DM1 | 6 | £1·50 |
|  | DM2 | 10 | 0·60 |

|  | *Grade* | *hours* | *rate per hour* |
|---|---|---|---|
| Wages | A | 8 | £1·00 |
|  | B | 5 | 0·80 |

The following actual data for the month of March concerning the prime cost of product Z are given:

*Stocks in hand at March 1*

|  | *Ref.* | *lb* | *price per lb* |
|---|---|---|---|
| Materials | DM1 | 85 000 | £1·40 |
|  | DM2 | 124 000 | 0·55 |

Finished product Z 15 400 units

There were no work in progress stocks at either the beginning or end of the month.

| Materials Ref. | Purchased lb | price per lb | Consumed lb |
|---|---|---|---|
| DM1 | 140 000 | £1·60 | 62 400 |
| DM2 | 220 000 | £0·65 | 103 000 |

| Wages: Grade | Paid hours | rate per hour | Idle time incurred — hours |
|---|---|---|---|
| A | 78 800 | £1·10 | 600 |
| B | 50 500 | 0·75 | 300 |

| Finished product Ref. | Produced units | Sold units |
|---|---|---|
| Z | 10 200 | 9 500 |

Stocks of raw materials are priced on an actual cost F.I.F.O. basis. Issues to work in progress are priced at standard. Finished goods are valued at standard prime cost.                                                    (ICMA)

5 J Limited makes a branded product and operates a standard costing system. Using the data given below for April, you are required, for direct materials, to:

(a) Calculate the cost variance;
(b) analyse the cost variance into price variance for each material and total, and usage variance;
(c) analyse the usage variance into mix variance and yield variance;
(d) write up the following ledger control accounts in the cost ledger: raw material stores, work in progress and finished goods.

The standard direct material mix for a batch to produce 1000 lb of the product is:

| Raw material | Quantity lb | Standard price per lb £ |
|---|---|---|
| A | 550 | 0·50 |
| B | 250 | 1·00 |
| C | 300 | 0·75 |

During April twenty batches were processed and the actual output of the product was 20 200 lb. The actual materials consumed were:

| Raw material | Quantity | Actual price per lb |
|---|---|---|
| | lb | £ |
| A | 11 800 | 0·45 |
| B | 4 900 | 1·00 |
| C | 6 100 | 0·70 |

You are to assume that there were no opening or closing stocks.                                    (ICMA)

6  The manufacturing division of a company producing one product operates a standard costing system with thirteen 4-weekly periods each year.

You are required to calculate for Period 3
(*a*)  The following cost variances:

direct materials price
direct materials usage
direct wages rate
direct labour efficiency
overhead expenditure
overhead capacity usage
overhead volume efficiency

(*b*)  the standard profit and the actual profit;
(*c*)  the reconciliation of the two profits given in answer to (*b*) above.

Data taken from the standard cost of the product and from the budget are as follows:

Standard prime costs per unit of product:
Direct materials:

| | | |
|---|---|---|
| A  3·36 lb at £120 per ton | = | £0·180 |
| B  0·0375 gallons at £24 per gallon | = | 0·900 |
| Direct labour — 15 minutes at £0·5 per hour = | | 0·125 |

|  | £1·205 |

Standard selling price per unit: £2·50

Budgeted labour force: 55 men, each working 40 hours per week

Budgeted fixed overhead: £286 000 per annum

Actual data for Period 3 were as follows:

*Production—30 000 units*

|  | Material A | Material B |
|---|---|---|
| Stock at end Period 2 | 15 tons | 580 gallons |
| Purchases for Period 3 | 55 tons | 1 210 gallons |
| Purchase price | £135 per ton | £22·6 per gallon |
| Stock at end Period 3 | 24 tons | 690 gallons |

| Direct labour: | |
|---|---|
| Actual hours | 8 700 |
| Wages paid | £4 320 |
| Fixed overhead incurred: | £22 600 |

Opening and closing stocks of work in progress and finished goods were identical.

All goods sold were at standard selling price. You are also advised that the direct material stock accounts are valued at standard prices and any price variance is transferred to the profit and loss account of the period in which the purchases are made.                  (ICMA)

7  GRO is a garden fertiliser produced by mixing three chemicals G, R and O in the proportions 5, 3 and 2 respectively; these proportions are not absolutely critical, and saleable GRO within the accepted tolerance is produced even when the proportions are varied within defined limits. The standard prices of the chemicals are:

G—60p per lb; R—50p per lb; O—72p per lb

The normal yield from the mixing process is 90%, the loss being due to evaporation and the removal of residual chemicals of no value which arise during the process. During May the output of GRO was 4 000 7-lb packets and 6 000 3-lb packets, the input materials being:

> 23 000 lb of G costing 63p per lb
> 17 000 lb of R costing 47p per lb
> 10 500 lb of O costing 73p per lb

You are required to calculate the material price, mix and yield variances. (ACCA)

8 The following information has been extracted from the budget of AB Ltd for Period 1.

| Product | Sales Quantity | Selling price | Standard cost |
|---|---|---|---|
| Alpha | 10 000 | £5 | £4 |
| Beta | 5 000 | £10 | £7 |

During the period, sales and average prices obtained were:

| Alpha | 9 500 | £4·90 |
|---|---|---|
| Beta | 5 700 | £9·80 |

You are required to prepare a statement reconciling actual sales margin with budget, showing the sales margin variance attributable to price, quantity and mix of sales. (ACCA)

# 14

# Decisions—Marginal Costing

What are we reporting? To whom are we reporting? Why should we be reporting? How are we to report?

The first and last of these questions have been the subject matter of Chapters 3 to 13. The second question has been an implicit and pertinent feature of the discussion and examination of each topic and chapter. Have we been certain why we have been reporting? We are reporting to management because their fundamental role is concerned with making decisions.

Those decisions involve, very often, choosing between alternatives, or between several courses of action, the objective of the ultimate choice being consistent with some known, acceptable, given or assumed objective, or set of objectives. The cost ascertainment methods and control systems we have examined have produced answers by comparing historical fact against forecast or budgeted possibilities. They have placed the onus for establishing the validity of figures and taking action on the shoulders of the manager. However, some management decisions can be more easily made by the use of a technique known as marginal costing.

## Why marginal costing?

Management decisions can be divided broadly into short-term and long-term. The long-term decisions are allied to the forecasting and budgeting process and are concerned with the wide range of opportunities the organisation may be facing or will have to face over the next, say, three to five years, or longer. The great majority of day-to-day decisions are short-term.

In the short-term, conventional cost ascertainment and control methods are found to be somewhat inadequate for decision formulation.

This is largely due to the inclusion of the fixed, or policy, or period costs in the general absorption or total cost systems we have examined.

For when day-to-day decisions are required in a conventional cost accounting system, they are often made without the detailed analysis necessary to realign the data. That realignment must be carried out if we are to avoid the possibility of under- or over-absorption of overhead.

### Illustration

In a department of a factory the forecast overheads of £20 000 are recovered on an hourly rate basis over a forecast of 40 000 production hours. The overheads are known to be £5 000 for fixed overhead and £15 000 for variable overhead. What change occurs in the rate per hour if production hours vary by 10%?

The following table demonstrates:

|  | *Production hours* | | |
|---|---|---|---|
|  | Normal | 10% Increase | 10% Decrease |
|  | 40 000 | 44 000 | 36 000 |
| Variable overhead | £15 000 | £16 500 | £13 500 |
| Fixed overhead | £5 000 | £5 000 | £5 000 |
| Total overheads | £20 000 | £21 500 | £18 500 |
| Combined hourly rate | £0·50 | £0·4886 | £0·5139 |
| Variable overhead rate per hour | £0·375 | £0·375 | £0·375 |
| Fixed overhead rate per hour | £0·125 | £0·1136 | £0·1389 |

This shows one of the major characteristics of cost, variability. Even with increasing or decreasing volumes, the truly linear variable costs are a constant per unit. Yet the fixed costs will decrease or increase per unit, as volume increases or decreases.

This phenomenon forms the basis of marginal costing—sometimes referred to as a short cut to executive decisions. It can, in a fairly simple and straightforward manner, give up-to-the-minute answers to management on such questions as:

1  Should a particular low-priced order be accepted?
2  What additional volume of business can make up for wage rises?
3  What are the products to concentrate on?
4  What product mix will maximise profits?
5  What increased volume is needed to offset a decline in market price?
6  At what volume of sales will an organisation start to show a loss?

These decisions can be made quickly and give marginal costing techniques an advantage over absorption or total cost methods.

### The concept and definition

For any given volume of output the total cost is comprised of variable or avoidable costs and fixed, or 'unavoidable', or 'policy' costs. If the volume increases or decreases by one unit, the variable costs will increase or decrease in direct proportion, whilst the total fixed costs will remain the same. Thus, marginal cost has been defined as:

'The variable cost of one unit of a product or a service; i.e. a cost which could be avoided if the unit was not produced or provided. *Note:* in this context a unit is usually either a single article or a standard measure such as the litre or kilogram but may in certain circumstances be an operation, process or part of an organisation.' (ICMA)

## *A simple example*

To establish a working arrangement of the technique we consider a basic set of information applicable to a factory making a single product from wood. The input direct material and direct labour details are as follows:

| *Cost standard per unit* | | £ | |
|---|---|---|---|
| *Direct material:* | Wood | 1·00 | |
| | Steel | 0·20 | |
| | Screws | 0·10 | |
| | Fittings | 0·30 | |
| | | | £1·60 |
| *Labour:* Grade 1 | 2 hours | 2·00 | |
| 2 | 1 hour | 0·70 | |
| | | | £2·70 |
| | | | £4·30 |
| Variable costs: £700 per 1000 units | | | £0·70 |
| Unit standard variable price | | | £5·00 |

These details would have been arrived at after much analysis and estimating. They have probably been subjected to comparison with actual costs over time, amended and revised, and can now be accepted with reasonable certainty: the firm is now prepared to accept that the unit standard variable cost is an effective value reflecting the best methods and organisation that can be applied under the known conditions.

The firm also knows that the best price it can obtain for its product in a highly competitive market is £7·00 per unit.

It is also aware that there are annual fixed costs amounting to £40 000 covering such items as management and supervision salaries and expenses, rates, electricity, telephones, advertising and so on, which it cannot avoid.

If we follow the methods advocated by an absorption costing system we need to forecast the volume of output, divide it into the value of fixed costs, and arrive at the absorption rate of fixed overheads thus:

$$\frac{\text{Forecast fixed costs}}{\text{Forecast output}} = \frac{£40\,000}{25\,000 \text{ units}}$$
$$= £1\cdot60 \text{ per unit}$$

If at the end of the year, it was found that only 23 000 units were produced and sold, the absorption cost system would then have revealed the following facts:

| | | |
|---|---:|---:|
| Actual sales: 23 000 at £7 per unit | | £161 000 |
| Costs of production for 23 000 units: | | |
| Unit variable cost | £5·00 | |
| Unit fixed cost | £1·60 | |
| | ——— | £151 800 |
| | £6·60 | |
| | | 9 200 |
| *Less:* under-recovery of fixed overhead: | | |
| 25 000 − 23 000 units at £1·60 per unit | | 3 200 |
| Actual profit | | £6 000 |

Management would have been puzzled by the complexity of the adjustment of profit for the under-recovery of fixed overhead. They would argue that since we are selling for £7 and costs are £6·60 then, surely, there is a £0·40 profit per unit; as we sold 23 000 units, profit must be £9 200. They would have overlooked the fact that the £0·40 per unit profit depends *on an output of precisely 25 000 units.*

A marginal costing system would not be complicated by

this calculation, for the very simple reason that fixed costs are regarded as *period* costs to be paid for out of any surplus arising from the sale of goods at their variable cost. The end-of-period calculation would be made as follows:

| | | |
|---|---|---|
| Actual sales: 23 000 at £7 per unit | | £161 000 |
| Variable cost of sales: | | |
| 23 000 at £5 per unit | | 115 000 |
| | | £46 000 |
| *Less* period fixed costs | | 40 000 |
| Profit | | £6 000 |

We may ask ourselves, why bother? Indeed, that could be a valid comment on the simple single-product organisation we have used above. But consider the more likely practical situation of a two- or three- or multi-product company; imagine the complicated calculation and basis needed to allocate, apportion and absorb the fixed period overhead costs; then, the subsequent detailed and complex calculation required to establish where, why and by how much that fixed cost is over- or under-absorbed. At that point we may realise the advantages that the technique of marginal costing offers to management.

### The cost–profit–volume relationship

It is possible to establish a relationship between cost, profit and volume that is not obscured or distorted by absorption costing methods.

We have seen that whilst the unit sales price and unit variable costs remain the same for varying volumes of output, the total fixed or period costs are fixed irrespective of volumes of output.

Also, in a conventional absorption system, when actual

volume differs from the forecast volume, under- or over-absorption of fixed costs occurs. Thus, the *true* actual unit cost is hidden by a complex relationship between unit costs and volume. Marginal costing, by contrast, keeps the two types of cost, variable and fixed, separate.

Because of the character of fixed costs, net profit cannot be established on a per unit basis; it can only be established for the total activity over a given period of time. None the less, the relationship between selling price and variable cost can be accepted as constant.

A fundamental relationship can be established:

Let $V$ = volume of business in units for the period
$s$ = sales price per unit
$v$ = variable cost per unit
$F$ = period fixed costs
$P$ = period profit

Then: $V(s - v) = F + P$

Taking the figures used for our single-product example above, we would obtain:

$$23\ 000\ (£7{\cdot}00 - £5{\cdot}00) = £40\ 000 + \text{Period profit}$$
$$£46\ 000 = £40\ 000 + £6\ 000$$

The cost relationship for a varying range of activity levels may also be shown graphically. Figure 88 illustrates the total cost position. We observe that total fixed cost is a constant sum over the range, whilst total variable costs increase directly in proportion to the increase in activity. Figure 89 shows the rather more complex cost per unit relationship resulting from the addition of fixed and variable costs over the range of activity. The table at the top of Figure 89 is the basis of the calculations, and the information is again that used above for the single-product organisation. We note that

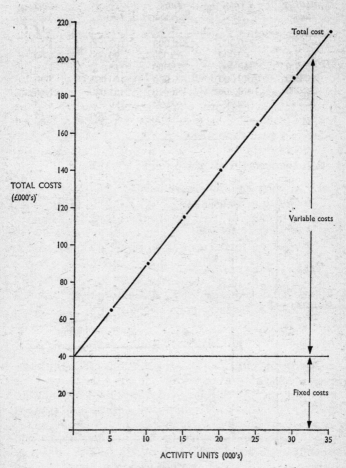

**FIGURE 88**

| Activity units | Total fixed cost | Total variable cost | Total cost | Cost per unit |
|---|---|---|---|---|
| 5 000 | £40 000 | £25 000 | £65 000 | £13·00 |
| 10 000 | 40 000 | 50 000 | 90 000 | 9·00 |
| 15 000 | 40 000 | 75 000 | 115 000 | 7·66 |
| 20 000 | 40 000 | 100 000 | 140 000 | 7·00 |
| 25 000 | 40 000 | 125 000 | 165 000 | 6·60 |
| 30 000 | 40 000 | 150 000 | 190 000 | 6·33 |
| 35 000 | 40 000 | 175 000 | 215 000 | 6·14 |

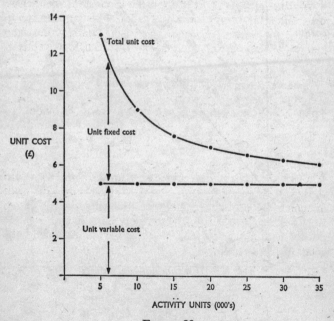

FIGURE 89

unit variable cost is a constant per unit, whilst unit fixed cost decreases as activity increases. Marginal costing avoids this rather complex relationship by putting aside the period fixed costs.

### Contribution or margin

The difference between the sales value and the variable cost is known as the 'contribution' or 'margin'. Thus:

$$\text{Sales} - \text{Variable cost} = \text{Contribution.}$$

We have seen that this relationship is constant whether we take it in total or unit form. We can use the contribution to evolve another relationship, between contribution and activity or volume and the total period fixed costs. Thus:

Let $F$ = Fixed costs for the period
$C$ = Contribution per unit $(s - v)$

Then $\dfrac{F}{C}$ = Volume in units at which no profit is made:

$$\frac{F}{C} = \frac{\text{£40 000}}{\text{£2}} = 20\ 000 \text{ units}$$

If we glance back at the table at the top of Figure 89 we see that at 20 000 units the unit cost is £7. That is also the price at which the product is sold and thus there would be no profit. Therefore, if the organisation wanted to finish the period with profits of £6 000, then we could amend the relationship as follows:

Let $F$ = Fixed costs per period
$P$ = Desired profit in period
$C$ = Contribution per unit

Then $\dfrac{F + P}{C} = \dfrac{\text{£40 000} + \text{£6 000}}{2} = 23\ 000$ units.

This, we observe, is the activity level used previously in the comparison of the absorption and marginal costing techniques.

We also note that this relationship is a re-arrangement of the one already discussed, viz:

$$V(s - v) = F + P$$

## The profit–volume ratio (PVR)

This is another way of expressing the relationship discussed above and is more usefully described as the *contribution/sales ratio*. We note that the relationship between sales and variable cost is a constant. Thus, the relationship between sales and contribution must also be a constant.

Let $s$ = sales price per unit
$v$ = variable cost per unit
$C$ = contribution per unit where $s - v = C$

Then $\dfrac{C}{s}$ = PVR

$\dfrac{C}{s}$ is a constant ratio which may be expressed in percentage terms by multiplying by 100. Let us now examine the manner in which we can use the ratio.

Fixed costs: £40 000.
Sales *less* variable costs equals contribution and is constant.
Thus, where no profits are made:

$$V(s - v) = F + P$$
$$C = £40\ 000 + 0$$

The relationship unit contribution : sales ratio is expressed as:

$$\frac{\text{Contribution per unit}}{\text{Profit–volume ratio}} = \frac{£2}{£2/£7}$$
$$= £2/£0{\cdot}285$$
$$= £7 \text{ per unit}$$

By reference to the table at the top of Figure 89 we observe that this refers to an activity output of 20 000 units which we may check as follows:

| | |
|---|---|
| Sales: 20 000 at £7 per unit | £140 000 |
| Variable costs: 20 000 at £5 per unit | £100 000 |
| Contribution | £40 000 |
| Less fixed costs | £40 000 |
| Profits | £ 0 |

### The break-even point

We note that it is possible to calculate the point at which the firm makes neither profit or loss, that is, where the contribution exactly equals the total of the period fixed costs. At that point the firm is said to have reached the break-even point. The sales value of that point is determined by multiplying the period fixed costs by the relationship between sales and contribution as follows:

Let $F$ = Fixed costs
$\quad s$ = sales price per unit
$\quad v$ = variable cost per unit
$\quad C$ = contribution per unit

Then: $F\dfrac{s}{s-v} = F\dfrac{s}{C}$

Using the same figures we obtain £40 000 $\times$ £7/£2 = £140 000, which is the figure arrived at in the discussion on profit–volume ratio, where we noted that the total unit cost and unit selling value were £7. We could relate these calculations back to the concept of the contribution or margin where at 20 000 units, contribution exactly equalled fixed costs. Thus 20 000 units at a unit selling price of £7 will also give us the break-even sales value of £140 000 arrived at above.

### The margin of safety

This is the relationship between the break-even point and the actual activity and indicates the extent to which a fall-off in activity could affect the profit capacity of the organisation. It is calculated as follows:

Let $P$ = profit for the period
$C$ = contribution per unit
$s$ = sales price per unit

Then $\dfrac{P}{C/s}$ is the margin of safety.

We have already discovered that the relationship between contribution and sales is known as the profit–volume ratio; therefore, margin of safety $= \dfrac{\text{Profit}}{\text{Profit volume ratio}}$. Thus:

$$\begin{aligned} \text{Margin of safety} &= \text{Profit/PVR} \\ &= £6\,000/0{\cdot}285 \\ &= £21\,000 \end{aligned}$$

This is the value of 3000 units selling at £7 per unit and the margin of safety over the break-even point of 20 000 units whose total value was £140 000, as calculated in our examination of the break-even point of sales.

*Graphical presentation and the break-even chart*

There is no one way of presenting the foregoing information in graphical form. All are founded on the assumption running throughout the discussions that the relationship between sales and variable costs is constant and based on the straight line relationship $y = a + bx$ where:

$y$ = costs
$a$ = fixed costs
$b$ = a constant cost
$x$ = the activity

For example,

$$y = £40\,000 + 20\,000\,(£5) = £140\,000$$

which, we have seen, is the break-even point. Alternatively:

$$y = a + bx$$
$$= 0 + 23\,000\,(£7)$$
$$= £161\,000$$

which is the total value of sales for 23 000 units.

These and all the other relationships may be brought together in a single graphical demonstration known as the break-even chart. Figure 90 illustrates the linear relationship between costs, profits and volume.

We note that the unbroken line shows the original relationships on the basis of

Fixed costs—£40 000 per period
Variable costs—£5 per unit
Sales price—£7 per unit

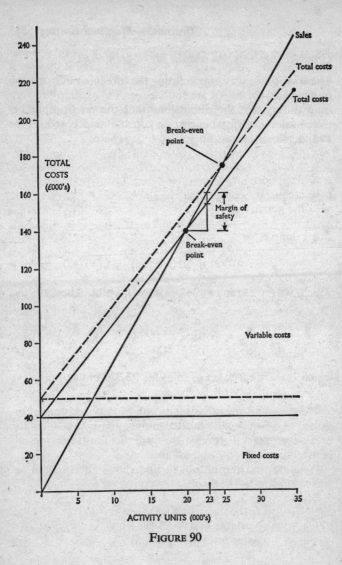

FIGURE 90

Break-even point can be read as 20 000 activity units at £140 000 sales revenue. At 23 000 activity units there is a £6000 vertical difference between the total cost line and the sales revenue line.

At 23 000 activity units there is a £21 000 vertical difference between the break-even point and the sales revenue line. This is the margin of safety.

If fixed costs increased to £50 000 per period as represented by the dashed line, then total costs would increase, giving us a new break-even point at 25 000 activity units and £175 000 sales revenue. This point is beyond the margin of safety and shows the danger that may exist if fixed costs increase, or if severe competition keeps sales price down, or again, if demand decreases such that the 25 000 units position is no longer viable.

The graph may also be simplified for presentation to production management, to whom the interaction of volume is important. This may be done with a contribution volume graph as shown in Figure 91. In this situation we show contribution and fixed cost lines on the basis that contribution per unit equals sales less variable cost—in this case, £7 − £5 = £2. The contribution line is thus:

$$y = a + bx$$
$$= o + b£2$$

Thus, for 35 000 activity units,

$$y = a + bx$$
$$= o + 35\,000\,(£2)$$
$$= £70\,000$$

From this form of presentation we are able to read the effect of declining production, increasing or decreasing fixed costs

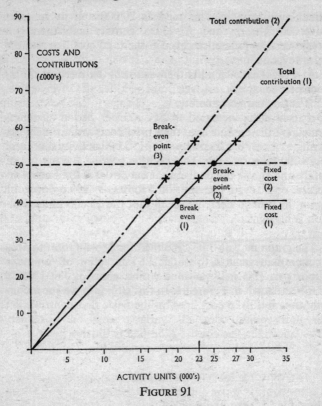

FIGURE 91

and changes in the relationship between sales price and variable cost per unit.

In Figure 91 the full line represents the information previously used. From it we can read the break-even point of 20 000 units. We can observe that at 23 000 units there is a vertical difference between the fixed cost line and contribution line of £6000. This represents excess of contribution over fixed costs and therefore, profit. The dashed line represents an increase in fixed costs to £50 000. We see that the new break-even point is now 25 000 units. If the firm is still to make £6000 profit, it will need to move to 27 000 activity units.

The broken line represents a change in the relationship between sales and variable cost, that is, a non-proportional change. For example, unit sales price increases by £1·50 and unit variable cost increases by £1. The contribution therefore increases by £0·50 to £2·50.

Thus, at the original fixed cost of £40 000 the break-even point would be 16 000 units, and to have £6000 profit would require 18 500 units. If fixed costs were to increase to £50 000, the break-even point would be 20 000 units, and £6000 profit would occur at 22 500 units.

Yet another presentation is shown in Figure 92. This graph takes the same information and illustrates the make-up of variable cost by element, adding on the fixed cost to arrive at total cost. The angle between sales and total cost beyond the break-even point is then also broken down into the constituent parts of retained profit, taxation and dividend. This style would clearly be more suitable for presenting information to senior management.

That, then, is the basis of the marginal costing approach, demonstrated with a single-product organisation and some simplified figures. We now look at some of its applications.

## The maximisation of profit, and the product mix decision

Perhaps the most interesting problem is that faced by multi-product organisations, facing limiting factors. Under those conditions they will need to optimise their product mix so as to produce the largest contribution. Given that fixed costs

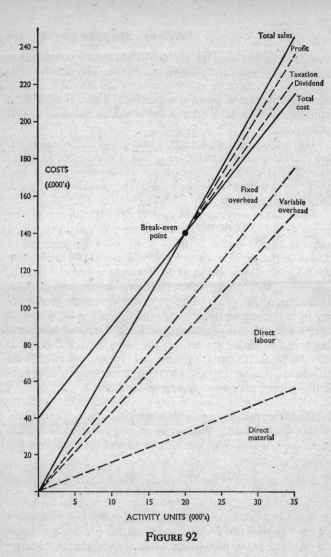

FIGURE 92

remain constant over the activity range, then to obtain that largest contribution will lead to maximised profit.

To demonstrate the application of the marginal costing technique we consider the following example:

### *Illustration*

Urban Industries Ltd manufacture three similar products known as 'Kay', 'Elle' and 'Emm'. Information concerning these products is as follows:

|  | Kay | Elle | Emm |
|---|---|---|---|
| Cost standard per unit: |  |  |  |
| Direct materials | (2)£8 | (2)£10 | (1)£6 |
| Direct labour (£1 per hour) | 5 | 2 | 3 |
| Variable overhead | 2 | 2 | 1 |
| Unit selling price | £21 | £19 | £14 |
| Forecast sales units | 10 000 | 30 000 | 40 000 |

The figures in brackets against direct material refer to the number of specially purchased springs used on each product. The supplier of these springs has informed the company that there will only be 100 000 available next year. The production manager also informs us that he cannot guarantee a larger work force than one hundred people, each of whom will be available for 2000 hours in the year. The fixed costs of the company are £150 000. There are no opening or closing stocks of any of the three products.

We are required to maximise resource utilisation as far as possible, to obtain maximised profit.

We observe that it will not be possible to produce all the forecast sales. We will not have sufficient production hours or special springs.

|  | Total | Kay | Elle | Emm |
|---|---|---|---|---|
| Forecast sales |  | 10 000 | 30 000 | 40 000 |
| Unit labour hours per unit |  | 5 | 2 | 3 |
| Total hours | 230 000 | 50 000 | 60 000 | 120 000 |
| Special springs per unit |  | 2 | 2 | 1 |
| Total springs | 120 000 | 20 000 | 60 000 | 40 000 |

The problem is thus to be resolved within the two constraints of production hours and special springs consistent with producing the largest contribution, and thus, a maximised profit.

Figure 93 shows the analysis. At items 1 and 2 on the first table we establish contribution per unit for each of the three products and then grade that contribution in order of the importance of its absolute value. If there were a sales constraint only, the company would then attempt to sell as many 'Kay' as possible, for it gives the largest unit contribution. However, two constraints face the firm: the number of production hours available and the number of special springs that will be available from the supplier.

Items 3 and 4 establish the contribution per production hour and the contribution per spring respectively, and grade them in order of their absolute value.

Thus, 'Elle' is number one in importance with respect to production hours, but, 'Emm' leads with respect to contribution per special spring. The contribution per hour or per spring is arrived at by dividing the number per unit required into the contribution per unit.

We then proceed to find which limitation, when applied, provides the largest absolute sum of contribution.

It will be noted that each schedule is adjusted line by line as the constraint takes effect. For example, in the production hours limitation schedule we find that, having used 60 000 hours for 'Elle', then 120 000 hours for 'Emm', only 20 000 hours are available for 'Kay', thus reducing the output from 10 000 units to 4000 units. By applying special spring availability to those adjusted figures, we find that we use 60 000 on 'Elle' and 40 000 on 'Emm', leaving none for Kay. Thus, product 'Kay' would not be produced and would leave the 20 000 production hours allocated to Kay under-utilised. This would raise another problem; but at least we have one

| | | | Kay | Elle | Emm |
|---|---|---|---|---|---|
| **CALCULATION OF CONTRIBUTION PER LIMITING FACTOR** | | | | | |
| 1. | Unit variable cost £ | | 15 | 14 | 10 |
| | Unit sales price £ | | 21 | 19 | 14 |
| 2. | Unit contribution £ | | 6 | 5 | 4 |
| | Contribution ranking | | 1 | 2 | 3 |
| 3. | Special springs per unit | | 2 | 2 | 1 |
| | Contribution per unit per spring £ | | 3 | 2·50 | 4 |
| | Contribution ranking | | 2 | 3 | 1 |
| 4. | Production hours per unit | | 5 | 2 | 3 |
| | Contribution per production hour per unit £ | | 1·20 | 2·50 | 1·33 |
| | Contribution ranking | | 3 | 1 | 2 |

**PRODUCTION HOURS LIMITATION**

| | Total | Kay | Elle | Emm |
|---|---|---|---|---|
| *Ranking No. 4 above* | | 3 | 1 | 2 |
| Forecast sales | | 10 000 | 30 000 | 40 000 |
| Production hours (per unit) | | 5 | 2 | 3 |
| Possible output (hours) | 200 000 | 20 000 | 60 000 | 120 000 |
| Adjusted sales | | 4 000 | 30 000 | 40 000 |
| Special springs per unit | | 2 | 2 | 1 |
| Possible spring use | 100 000 | — | 60 000 | 40 000 |
| Adjusted sales | | — | 30 000 | 40 000 |
| Contribution per unit | | | £5 | £4 |
| *Total contribution* | £310 000 | | £150 000 | £160 000 |
| *Underutilised Production Hours* | 20 000 | 20 000 | | |

**SPECIAL SPRINGS LIMITATION**

| | Total | Kay | Elle | Emm |
|---|---|---|---|---|
| *Ranking No. 3 above* | | 2 | 3 | 1 |
| Forecast sales | | 10 000 | 30 000 | 40 000 |
| Special spring—per unit | | 2 | 2 | 1 |
| Possible spring use | 100 000 | 20 000 | 40 000 | 40 000 |
| Adjusted sales | | 10 000 | 20 000 | 40 000 |
| Production hours per unit | | 5 | 2 | 3 |
| Possible output hours | 200 000 | 50 000 | 30 000 | 120 000 |
| Adjusted sales | | 10 000 | 15 000 | 40 000 |
| Contribution per unit | | £6 | £5 | £4 |
| *Total contribution* | £295 000 | £60 000 | £75 000 | £160 000 |
| *Underutilised springs* | 10 000 | | 10 000 | |

FIGURE 93

idea of how to utilise resources as far as possible to produce a total contribution of £310 000.

The technique is now applied similarly to the special spring limitation condition giving a total contribution of £295 000 which, although only requiring the use of 90 000 springs, fully utilises the 200 000 production hours.

No mention has been made of the fixed costs of £150 000. These have to be paid at any activity level, irrespective of any constraint or limiting factors. Thus, maximising contribution less the fixed costs in total, leads to a situation where profits are also maximised.

This example is fairly simple. Under more practical operating circumstances the limitations may be more than two, and may all operate in different directions and give rise to different cost characteristics. For that purpose, a mathematical technique known as linear programming has been developed. An explanation of this technique is usually found in books written for the study of management accounting. It is not within the scope of this text.

## Sales volume and the pricing decision

Probably the greatest area of misunderstanding occurs between sales and accounting departments in connection with the relationship between costs and selling prices. The dichotomy runs something like this: 'accountants have no understanding of competitive pricing'; 'sales have no regard for costs'. The root cause of this long-standing disagreement may be traced back to the use of absorption or total costing as the basis for reaching decisions.

The following example shows how the technique may be used in a straightforward decision situation.

### Illustration

The Makem Manufacturing Co. produces 10 000 units per annum by employing 50% of the factory capacity. The selling price of the unit is £5, and the total costs were:

| | |
|---|---|
| Materials | £10 000 |
| Wages | £20 000 |
| Fixed overhead | £10 000 |
| Variable overhead | £4 000 |
| | £44 000 |

Variable overhead maintains a constant ratio to the number of units produced.

The company accepts an order for an additional 10 000 units at a selling price of £3·87½ each.

The increased volume of purchases reduces the material prices by 2½%. Wage rates remain constant, but due to the employment of new workers there is a drop in labour efficiency of 5% on all production.

We are required to prepare a statement showing the variation of net profits resulting from the acceptance of the order (ICMA).

There would be a great temptation, with an absorption system, to say that the order should not have been accepted at £3·87½. After all, 10 000 units cost £44 000 to produce, and, therefore, £4·40 per unit. This single point does as much as anything to point out the fallacious base of pricing from such a system. The comparative situation is demonstrated in Figure 94, from which we observe that the additional units increase total contribution by £3250 and thus profits from £6000 to £9250. This shows that even at a selling price at or near to the unit variable cost, there is something to be gained.

At 50% capacity   —   10 000 units

| Revenue at £5·00 per unit | | | £50 000 |
|---|---|---|---|
| *Costs:* | *per unit* | *Total* | |
| Materials | £1·00 | £10 000 | |
| Wages | 2·00 | 20 000 | |
| Variable Overhead | 0·40 | 4 000 | |
| Total Variable Cost | £3·40 | | £34 000 |
| Contribution | 1·60 | | 16 000 |
| *Less* Fixed Costs | | | 10 000 |
| *Profit* | | | £6 000 |

Break-even units = Fixed Costs/Contribution per unit
      = £10 000/£1·60 = 6250

Profit units   10 000 — 6250 = 3750 at £1·60 = £6000

At 100% capacity   —   20 000 units

| Revenue at £5·00 per unit for 10 000 units | | | 50 000 |
|---|---|---|---|
| at £3·87½  ,,   ,, ,, 10 000   ,, | | | 38 750 |
| | | | £88 750 |
| *Costs:* | *per unit* | *Total* | |
| Materials £1·00 less 2½% | £0·975 | 19 500 | |
| Wages £2·00 plus 5% | 2·10 | 42 000 | |
| Variable Overhead | 0·40 | 8 000 | |
| Total Variable Costs | £3·47½ | | 69 500 |
| Average and total contribution | 0·962 | | £19 250 |
| *Less* Fixed Costs | | | 10 000 |
| *Profit* | | | £9 250 |

Break-even units on average contributions
      = £10 000/£0·962 = 10 389
   Profit units   20 000 — 10 389 = 9611 at £0·962 = £9250
Reconciliation of profit change:
   Profit change £6000 to £9250 =                                £3 250
Accounted for by:

(a)   Additional contribution

| | | |
|---|---:|---:|
| Additional unit selling price | £3·875 | |
| Old unit variable costs | 3·400 | |
| for 10 000 units at | 0·475 | £4 750 |

(b)   Less overall increase in variable cost

| | | |
|---|---:|---:|
| Old variable cost | £3·400 | |
| New variable cost | 3·475 | |
| for 20 000 units at | £0·075 | 1 500 |
| | | £3 250 |

FIGURE 94

### The stock valuation decision

We have noted that the marginal cost concept is that the variable cost of a product is a 'true' cost, and that fixed costs are period or policy costs *not* to be absorbed in product costs. It follows that fixed costs are a charge against the sales in each accounting period, and that no inclusion of fixed costs in stock valuations should be made. The effect is more pronounced when examined in the case of an organisation with seasonal or production cycle fluctuations.

There may perhaps be some disadvantage in the fact that when stocks of goods and work in progress are built up, the marginal method may, if incorrectly presented, show a worse trading position than other more orthodox methods. But marginal costing systems can show the disadvantageous effects that more orthodox methods may conceal. Stock valuation has always been a rather thorny and vexing problem. There is much to be said for claiming that fixed costs are a charge against the period and thus omitting them from the valuation of stock.

*Illustration*

|  | Units | Variable Cost Basis £ | Total Cost Basis £ |
|---|---|---|---|
| Opening stock | 1 000 | 5 000 | 6 600 |
| Production | 24 000 | 120 000 | 158 400 |
|  | 25 000 | 125 000 | 165 000 |
| Closing stock | 2 000 | 10 000 | 13 200 |
| Cost of sales | 23 000 | 115 000 | 151 800 |
| *Plus* fixed costs |  | 40 000 | — |
|  | 23 000 | 155 000 | 151 800 |
| Sales at £7 per unit |  | 161 000 | 161 000 |
| Profit |  | 6 000 |  |
| Sales *less* total cost |  |  | 10 800 |
| Under-recovery of fixed overheads: |  |  |  |
| 2000 units at £1·60 | 3 200 |  |  |
| Stock change: |  |  |  |
| 1000 units at £1·60 | 1 600 | — | 4 800 |
| Profit |  | 6 000 | 6 000 |

## The case for and against marginal costing

In this chapter, a fairly simple examination of the technique has been made and an attempt to demonstrate a few of the problems that can be solved. The merits may be said to be:

1  Marginal costs are simple to compute, being the variable costs only. The necessity to apportion fixed costs disappears.
2  Responsibility for control is more easily apportioned, since only variable costs over which they have control are presented to each level of management.

3 All levels of management are more readily able to see the effects of their decisions—sometimes before an action is taken.
4 The importance of the volume of output is more readily appreciated. The highly unsatisfactory position with respect to orthodox overhead recovery is avoided.

The demerits may be said to be:

1 It is often impossible to separate some expenses into fixed and variable in the short term.
2 There is the danger that, unless fully explained, marginal cost may be mistaken for total cost and used as the wrong basis for a decision, for example, in price reconstruction.
3 It may be difficult under many circumstances to deduce the contribution made by some production units. Thus the effectiveness of the system is lost.

Overall, many of the arguments used may be said to be true of all the methods and techniques of cost accountancy. But, like all things, methods and techniques should only be used when and where they will provide the analysis and information that will prompt the action that management can take to achieve a desired result.

### Exercises

1 You are required to present a report to the Managing Director of the Z Manufacturing Co Ltd forecasting profit and loss for the coming year based on the information given below. In the report you should include a budgeted profit and loss statement for the company for the year, and discuss the proposal by the sales director to reduce prices and increase revenue. You should also

suggest possible alternatives which the sales director could adopt.

> *Profit and Loss account—current year (£000's)*
>
> | Sales | | 6000 |
> |---|---|---|
> | Costs: | | |
> |  Direct material | 2400 | |
> |  Direct wages | 1500 | |
> |  Variable overhead | 3000 | |
> |  Fixed overhead | 1300 | 5500 |
> | | *Profit* | 500 |

The sales director has suggested that in order to expand sales, the selling price of the company's product should be reduced by 10%. The resultant sales revenue would be 20% up on the current year.

As management accountant you have forecast the following changes for the next year as compared with the current year:

Direct materials will increase by 5%.
Direct labour rates will increase by 10%.
Fixed overhead will increase by £300 000.

(ICMA adapted)

2  The board of directors of KF Ltd, manufacturers of three products A, B and C, have asked for advice on the production mix of the company. You are required to prepare a statement to advise the directors of the most profitable mixture of the products to be made and sold. The statement should show:

(a) the profit expected on the current budgeted production

(b) the profit which could be expected if the most profitable mixture was produced.

You are also required to direct the director's attention to any problems which are likely to arise if the mixture in (*b*) above were to be produced. The following information is given:

| Data for standard costs per unit: | Product A £ | Product B £ | Product C £ |
|---|---|---|---|
| Direct material | 10 | 30 | 20 |
| Variable overhead | 3 | 2 | 5 |

| Direct labour: Department | Rate per hour | Product A hours | Product B hours | Product C hours |
|---|---|---|---|---|
| 1 | £0·50 | 28 | 16 | 30 |
| 2 | 1·00 | 5 | 6 | 10 |
| 3 | 0·50 | 16 | 8 | 30 |

| Data from current budget: | units | units | units |
|---|---|---|---|
| Production in thousands of units per year | 10 | 5 | 6 |
| Selling price per unit | £50 | £68 | £90 |

Fixed overhead per year: £200 000

| Forecast by sales director of possible sales for next year, in thousands of units | units | units | units |
|---|---|---|---|
| | 12 | 7 | 9 |

However, the type of labour required by Department 2 is in short supply and it is not possible to increase the manpower of this department beyond its present level.
(ICMA)

3 As cost consultant to a Mexican farmer who grows summer vegetables and exports them to the USA, you are required, using the information given below, to

    (*a*) Calculate the profit or loss per box of each type of vegetable that your client will obtain from operating the farm on the present basis.

(*b*)   advise your client of the area to be cultivated with each line to produce the largest total profit, and of the amount of the largest total profit.

The farmer owns 240 acres of land on which he grows staked tomatoes, ground tomatoes, cucumbers and green beans. Of the land, 70 acres are unsuitable for staked tomatoes or green beans but are suitable for cucumbers or ground tomatoes. On the remainder of the land any of the four crops may be grown. There is an adequate supply of labour for all kinds of farm work.

Marketing policy requires that each season the farmer produces all four types of vegetables, with not less than 5000 boxes of any one line.

It is decided that the area devoted to any one line should be in terms of complete acres and not in fractions of an acre. You may assume there are no other physical or marketing limitations. Details relating to production, market price and direct and fixed costs are given below:

|  | Staked tomatoes | Ground tomatoes | Cucumbers | Green beans |
|---|---|---|---|---|
| Acreage at present devoted to each line | 105 | 50 | 60 | 25 |
| Summer season's yield in boxes per acre | 700 | 200 | 150 | 300 |
| Weight per box in lb | 50 | 60 | 80 | 36 |
| Market price per box in dollars | 3·86 | 3·86 | 4·56 | 5·68 |
| *Costs: (in dollars)* | | | | |
| Materials per acre | 189 | 74 | 63 | 108 |
| Labour:   growing per acre | 224 | 152 | 93 | 132 |
| Harvesting and packing per box | 0·80 | 0·72 | 1·00 | 1 20 |
| Transport and export per box | 1·30 | 1·30 | 1·00 | 2·40 |

*Fixed overhead incurred each season (in dollars)*

| Expense | Basis of apportionment to products |
|---|---|
| Cultivation: | |
|   growing | 36 000—direct labour hours incurred |
|   harvesting | 12 000—direct labour costs incurred |
| Transport and export | 12 000—weight produced |
| General administration | 40 000—number of boxes produced |
| Notional rent | 12 000—number of acres cultivated. |

(ICMA)

4   Gadgeting Ltd manufactures a single product which is marketed in three grades of finish, viz: Presentation, De Luxe and Standard. The variable cost of the basic unit is £6 and the cost of finishing and packing is as follows:

| | |
|---|---|
| Presentation model | £4 |
| De Luxe model | £2 |
| Standard model | £1 |

The selling prices are:

| | |
|---|---|
| Presentation model | £15 |
| De Luxe model | £12 |
| Standard model | £10 |

The marketing manager has estimated demand for the next year as follows:

| | |
|---|---|
| Presentation model | 20 000 |
| De Luxe model | 30 000 |
| Standard model | 40 000 |

The production manager has estimated the production capacity of the factory at 150 000 hours per annum. Fixed costs have been estimated at £100 000 for the next year.

An enquiry has been received from a manufacturer, Green, who is considering using the basic unit as a sub-assembly in his own product and at an acceptable price would be willing to buy 30 000 units per year. The company's profit objective for next year is £300 000. You are required to:

    (*a*)   calculate the lowest price which could be quoted for the supply of the 30 000 units to Green.

    (*b*)   comment upon any business policy matters you consider relevant in the circumstances.   (ACCA)

5  XYZ Ltd manufactures three products, X, Y and Z, the unit variable cost details of which are:

|  | X | Y | Z |
|---|---|---|---|
| Direct material | £29·3 | £18·6 | £47·5 |
| Direct labour: | *hours* | *hours* | *hours* |
|   assembly | 5 | 8 | 10 |
|   machining | 4 | 3 | 5 |
| Variable overhead | £5·80 | £5·60 | £4·50 |
| Selling price per unit | £50 | £40 | £75 |

Owing to the difficulties of providing supervision, canteen facilities and transport, the company is restricted to a forty-hour working week. Assemblers are paid 50p per hour and machinists 60p per hour. The company plans its production and marketing operations in relation to the four-week periods which are used for accounting purposes.

The labour force expected to be available for each of the first two periods of the forthcoming year are:

|  | Assemblers | Machinists |
|---|---|---|
| Period 1 | 97 | 60 |
| Period 2 | 127 | 63 |

but no guarantee is given to them that their services will necessarily be required, and only time spent on production is paid for.

Marketing management have estimated demand for Period 1 to be 800 of each product, increasing by 10% cumulative per period throughout the year. No stocks of finished products or work in progress exist at the beginning or end of any period. The company's fixed overheads for the coming year are expected to be £1000 per week.

You are required to:

(a) prepare statements showing the most profitable production plan for the company to pursue for each of the two periods in question, and the profit for each of the two periods.

(b) explain briefly the principles you have applied in making your proposals. (ACCA)

# For Further Reading

*Job Evaluation and Merit Rating* (pamphlet)
(Trades Union Congress)

*Production Control in Practice*
K. G. Lockyer (Pitman)

*Production Management*
H. A. Harding (Macdonald and Evans)

*The Techniques of Production Management*
Ray Wild (Holt)

*Work Study and Related Management Services*
(Metric Edition) D. A. Whitmore (Heinemann)

# Index

# Index

## TEACH YOURSELF BOOKS

## MANAGEMENT ACCOUNTING

### Brian Murphy

The role of the management accountant is to present management with the best possible financial information upon which they can base their decisions, and to establish control systems to ensure that the best use is being made of the concern's resources.

This book describes the main systems and techniques which are at present available to the management accountant. Topics covered include historical and standard costing, budgetary control, financial planning and marginal costing. Working examples are included throughout and a number of practical exercises are given in each chapter.

The author is Principal Lecturer in management accounting at Huddersfield Polytechnic.

Published in USA by
David McKay Company, Inc.

| UNITED KINGDOM | 95p |
| AUSTRALIA | $3.05* |
| NEW ZEALAND | $3.05 |
| CANADA | $3.25 |

ISBN 0 340 12495 4

*recommended but not obligatory

# TEACH YOURSELF BOOKS

## UNDERSTANDING STATISTICS

### Martin Leonard

Modern society demands, and gets, more and more information about itself. Every day a vast quantity of this information is hurled at the public, much of it in the form of statistics.

This book will help you understand that information, the way it is collected, prepared and presented, whether it is information on the sales of pop records, crime, politics, business or any of the other numerous areas where statistics are used. It does so without using complicated mathematics.

If you distrust all statistics, from opinion polls to the hit parade, from the cost of living index to population projections, this book will tell you which ones you can trust and how far you can trust them. In an age when skill with figures is as important as skill with words this book is essential.

| | |
|---|---|
| UNITED KINGDOM | 95p |
| AUSTRALIA | $3.05* |
| NEW ZEALAND | $3.05 |
| CANADA | $3.25 |

ISBN 0 340 18259 8   *recommended but not obligatory

TEACH YOURSELF BOOKS

## OPERATIONAL RESEARCH

**M. S. Makower & E. Williamson**

Operational Research is the application of scientific method to management decision-making. It is being used to tackle a wide variety of problems, ranging from space-exploration to the control of supermarket stocks.

This book introduces and discusses some of the more important techniques which have been developed to help solve such problems. These include forecasting methods, the theory of queues, linear programming, and network analysis. Explanation and illustration of these techniques is carried out through worked examples, and each chapter ends with further exercises (and solutions) to enable the reader to test his understanding of the methods described.

Operational Research is a fascinating and increasingly topical subject. Those with a slight taste for numbers and at least some recollection of school mathematics should follow with ease the ideas presented.

An introduction to OR for business and management students and for all those involved in forecasting, planning, and decision-making.

| UNITED KINGDOM | £1.25 |
| AUSTRALIA | $3.95* |
| NEW ZEALAND | $3.95 |
| CANADA | $4.95 |

ISBN 0 340 20232 7    *recommended but not obligatory

TEACH YOURSELF BOOKS

## CRITICAL PATH ANALYSIS

### Douglas W. Lang

This comprehensive introduction to the increasingly important field of Critical Path Analysis has been developed from experience in consultancy and teaching.

CPA is the organised application of systematic reasoning to the planning and control of practical situations consisting of many separate, and often simultaneous, jobs. Usually CPA techniques can usefully be applied to any complicated project, large or small, for example, planning a product launch or building a house or factory, and one particular benefit of CPA is that it highlights the sequence of jobs which will determine the total time of a project.

This is a book for both students, and managers involved in project planning. The text is illustrated with numerous practical examples, exercises and case studies and chapters include questions on the techniques described.

Douglas W. Lang is Lecturer in Quantitative Aspects of Management at the Polytechnic of Central London.

Published in USA by
David McKay Company, Inc.

| | |
|---|---|
| UNITED KINGDOM | £1.75 |
| AUSTRALIA | $5.65* |
| NEW ZEALAND | $5.50 |
| CANADA | $5.95 |

ISBN 0 340 21278 0

*recommended but not obligatory

TEACH YOURSELF BOOKS

## ECONOMICS FOR EVERYONE

### K. Norris & J. Vaizey

The important role economics plays in our lives is becoming increasingly apparent and a knowledge of economic principles is necessary to understand fully much of what is written in the press and spoken on radio and television.

In this book Dr. Norris and Lord Vaizey have written a straightforward and vigorous introduction to the whole field which discusses such questions as

What is economics about?
What is meant by full employment?
What causes inflation and how can it be controlled?
What is the money supply?
How can the economy be managed?
What is meant by the balance of payments?
What determines relative pay?
How do firms set their prices?
How do banks create money?

ECONOMICS FOR EVERYONE gives the understanding and background the intelligent layman needs if he is to make sense of day to day events and is a useful introduction to more advanced material.

Lord Vaizey is Professor of Economics and Dr. Norris Reader in Economics at Brunel University.

| | |
|---|---|
| UNITED KINGDOM | £1.50 |
| AUSTRALIA | $4.90* |
| NEW ZEALAND | $4.70 |
| CANADA | $4.95 |

ISBN 0 340 21905 X    * recommended but not obligatory

# TEACH YOURSELF BOOKS